AF552661

EXPORT MANAGEMENT

Encyclopaedia of Commerce and Management Series

EXPORT MANAGEMENT

Edited by
Asit K. Ghosh
Prem Kumar

ANMOL PUBLICATIONS PVT. LTD.
NEW DELHI - 110 002 (INDIA)

ANMOL PUBLICATIONS PVT. LTD.
4374/4B, Ansari Road, Daryaganj
New Delhi - 110 002
Ph.: 23261597, 23278000
Visit us at: www.anmolpublications.com

Export Management

ISBN 81-7041-363-X

PRINTED IN INDIA

Published by J.L. Kumar for Anmol Publications Pvt. Ltd., New Delhi - 110 002 and Printed at Mehra Offset Press, Delhi.

Preface

The dimensions of management in the corporate field are ever changing according to the continuous development of science, technology and the economics of business. Over the past four decades, the boost given to science and technology during the Great War years has resulted in spill-over benefits for industries and manufacturing sectors in almost all countries. The widespread use of electronic data processing (EDP) or computer technology in modern management applications in both office and factory is a direct outcome of the earliest applications of the computer for defence purposes in Germany, the U.K. and U.S.A. during the Second World War. With the end of the War came a remarkable decades-long spurt in consumer goods industries including television, audio-visual teaching methods, fuel-efficient engines for various civil and industrial use and a vast range of home products. The age of the modern enterprise began with the new economic climate created by the spread of education, rising expectations of the new generations of people and the resultant ever-increasing national and international markets.

It was in the context of the new era of management science that the present concept of a series of books on current management theory, practice and applications were formulated. The objective is to present the most representative as well as contemporary thinking, ideas and deliberations under various useful heads such as general, marketing and sales, personnel project and production management, material management, financial management, organisation theory and behaviour, industrial psychology, rural development, government and business including public enterprises management, and economic and business policy. The comprehensive coverage has been attempted to include within these volumes the contributions made by academicians, professional managers, senior executives and other management experts over the past decade to current perspectives in management science.

The work of compiling these volumes has been a gigantic task. Thousands of articles, papers and communications from numerous sources have been studied and sifted. Seminar, conference and discussion papers were obtained from various libraries and other sources to cull material of high quality and standing relevance for the benefit of not only students and scholars of management but also professional executives, managers and corporate planners and policy-makers. This compilation would not claim to be perfect in many respects; but is only an overview of current thinking and applications in the present business world.

We gratefully acknowledge the various libraries and their librarians for assistance in putting together these papers. We are especially grateful to the respective authors and organising colleges, universities and institutions for their papers as well as copies of presentations at seminars, conferences and discussions. Many of the authors included here could not be traced to their present position as their papers are a few years old and there in high mobility among managers and academicians alike. However, we are grateful to all of them. Finally, we have a word of appreciation for the support services, including typing and collating, provided by the publishers.

EDITORS

Contents

Contents

1

NEW AND EMERGING TECHNOLOGIES IMPACT ON DEVELOPING COUNTRIES

The Introduction of new technologies has traditionally been an issue of controversy. Cursed as a threat to values and patterns of life by some, they are hailed as the key to a better and more prosperous future by others. This controversy also accompanies the rapid technological change the world is witnessing today. It is in particular the emergence of a series of fundamentally new technologies such as microelectronics, biotechnology, material technology, laser technology and sea-bed mining which fuels the debate on the potentially wide-ranging implications of the new technologies. So far, however, attempts to assess the socio-economic impact of these technologies are mainly confined to the industrialised countries, where developed, perfected and first applied. Little systematic knowledge is available about the consequences, which can be expected for developing countries. However, given the far-reaching implications these technologies may have for these countries, such an assessment is of crucial importance.

In view of this, UNCTAD-VI at Belgrade requested the Secretary-General of UNCTAD to prepare proposals for work on new and emerging technologies to be submitted for consideration to the fifth session of the Committee on Transfer of Technology. Contained in a secretariat report, entitled, *New and Emerging Technologies: Some Economic, Commercial and Development Aspects*, these proposals were discussed at the recent session of the Committee. This article presents some key observations and suggestions of the report on new and emerging technologies.

SOME NEW TECHNOLOGIES

Micro-electronics is essentially concerned with the production, processing, transmission and storage of information which in turn is used in the production of goods and services. It is a science-based as well as capital-intensive technology, which developed as the fruit of more than three decades of basic and applied scientific research, benefiting from the direct and indirect support of the governments of the most advanced industrialised countries.

Micro-electronics has made an unprecedented inroad into modern production processes in practically all sectors of economic activity. There are numerous examples of its application. It is used in agriculture for irrigation, cattle monitoring and crop control. In industry, operations are increasingly monitored and controlled with the help of micro-electronics. In services, the technology is used in banking, insurance, transport, engineering and construction. Micro-electronics has also profoundly affected the informatics and telecommunications industries and the combination of these two has led to the rise of telematics and the growth of transborder data flows which permit access to information irrespective of location.

The incorporation of micro-electronics in products have increased the latter's efficiency, reliability and flexibility in performing additional, more varied and improved functions. At the same time, it has caused product differentiation to become more pronounced and the specifications of goods more complex. With micro-electronics, production processes have become highly automated, as is illustrated by applications such as numerically-controlled machine-tools, industrial robots, computer-aided manufacturing.

Biotechnology involves the practical application of biological organisms, systems or processes to manufacturing and services industries and/or their use in the transformation of natural compounds. This technology has emerged from the latest advances in molecular biology, biochemistry, microbiological genetics and biochemical engineering. The principal techniques used in biotechnology—which include recombinant DNA technology or genetic engineering, cell fusion and new bioprocessing engineering—hold the promise of solving a broad range of problems relating to the production of synthetic fuels, recovery of raw materials, novel methods of crop fertilisation, plant and animal breeding, pest control and waste treatment, and of improved production methods for a number of products, such as pharmaceuticals, feedstuffs and petrochemicals. At present it is difficult to assess the economics of biotechnology applications because most of them have not yet moved from the laboratory stage to actual production.

Materials technologies have made remarkable advances in many fields. The materials embodying these technologies—such as fine ceramics, optical fibre, plastic and fibre-reinforced composite materials—allow improvements in the quality of many existing products and lead to a reduction in manufacturing costs through a saving of energy and materials and through weight reduction. They stimulate the development of new products and help to expand the scope for manufacturing activities in small and medium-sized markets. Some of these new materials are already beginning to replace traditional materials, as in the case of optical fibres, which have begun to replace copper in telecommunications. The same is true in the cases of fine ceramics, plastics and composites, which can be substituted for steel and aluminium in the construction of buildings, highways and cars.

EFFECTS ON DEVELOPING COUNTRIES EXPORTS

New and emerging technologies are likely to have a dual effect on the export performance and possibilities of developing countries. While the competitive position of many developing countries' exports in world markets may be eroded by these technological changes, it is also true that new technologies offer new production opportunities which, if seized in time and properly exploited by developing countries, would improve their export performance. Which of the two possibilities applies, and for which products and countries, is a question of great policy relevance for developing countries.

The vast majority of these countries depend for the bulk of their exports on a small number of primary and semi-processed commodities, ranging from food, tropical beverages and agricultural raw materials to ores, metals and vegetable oils. Commodity producers are likely to be affected in two ways. On the one hand, the application of new technologies creates new and more efficient production processes for existing products, which economise the quantity of energy used and raw materials inputs per unit of output. They also create greater flexibility regarding commodity inputs, making it possible to substitute one commodity for another if market conditions make this economic. Furthermore, the application of new technologies leads to the creation of new, final and intermediate products, some of which can be substituted for primary commodities. Thus, for example, high fructose corn syrup produced with the help of biotechnology is replacing sugar in certain uses. Ethanol produced by biomass technology may continue to become economically attractive as a substitute for petroleum, whereas ceramic, plastic and other composite materials are finding their way into the manufacture of automobile parts, replacing steel, aluminium and other metal products. Many of these developments have negative effects for the commodity exports of developing countries, although some new product applications may also engender a new demand for selected commodities.

Exports of manufactures have been a dynamic factor in the rapid growth and development of a number of developing countries such as, to name only a few, Brazil, Mexico and the Republic of Korea. Their exports have succeeded in making inroads into the markets of developed countries since the mid-'sixties. This group of countries is also likely to be affected by the emergence of new technologies. The cost-reducing application of micro-electronics, particularly through increased automation, has permitted significant improvements in labour productivity, thereby changing the composition of costs in favour of countries in which labour is relatively scarce. Moreover, many off-shore assembly operations, which were profitable in some developing countries, mainly because of low absolute costs of both unskilled and skilled labour, are now being transferred back to the home country or other developed countries as automation makes it possible to centralise the location of production and thus reduce costs.

The risk that comparative advantage may shift away from developing countries reflects the fact that automation permits not only labour cost reductions, but also improved quality control and management practices. Developing countries whose competitive edge on world markets was based on conventional technology, low labour cost and an abundance of natural resources, could be in danger of losing this advantage with respect to a wide range of exports such as fibres, textiles, apparel, shoes and leather articles, consumer electronics and electrical machinery. An example is the automation of garment manufacturing, whose production process was hitherto characterised by separate and skilled labour operations but which is now moving towards electronically-based technologies for grading, laying out, cutting and even sewing functions. Markets for the manufactures exports of developing countries may also be adversely affected as a result of the influence the new technologies may have on the level and composition of demand and on the specifications of products, particularly if these countries do not adjust their production capacity to changes in demand in the international markets, which are created by the emergence of these technologies.

The impact of the developments outlined above on exporters in developing countries is not uniform but depends on a number of factors. Transport and tariff barriers facing developing countries' products, as well as the speed and industrial pattern of the diffusion of the new technologies in the North play a decisive role. For some product-groups, the introduction of new technologies has not been as rapid as had been expected owing to technical, institutional and structural obstacles, which have affected the pattern and depth of their diffusion in the North. The extent and speed of the transfer of the new technologies and their applications to developing countries and of their absorption by them are of course also crucial.

In general, the transfer of the new technologies enables developing countries to produce and export a wider range of goods than would otherwise be the case. It furthermore provides them with possibilities, which could at least partially offset the threatened displacement of certain of the products they export to developed countries as a result of labour-saving innovations.

In the *first* place, since some of the new technologies economise not only on labour generally but also on factors such as higher skilled labour that are relatively scarce in some developing countries, they diminish one of their disadvantages in competing in external markets. Examples are numerically-controlled machine-tools and computer-aided design, which embody skills in the equipment itself, making it possible to employ less qualified personnel to carry out the required functions. On the other hand, the same technologies may be creating the need for other skills that are in scarce supply in some developing countries.

Secondly, some of the applications of new technology are in fields that are primarily of interest to developing countries. Cases are the use of recombinant DNA for the production of vaccines and drugs needed in tropical medicine, the development of new seed varieties suited to arid zone agriculture and improved recovery of ores in mining operations, which could give a boost either to trade among developing countries or between them and developed countries.

Thirdly, transfer of the new technology to developing countries could in principale make a positive *indirect* contribution to the exporting capability of developing countries through improvement in general productive efficiency of the domestic economy. Of particular relevance are the possibilities afforded by the application of micro-electronics and computerisation technology for streamlining the operation of services that are essential for the export sector as communications, banking and insurance. Transferred to developing countries, the advances in information technology, including telematics, could help to improve the state of knowledge of would market conditions and decrease the distance between developing country suppliers and their customers, thereby improving their capacity to service overseas market efficiently.

QUESTIONS FOR EXAMINATION

It is thus evident that developing countries can expect a variety of potential benefits from the new technologies. Hence they need to investigate the options they have for acquiring them. The report examines some of the questions which require further examination in this regard.

One such question is:

How soon after the initial commercial exploitation of a technology in the country where it is a first developed would one expect its transfer to developing countries to take place? The answer depends on a complex of a considerations and varies according to the particular technological application. Among the factors involved are:

The size of the home market and the rapidity with which it becomes saturated; the rate of product turnover and diffusion of the technology in the home country and other developed country markets; and the influence of government policies on access to technology. The availability of a large domestic market such as that of North America can mean that the technology-holding firm has a sufficiently large outlet in which to capitalise on its known-how, and that it does not feel impelled in the initial period to search for overseas opportunities, particularly in what are perceived to be risky environments of developing countries.

The rate of diffusion of new processes and products depends in part on the degree of competition among holders of technology and on the rate of innovation. This influences not only their accessibility but also the terms of their acquisition. A rapid turnover of new processes or products increases their rate of obsolescence and shortens the time span required before the exploitation of a technology in the relatively less attractive markets of developing countries becomes profitable. The rate of obsolescence of innovations in micro-electronics has until recently been characterised as quite rapid, although there are signs that this may be changing. Other things being equal, the cost of transferring these technologies should decline as they become more mature.

An interesting feature of the behaviour of many of the leading innovators in the newly emerging technologies has been an aversion to patenting because of the amount of disclosure it permits to potential competitors. Moreover, it has been suggested that among some patent-holders cross-licensing and pooling of patents has been practised in order to block entry of competitors. High technology has engaged the interest of virtually all industrialised country governments and many developing country governments. Anxious to protect what they perceive to be national interests, some governments have taken steps to restrict the spontaneous rate of diffusion of these technologies to other countries. On their side, governments of developing countries whose economies are large enough to provide attractive domestic markets to potential investors may be expected to erect taiff barriers and provide other inducements in order to foster the creation of "infant" industries based on some of the new technologies.

A second question concerns the degree of diversity of the channels and sources available for the transfer of the new technology. What will be the relative importance of direct foreign investment of the traditional kind by transnational corporations in majority-owned subsidiaries as distinct from technology transfer *via* other form such as pure licensing, consultancy agreements and other arrangements and from other types of suppliers such as sellers of equipment and components and firms from other developing countries?

It is difficult to even speculate on this question without further research, but it is obviously relevant to an understanding of the options open to developing countries in acquiring the new technology. However, two of the more interesting trends that may be emerging with implications for technology transfer can already be mentioned. One concerns the possible impact of the "information revolution" on the location of production, both in general and in the new fields opened up by the emerging technologies. On the one hand, the reduction of the cost and the increased availability of information about sources and markets may mean that it is no longer as necessary for production to be physically contiguous to certain kinds of markets where customer servicing and close contact with consumers was formerly necessary. On the other hand, the information revolution may stimulate technology transfer to developing countries by reducing the risk and uncertainty associated with it, and by increasing the speed with such transfers occur. The relative importance of these two kinds of tendencies is a matter for further investigation.

The second possibly significant trend concerning access to and transfer of the new technologies relates to the reaction of manufacturing firms in newly industrialising countries to the threatend erosion of their competitive advantage as a result of the emergence of these technologies, particularly in micro-electronics. In order to keep abreast of and gain access to the latest developments which, as mentioned previously, are taking place very fast and are subject to secrecy, firms from some of these countries-notably the Republic of Korea and Singapore—have begun establishing small research and manfacturing subsidiaries near Silicon Valley and other areas in the United States where many of the latest innovations are being produced.

Once some of the know-how and experience has been acquired, it is transmitted back to the parent companies through movevent of personnel and other means. Part of the increasingly significant transfer of technology to other developing countries by firms in newly industrialising countries is also motivated by the impact of micro-electronics and automation. Since labour costs in some of these countries are lower than in the newly industrialised countries, the shift of export-based manufacturing to the former the latter may permit a partial offsetting of the erosion of the labour cost advantages caused by automation in developed countries. As the new technologies become more widely diffused, standardised and understood, one may expect at some stage to see them being transferred increasingly from newly industrialised to other developing countries. These are hypotheses, however, that still need to be tested, the report points out.

TECHNOLOGY UTILISATION AND ASSIMILATION

Some of the new technologies, such micro-electronics and informatic, have already found entrance into many developing countries and are used in a number of different ways in a veriety of economic sectors. Little, however, is known about how the introduction of these technologies affects technological development in developing countries. Until an assessment of this impact is made, no basis will exist for promoting the rational use of these technologies apart from considerations of private commerical profitability. In particular, it will be the marketing strategies of foreign technology suppliers rather than socio-economic and technological considerations of the recipient countries, which will tend to determine the pattern of diffusion of the new technologies. This is all the more critical if the new investment necessary for utilisation of these techniques is quite large on account of their "systemic" or "packaged" nature.

In their efforts of utilise and assimilate the new technologies, governments and entrepreneurs of developing countries are facing some critical questions. One question is that of when and to what extent existing production operations in individual sectors of the economy should be replaced. Any decision on such a matter entails a host of consequences, which must be carefully assessed, including its financial implications and the new requirements for skilled labour. The problem may be illustrated by the case of micro-electronics, whose introduction, tempting as it would seem for many production processes, demands a number of careful cost/benefit evaluations. For example, the cost of the hardware, which has witnessed a sharp decline in recent years, must be considered in relation to the cost of software which remains high and is expected to reach 95 per cent of the product cost in a not too distant future. It must also be borne in mind that for existing enterprises the introduction of micro-electronics implies—in addition to its direct costs—an indirect cost element due to the restructuring, which is required within these firms if they are to benefit from the new technology. These indirect costs arise mainly for two reasons:

First, because the introduction of micro-electronic based systems is associated with the replacement of older electronic, electro-mechanical and mechnical equipment, the scraping of which may be quite costly, especially if investment in it has not been amortised.

Secondly, micro-electronics often requires systems within the firm to be made compatible. This also may not be cheap since it obliges the enterprise to modify not only production methods, but also management and marketing practices, after-sales service methods and personnel policies including retraining programmes.

Another issue relates to the fact that developing countries will need to devote resource to R&D for adaptation and minor modifications to enable them to assimilate the new technologies. Given the newness of these technologies and the rapidity with which technological changes are taking place throughout the would, developing countries must study carefully all the implications of introducing the new technologies, notably as regards the rational allocation of R&D resources, policies of manpower development and the organisation of skills from various disciplines.

2

KEY ASPECTS OF EXPORT MANAGEMENT

We generally think of exports as a series of business transactions involving the supply and shipment of various types of commodities and materials. This is, of course, true of 95 per cent of our export business. These exports are subsidised by Government through various incentive schemes and other measures, which induce manufacturers to export more, thereby earning foreign exchange for the country. It is a sad reflection of our times that these incentives are necessary. Despite higher productivity, we are still not in a position to export economically at world market prices, as any gains achieved by increases in efficiently are more than offset by the upward spiralling costs of materials and labour.

Even with these incentives, the time had case when India's traditional lines of exports such as texitiles, tea, jute, cotton and coffee will be greatly reduced because of increasingly still higher competition from other countries in fields in which we were once supreme. To offset this trend, we have in the past few years, entered the field of non-traditional exports like manufactured goods and engineering products, but the latent fear of all manufacturers and exports has been that these products may not be competitive enough in quality and price for sustained and continuous foreign exchange earnings. From a long term point of view, this fear should stimulate our exporters and manufacturers to greater efforts. We have, to think in terms of diversifying the aspects of our export trade and to tackle the problem from a wider perspective. The orientation of our thinking should, be flexible enough to recognise export outlets and opportunities which are not readily apparent on the surface.

One of the ways of doing this is to consider the feasibility of exporting *components and parts* to industries that are now being set up in developing countries. This is, in effect, a form of sub-contracting which could usefully be employed on such items as say, unfinished castings, forgings and stampings which could be machined and finished by the nascent industry in the developing country.

An extension of this *sub-contracting principle* can perhaps better be achieved by supplying parts or components to subsidiaries or associates of overseas collaborators of Indian manufacturers, who may have started a *joint-venture* in a developing country. However, one must be realistic about this, as it is obviously not always in the interest of the overseas principal to allow the India-based Company to supply component parts to a third country where he can perhaps export more profitably.

Nevertheless, mutual agreements can sometimes be worked out. For instance, the foreign exchange so earned by the Indian company can in turn be used to import components or raw materials from the parent firm. From a long-term point of view this approach may, in fact, turn out to be economically advantageous to the foreign Principal.

The logical extension of this type of collaboration may very well lead to the formation of tripartite joint-venture which perhaps has received serious attention so far. It may sometimes happen that, for political or balance of trade reasons, the stabilising catalytic influence of an Indian partner may be acceptable to all parties, whereas a straight-forward bilateral agreement between a foreign principal and the local entrepreneur in a developing country, might not receive the blessing of this Government. Form India's point of view, it is, however, preferable to consider the setting up of direct joint-ventures in developing countries in Africa and West Asia where we can supply our own know-how and management skills.

Equity participation in these joint-ventures can only be made by providing indigenously manufactured machine tools and equipment, as no foreign exchange would be permitted to be sent out of the country. Nevertheless, there are, at this moment, some 35 to 40 joint-ventures with Indian collaboration, operating in various parts of the world. The majority of them are in Africa.

The advantages of setting—up such joint-ventures lie in the fact that profits can be made in the following way:

We can derive payments in foreign exchange for know-how,

We can obtain royalties on the products that are being manufactured,

We can repatriate dividends on equity shares, and

Last but not least, we can, for the next decade or so, hope to export component parts and materials to the industries that are being set up, thereby ensuring a steady source of foreign exchange earnings and continuous work for our factories.

The Ministry of Commerce, was considering in what manner Indian entrepreneurs may benefit by way of import entitlements from foreign exchange earned through know-how, royalty and other such fees. That the Government of India is fully aware of the need to assist Indian parties undertaking collaberation or investments abroad was evidenced from the statement of Finance Minister where he said:

"Some fiscal encouragement needs to be given to our industries to encourage them to provide technical know-how and technical services to newly developing countries. I propose, therefore, to provide for a concessional rate of tax on dividends received by an Indian company from a foreign company on shares alloted to the Indian company in consideration for supplying technical know-how or rendering technical services. This concessional rate of 25 per cent will also be charged on royalties, commissions, fees etc., received by an Indian company from a foreign company for supply of technical know-how and technical service."

Another avenue open for exploration is the possibilities of exporting our engineering and technical skills. Development plans for various countries particularly in Africa, will entail a widespread use of project consultants as well as the employment of management personnel with experience. As an example, geogogical surveys, water well drilling programmes, irrigation schemes, dam construction, hydro-electric projects, air conditioning installations and the processing of agricultural products are projects which we, in India, are familiar with, having learnt our expertise the hard way. We have learnt at the hands of our foreign associates for over half a century and there is a wealth of talent, skills and know-how in our own country which has a great export potential if properly harnessed and applied. We have given insufficient thought to this aspect of technical consultancy not merely in the manufacture or production of goods but in the design and installation of engineering systems and processes.

Let us see another aspects and that is how best to show the rest of the world what we can offer them in the way of goods, products, technical services and engineering skills. Usually, it is through holding of International Fairs in India, participation in Fairs and Exhibitions abroad, sending out of trade delegations consisting of Government and representatives of trade and industry where we could tell the world what we produce and can offer them. While these are useful aids, they lack intelligent and long-term planning with the result that the fairs and exhibitions in this country tend to look more like the traditional Indian bazaar than act as a shop window of the country's development and degree of sophistication.

But no amount of exhibitions or sending of delegations abroad can give the peoples of other countries more than a second-hand idea of our capabilities. What is essential is that foreigners come here to see for themselves our factories, our methods and processes, the type of special skills we possess and the degree of sophistication we have achieved. I experienced this sort of impact, when I was invited by the Canadian Government to be their guest for what was termed "Operation World Markets"—part of their *export derive* for machinery and equipment. I visited plants and factories along with six other persons from India and about 200 other representatives from over 50 countries in Europe, Asia, Latin American and the West Indies.

In this way, one got an opportunity to see numerous factories and plants were again everything was so well organised that there was always sufficient time to be briefed initially on the particular company being visited and to have a general discussion and make necessary contacts at the end of the tour of the plant. It was amazing how much was achieved both by our hosts and the invitees in the space of 6 days—due mainly to the excellent pre-planning and clock-work efficiency of the Canadian Trade Ministry. The cost of the Canadian Government was mainly in their own currency in the return air fares, the transport charges between cities and the overnight stay in hotels, while the individual companies and chambers of commerce played host to the visitors during the day and often looked after entertainment in the evenings. Almost every country sent official and unofficial representatives and this 6-day visit resulted in billions of dollars worth of export orders, and also led to collaboration ventures, etc., although it was intended to be primarily a "See Canadian Industry" operation. A few weeks later, Canada put on a trade fair where they secured valuable orders for consumers and other products. An important feature here was that the invitation to each individual was from the Minister of Trade & Commerce, which lent great weight to the invitation. An operation of this nature organised by both Government and Industry would, to my mind, be far more effective as a means of promoting exports than all the other measures.

Finally, good publicity and the right type of Public Relations are essential in the context of developing exports and attracting interest of other countries to our own. We take great pains to illustrate our industries, factories and products in beautiful blow-ups of photographs which are displayed at exhibitions fairs and through other media but it seems that proper care is not taken always to depict the modernisation and sophistication of our industries, plants and products. The need is for a more flexible yet *pragmatic approach on the subject of exports*. We must continually seek different and new approaches, whilst at the same time modifying our attitudes to the shift of outside opinions in order to keep a public image abroad of which we can be proud.

INDIA'S SMALL INDUSTRY EXPORTS

In many countries, small industries are responsible for a large proportion of their countries' foreign exchange earnings. It is not always possible to give precise statistics because there are often no precise definitions abroad of small scale industry, as there is in India. Authoritative figures, however, how that in Japan, for instance, 67 per cent of that country's export trade is accounted for by small scale industries. It is probable that nearly 50 per cent of U.K.'s exports are achieved by what in India, would be classified as small scale industries.

In other countries, small scale units do export not because of Government compulsion or of financial incentives but because they find that, in the long run, it pays them better to export their products than to sell them in the home market. One of the firms in the U.K. which makes highly competitive consumer products with 25 employees and a capital of about Rs. 1 lakh, exported 80 per cent of its output simply because more profits were made by exporting than in the domestic market. Much of the world's. trade is conducted through comparatively small importing merchants abroad and it is frequently found that these merchants prefer to deal with smaller manufacturers upon whom they feel they can rely for personal attention much more than on large producers. If the Indian manufacturer wishes to import raw materials and machinery, or wishes to go abroad for study or on holiday, or if his family want the benefits of imported items, then that manufacturer must help to earn the necessary foreign exchange. Just because he is classed as a small scale industry does not mean that he can expect his bigger brothers in industry to do all the work for him. There is really no reason why Indian small scale industries should not emulate their counterparts in other countries. A survey showed that, in general, the quality of products made in the Indian small scale sector was suitable for overseas markets and that prices, generally, were suitable also.

The main definiency of Indian small industry is in the field of export know-how. Many small industries believe that all they need to know is at what prices competing products sell, in overseas markets and to have lists of names of importers to to whom they can just write a latter. Much more is needed;

This includes knowledge of what products are most suitable for which overseas markets; how to present those articles properly in the way of sales leaflets, catalogues, and packaging. It also includes knowledge of how to price the articles in a way acceptable to the foreign buyer, how to write attractive sales latters, how to ship the goods and prepare the shipping documents in a way which will give the importer no trouble, and how to arrange payment.

LESSONS FROM JAPAN

1. Need for Marketing Strategy

The success of the Japanese export programme was due largely to the highly developed *merchandising sense* of Japanese business, large and small. This sensitivity to the needs of foreign consumers *in terms of product, design, colour and quality* does not seem to exist widely among Indian proprietors of small industry. These skills must be developed if Indian small industry is to compete in the world markets.

2. Strengthening of Distribution Channels-Export Houses and Indent Houses

The Export House system of Japan has been a major factor for the success of Japanese foreign trade. They provide the necessary facilities for thousands of manufacturers on a scale which no individual firm could develop. Indian small industries should establish Export Houses with sufficient capital and competent trained personnel. There should be no more than 12 Export Houses for all India, and they should operate on a regional basis, such as Madras, Calcutta, Bombay, Delhi and other commercial centres. They should be organized in such a manner that there are three departments dealing respectively with domestic sales, exports, and imports. There should be no competition among Export Houses in foreign countries. Indent Houses (large general wholesalers in major foreign commercial centres) should be used extensively in collaboration with Export Houses.

3. Direct Contact with Foreign Markets

The Japanese practice of having merchant vessels stocked with the products of small manufacturers and going from one market to another could be effectively used by Indian manufacturers.

4. Encouragement of Export Drive

The desirability of tax concessions, import privileges and other forms of Government subsidy for those firms which are contributing substantially to India's foreign trade should be examined.

5. Encouragement of Foreign Collaboration

The investment environment in India cannot be considered favourable when contrasted with countries such as Malaysia, and Brazil. The obstacles placed in the way of investment and foreign capital should be eliminated and a generally favourable environment created.

FACTORS LIMITING EXPORTS & PROBLEMS FACED BY SMALL INDUSTRY

1. Internal Sellers' Market

The Sellers' Morket in India has been a major factor for the lack of export effort by business in general and small business in particular. Inferior merchandise is sold with little difficulty in the Indian market and the poor design and quality of this merchandise makes it difficult to sell them abroad where it has to compete with the products of countries who are more sophisticated industrially.

2. Heavy Tax Burden

A revision of the Indian tax system which would be designed to encourage export is highly desirable.

3. Poor Management of Small Units

General management in small industryi s not competent to compete in world markets. One man control, lack of delegation and administrative bottlenecks are evidence of this poor management. This situation is contrasted with the current Trends in small industry management in Japan, which includes greater use of consultants and the willingness to include non-family members at the higher levels of management.

4. Bottlenecks in Raw Materials

Small manufacturers have difficulty in obtaining raw materials and power. Small industries should be given greater opportunity to import the necessary raw materials when there is a reasonable certainty of their selling abroad and obtaining foreign exchange. The import entitlements currently provided by the government may be more extensive.

5. Bottlenecks in Technical Know-how and Semi-skilled Labour

The high rate of absenteeism among semi-skilled labourers, and the relative lack of technical skills which exist in the small sector are unfavourable factors.

6. Other Reasons for the Low Volume of Exports by Small-scale Industry

(a) Lack of modern marketing techniques,

(b) Poor packaging and product design,

(c) Poor brand policy,

(d) Lack of knowledge foreign markets by the small manufactures.

Japanese manufacturers obtain prompt and adequate market information of all major foreign markets from JETRO (Japanese Export Trade Organization—a market research organization sponsored jointly by the Japanese Government and Japanese industry).

7. Poor Understanding of Cost Accounting

Many Indian products are not priced realistically in world markets.

SMALL INDUSTRIES HAVING EXPORT POTENTIAL

These may be grouped into three major categories:

(a) Industries which had increased export sales each year.

(b) Industries which may be considered to be progressive because of exports which increased as compared with previous years.

(c) Industries whose sales decreased in comparison with previous years.

Traditional items of India's export trade such as tea, cotton, jute, cashew, spices and mica, are excluded. Also those products which are mainly in the large scale sector are excluded.

(a) Promising Exports

1. Oil cakes (including deflated groundnut meal)
2. Fruits and vegetables, fruits, fresh or dried
3. Groundnut Oil
4. Cotton piecegoods, handloom products
5. Coir manufactures (excluding fibre and yarn)
6. Coir mats and mattings
7. Lemongrass Oil
8. Prawns
9. Bristles
10. Plants and parts of plants for use in dyeing and tanning
11. Animal casing
12. Canned fish
13. Sewing machines and parts
14. Candles, tubes and articles of inflammable materials
15. Umbrellas, walking sticks and similar articles
16. Palmar.sa oil
17. Leather manufactures
18. Artificial leather.

(b) Progressive Exports

1. Geat skins and kid skins, undressed
2. Gums, resins

3. Lac
4. Carpets, floor rugs, mats and matting
5. Caster oil
6. Groundnut oil
7. Footwear
8. Handicrafts (such as artware)
9. Fruits
10. Vegetable oils (non-essential)
11. Household utensils of iron and steel
12. Meat, fresh, chilled or frozen
13. Soap and other cleansing preparations
14. Plastic goods
15. Linseed oil
16. Cutlery, including table and kitchenware.

(*c*) *Stagnant Exports*

1. Leather and leather manufactures
2. Hindes and skins, tonned or dressed
3. Leather undressed
4. Bones for manufacturing purposed
5. Plant, seeds, flowers mainly for use in medicine or perfumery
6. Opinum crude
7. Dressed and finished leather
8. Palm fibre
9. Sandalwood oil
10. Silver, platinum, gems and jewellery
11. Bidi leaves

12. Travel goods, handbags and similar articles
13. Coir fibre
14. Dry batteries
15. Niger seed.

Industries which may be considered to have prospects for export trade includes the following:

Bristles
Canned fish
Sewing machines
Carpets
Vegetable oils
Footwear
Household utensils or iron and steel
Meat—fresh, chilled and frozen
Soap and other cleansing preparations
Plastic goods
Silver
Platinum
Gems and jewellery
Bicycles
Preserved Fruit and Vegetables
Industrial and scientific instruments
Machine tools.

Studies of specific foreign markets by existing organizations in India that are concerned with small industry should be made. The Export Promotion Councils, Ministry of Commerce, Federation of Associations of Small Industry in India, and other associations with similar objectives could undertake these efforts if they are backed by sufficient funds and provided with experienced personnel. Various trade associations can play an important role in promoting exports. Such associations, with the help of the Government can encourage standardisation of products, advocate a high degree of integrity among industrialists, thus ensuring satisfactory dealings with foreign buyers. They can also encourage either voluntary or mandatory quality control system.

Use of samples in foreign markets through participation in foreing trade fairs by Indian manufacturers. Strengthening of existing export incentives—import entitlement—based on a company's export volume—ranging from 20 per cent up to 75 per cent of the rupee value of the exports are worth examining.

3

EXPORT FINANCING MECHANISMS

L.S. SARMA*

In view of the persistently high level of imports necessary to sustain the economies of the developing countries and their increasing external debt-servicing payments, the promotion of exports is of paramount importance to them. The task of increasing their export trade is, however, rendered extremely difficult by tariff barriers, import restrictions, and the formation of economic communities in different regions of the world. The developing countries have therefore been actively adopting various export promotion strategies, and intensifying measures for achieving a stronger growth of their traditional and non-traditional exports, particularly since the early 1970s.

A. TRADITIONAL AND NON-TRADITIONAL EXPORTS

One of the major problems facing the developing countries with regard to achieving export expansion is the commodity composition of their external trade. The bulk of their export earnings is accounted for by traditionai exports, which mainly consist of primary products. In the case of some developing

*L.S. Sarma is Adviser (Export Credit Guarantee and Insurance) to the Development Bank of Mauritius.

countries with long-established manufacturing capacities, however, the traditional exports also cover various items of manufactured goods such as cotton textiles. There are inherent limitations to the growth potential of traditional export products, which may be summarized as follows:

(a) Inelasticity of international demand for many of the products;

(b) Continuously rising domestic demand resulting in limited availability of products for export;

(c) Higher domestic prices in respect of several commodities compared with international prices, which weakens the effort to export;

(d) Growing competition in world markets as well as emerging substitutes;

(e) Quantitative and other restrictions imposed by the developed countries.

In view of these limitations, it became imperative for developing countries to launch industrialization programmes for the long-term expansion of new exports of processed and manufactured goods.

While efforts to improve exports of traditional items are continued, it is the export of non-traditional items like light engineering products, chemicals, garments and also agro-based industrial products, which could more quickly contribute to an appreciable rise in the foreign exchange earnings of developing countries. The more industrialized of such countries have already been achieving a higher export growth rate in this way, and from the export of capital goods as well in some cases. The non-traditional export items comprise many dynamic product groups whose export growth can be sustained without being adversely affected by a temporary fall or rise in domestic demand and which have good potential markets abroad. The experience of some developing countries has also shown that traditional products like coffee, tea, cashew nuts and spices can be turned into non-traditional or dynamic export products by processing them so as to realize a higher unit value, or can be produced as finished products, like instant coffee and tea, and powered spices, instead of being exported in raw and bulk form. However, in endeavouring to promote their exports of manufactured products, the developing countries are faced with the problem of offering credit to the overseas buyers, which does not normally arise in the case of their traditional exports.

B. THE IMPORTANCE OF EXPORT CREDIT

Competition in world markets, both for consumer and capital goods, is becoming increasingly intensified and, in this situation, the bargaining power has shifted from the seller to the buyer, who tends to dictate terms in regard to price, quality and delivery schedules and above all, insists on appropriate credit terms. The availability of an adequate supply of credit at reasonable cost, therefore, greatly facilitates the task of the exporter and serves as an incentive to augment his export efforts. The difficult foreign exchange position in many countries makes it imperative for importers to ask for credits of varying duration, and the credit terms offered often influence the buyer's choice of supplier and thus the source of supply.

Export Credit

Its availability and cost has thus become an important tool of export promotion in developing countries. Owing to the inability of any exporters to finance large-scale export transactions on credit terms in many overseas markets from their own resources, they are constrained to turn to their governments and financial institutions for assistance in this regard. Even the leading exporting countries like the United States, the Federal Republic of Germany and Japan have been increasingly developing comprehensive systems and institutions for the provision of export finance. While effecting structural changes in exports from primary products to semi-manufactured and manufactured goods, it is necessary for developing countries to introduce suitable export financing systems, and the export financing mechanisms so evolved should embrace the two essential aspects of credit:

Its availability and its cost.

1. Availability of Credit

The question of availability needs to be viewed from the standpoint of manufacturer-exporters as well as of merchants or traders engaged in export business. The experience in many developing countries has indicated that whereas well-established exporters of undoubted means and standing are largely able to secure their credit requirements from the commercial banks, the "second line" borrowers—the small and medium exporters—have difficulty in obtaining the necessary credit. Banks may grant credit against LC's to these exporters, but they are not eager to make credit available against firm orders, except when export credit guarantees are forthcoming. Further, in the case of new markets for traditional goods or new non-traditional export lines, there is a natural hesitation and caution on their part because, in their view, the risk involved in more than ordinary. The essence of the problem is not merely adequate security, but assessment of the risk on the basis of information about markets and overseas buyers. The situation is different in developed countries, where commercial banks play an active role in export promotion. They have set up very useful information systems regarding the export potentialities and import regulations of various countries and the creditworthiness of overseas buyers. The banking system in developing countries, therefore, need to be staffed with more trained personnel to provide similar services for effective export growth, and the banks should also ensure that no worthwhile export order languishes for want of credit.

2. Cost of Credit

The cost of providing financial assistance to the exporter is as important as the availability of credit. Concessionary rates of interest on export credit have been regarded as one of the effective incentives for export promotion, the intention being to strengthen the competitive ability of the exporter in international markets. Any reduction in the cost of credit will help to scale down the cost of production and to assist the exporter in either granting extended credit to the overseas buyer at a lower rate of interest or in reducing his selling price.

In any scheme designed to reduce the cost of export finance, it will be necessary to set a ceiling on the rates of interest charged by banks to exporters at various stages of their operations. If a ceiling on the interest rates is to be effective without constraining the availability of credit to the exporter, due consideration needs to be given to:

(a) The provision of an adequate refinancing facility to banks;

(b) The maintenance of a reasonable spread between the cost of raising funds by banks and their lending rates.

A satisfactory margin can be assured to banks if they are granted refinancing facilities at a cheaper or concessional rate, so that the quantum of spread between the borrowing and lending rates offers the banks a sufficient incentive to lend to the export sector.

C. FINANCIAL NEEDS OF EXPORTERS

To a limited extent, the exporter may be able to meet the financing needs of an export transaction through the advance payment he secures from the overseas buyer and the credit allowed to him by his suppliers, supplemented by his own funds. However, the major portion of export finance required for the execution of sales contracts or orders needs to be provided by the commercial banking system and other financial institutions. The commercial banks play a very important role in the provision of the working capital finance required by exporters, and in more developed countries, there are also specialized institutions, such as development bank and export/import banks that provide export financing facilities to meet the diverse needs of exporters.

Export credit may be classified from two main standpoints—the stage at which it is provided, and its duration. Firstly, the credit extended for facilitating production, processing or packing of export goods up to the point at which they are placed on board the ships or other means of transportation is termed the *pre-shipment credit*. The financing of export goods from the stage of shipment to the date of realization of the export proceeds is known of the *post-shipment credit*. Secondly, credit is also viewed in terms of duration—short, medium and long term. Short-term credit generally implies accommodation for a period of 90 days, but may extend for longer. Medium-term credit covers a period of over 180 days up to five years, whereas long-term credit usually relates to periods of more than five years. This categorization, however, may from country to country.

Short-term financing is of vital importance to developing countries because of the type of products that most of them sell abroad. The traditional products comprising primary commodities and the non-traditional manufactures and consumer goods are generally exported on a short-term repayment basis. The other non-traditional items of a complex and sophisticated nature, such as engineering goods and industrial projects, need medium and long-term export financing and are often called "term exports." In view of the diversity in the stages of economic development of developing countries and also the widely differing export trade patterns and economic systems, it is rather difficult to structure export credit schemes that are suitable to all countries. However, based on the experience of some of the leading developing countries, which have been successfully operating export financing schemes, a broad framework of export financing mechanisms and their various aspects will be outlined in this chapter. The finacial assistance required from commercial banks for the different categories of exports is shown on page 44.

D. SHORT-TERM FINANCE

1. Pre-shipment financing

The exporter needs pre-shipment finance for securing the raw materials and other inputs required for the execution of an export order and also to arrange for the shipment of these goods to the foreign market. Banks in developing countries, which have introduced export finance systems, have adopted flexible schemes of pre-shipment financing to provide timely financial assistance to exporters against their export orders or contracts at reasonable cost and in adequate measure.

(a) Definition of Pre-shipment Credit

It is difficult to define pre-shipment credit precisely enough to convey its manifold aspects. However, it may be defined as any loan or advance granted, or any other credit provided, by a financial institution to an exporter for financing the purchase, processing or packing of goods, on the basis of letters of credit opened in his favour by an overseas importer of the goods, or upon a confirmed and irrevocable order for the export of the goods, or any other evidence of the placement of an order with the exporter. The maximum period for which any loan or advance may be granted or any other credit facility may be provided does not usually exceed 180 days, or such extended period as the central bank of the exporting country may allow. The pre-shipment credit ordinarily means a packing credit loan or an advance granted to an exporter. There are normally two ways open to an exporter to obtain finance at the pre-shipment stage:

Anticipatory letters of credit and packing credits.

(i) Anticipatory letters of credit

These are also called the red clause letters of credit. A red clause LC is a normal LC, which contains a special clause (usually typed in red) authorizing the negotiating/advising or confirming bank:

To make immediate payment to the exporter in full or in part of the amount of the LCs, or

To make payment to the exporter from time to time as per the terms provided therein and against specified documents and/or fulfilment of specified conditions, *e.g.*, an undertaking from the beneficiary to the effect that the amount drawn will be utilized for payment of the cost of raw materials to be consumed by him (exporter) from time to time, and that the relevant shipping documents will be presented to the bank for negotiation within a specified period.

The red clause LC is generally opened to enable the exporter to procure materials and execute the foreign buyers' order without locking up too much of his own funds. The advance made to the exporter is of course at the risk of the opening bank and is restricted to the amount authorized in the red clause LC. The bank must ensure that there are proper instructions on the red clause LC as regards reimbursement of the amount to be advanced to the .exporter. Generally, the reimbursement of the pre-shipment advance under a red clause LC is provided by the negotiation of a clean draft under the LC, in which case the invoice submitted at the time of the negotiation of the documents should show a deduction to the extent of the drawings already made. Before advancing against a red clause LC, it is advisable to ensure that the bank will be in a position to negotiate/purchase the bills drawn under the LC. This can be ascertained by reviewing the LC and ensuring that its terms and conditions are not violating any Exchange Control Regulations/Stipulations within the sanctioned limit of the bank.

(ii) Packing Credits

Foreign buyers do not generally establish red clause letters of credit. As a result, the exporter has to approach his own bankers to grant him the pre-shipment facility by way of a packing credit. As already defined above, a packing credit is essentially a loan or advance granted by a bank to an exporter to assist him in buying, processing, packing and shipping the goods. These advances are made by commercial banks in different forms. The concept of the packing credit has been pioneered in the Indian system of export credit provision and is emphasized in this chapter because of its special relevance to the needs of many exporters in developing countries who operate at low cash flow levels.

(b) Forms of Advances

The three main forms of financing the exports at the pre-shipment stage are:

> Loans, overdrafts and cash credits. All three forms are prevalent in different parts of the world. Overdrafts are most common in the Federal Republic of Germany, France, Italy, Switzerland and the United Kingdom. In the United States and Japan, term loans for short periods are the main form of short-term financing. The cash credit system, which is more or less like the overdraft, is widely used in countries such as India. The main features of the systems—their advantages and disadvantages—are briefly summarized below.

(i) Loans

In a loan account, the entire amount is paid to the borrower at one time, either in cash or by transfer to his current account. No subsequent debit is ordinarily allowed, except by way of interest and other expenses incurred for the protection of the security. Repayment is generally stipulated by instalments. There is usually a condition that, if an instalment remains unpaid, the entire amount of the loan will become due. The security may be personal or in the form of shares, debentures, government bonds, immovable property, and goods. The main advantage of the loan system is that the loans are for predetermined short periods and have a built-in programme of repayment. They are automatically reviewed by banks on the due

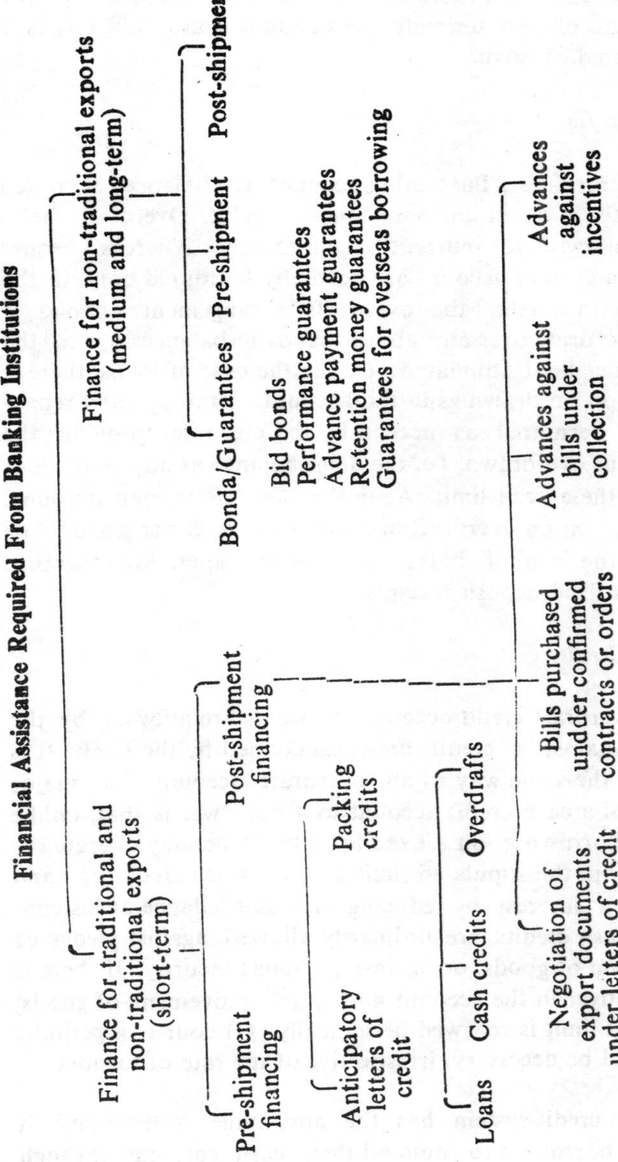
Financial Assistance Required From Banking Institutions
Finance for traditional and non-traditional exports (short-term)
Finance for non-traditional exports (medium and long-term)
Pre-shipment financing
Post-shipment financing
Bonda/Guarantees
Pre-shipment
Post-shipment
Anticipatory letters of credit
Packing credits
Bid bonds
Performance guarantees
Advance payment guarantees
Retention money guarantees
Guarantees for overseas borrowing
Loans
Cash credits
Overdrafts
Negotiation of export documents under letters of credit
Bills purchased undder confirmed contracts or orders
Advances against bills under collection
Advances against incentives

dates. The main disadvantage of the system is its inflexibility, and the need for borrowers to negotiate fresh loans every time. Verification of the ultimate use of funds is also difficult, as in the cash credit system.

(*ii*) *Overdrafts*

An overdraft is a fluctuating account, the balance of which is sometimes in credit and sometimes in debit. Overdraft facilities are allowed for current accounts only. Whereas cheques drawn on a current account are normally honoured only if the balance is in credit, the overdraft arrangement enables a customer to draw over and above his own balance up to the extent of the limit stipulated. Unlike the case of loans, there is no restriction on drawings in the account. Drawings and repayments are permitted as needed by the customer, provided the total amount overdrawn, *i.e.* the debit balance at any time, does not exceed the agreed limit. As in the case of a loan account, the security in an overdraft account may be either personal or tangible in the form of shares, government paper, life insurance policies and fixed deposit receipts.

(*iii*) *Cash Credits*

In an overdraft credit account, drawings are allowed by the borrower anainst a credit limit sanctioned by the bank. It is operated in the same way as an overdraft account. The major advantage of a cash credit account to a borrower is that, unlike the person borrowing on a fixed loan basis, he may operate the account within the stipulated limit as and when required, and can save on interest by reducing the debit balance at his convenience. Cash credits are ordinarily allowed against pledge or hypothecation of goods, or against personal security. If there is a good turnover in the account and quick movement of goods, a cash credit limit is renewed periodically. Of course, a periodic review would be necessary, irrespective of the rate of turnover.

The cash credit system has the advantage of flexibility. It enables the borrowers to route all their cash earnings through the account and keep drawings at the minimum level, thereby minimizing interest charges. As against this, because of the emphasis on the security aspect and the roll-over nature of the credits, the banks may find it difficult to ensure the end-use of funds, unless security for pre-shipment credits is segregated from the security offered for domestic credits.

While each system has its advantages and disadvantages, it is preferable for the choice of one or the other to be governed by the circumstances prevailing and the type of transaction. In the case of pre-shipment finance provided by banks in leading developing countries, the packing credit advances are granted to exporters by way of loans. For certain products, which are exclusively destined for exportation, pre-shipment credit may be given without firm orders or LCs, which may be preduced at a later date. In such cases, pre-shipment credit may by extended on a running account basis, as in the case of cash credit or overdrafts.

(c) Operational Mechanisms for Pre-Shipment Financing

Pre-shipment finance or packing credit is essentially working capital made available for the specific purpose of purchase/ processing/manufacturing of goods meant for export. All costs prior to shipment would be eligible for financing under packing credits, which are, in some respects, different from other types of working capital advances made for the domestic trade. Two essential features of such credits are the existence of an export order, and the liquidation of the advance out of the proceeds of the relative export bills. The cost of production of a number of products may be, at times, in excess of the world prices and thus various types of incentives, *viz.* cash subsidies and duty drawbacks may be given to exporters by their governments to enable them to compete in world markets. Cases may therefore arise of packing credits granted without margins and occasionally even in excess of the export prices. In the case of working capital advances for domestic trade, it will be ensured that the security charged to the bank does not suffer from defects such as non-marketability, lack of domestic demand, liability to wide fluctuations in prices, or difficulties in assessment of value. These considerations are not applicable when finance has been provided against goods meant for export against firm export orders. As these goods are sold forward at a fixed price, the considerations of local demand, marketability or price fluctuations do not apply in the same way as in the case of goods meant for domestic sale. Accordingly, the banks will entertain applications for packing credits regardless of some of the above defects, provided the borrower is of good standing and reliability.

Besides the usual requirements like the integrity, expertise, experience and creditworthiness of the exporter, the following points will usually be examined by the banks when considering proposals for export packing credits.

(i) The capacity of the exporter to execute the orders within the stipulated delivery schedules;

(ii) The financial viability of the export contract, in the event that the export business results in a loss, other the exporter has the ability to absorb such a loss;

(iii) Whether the quantum of finance asked for commensurate with the company's export turnover;

(iv) Whether appropriate arrangements have been made for the import to raw materials/components and, where relevant, the domestic purchase of such inputs;

(v) The spread of risk—the risk may be said to be well spread when goods are exported to a large number of overseas buyers residing in different countries;

(vi) Whether the exports are covered by irrevocable letters of credit, and if not, the status of overseas buyers must be ascertained;

(vii) The status of the issuing banks, where exports are covered by letters of credit;

(viii) The status of the buyer's country—both economic and political conditions in the buyer's country—may need examination to ensure that the proceeds of exports would be received in accordance with the terms of the relative orders;

(ix) The availability of security and whether appropriate export credit insurance cover is available;

(x) Whether the exchange risk has been covered, if necessary by making forward contracts, or by providing a suitable cushion within the price;

(xi) Whether export trade control and exchange control regulations in force have been complied with;

(xii) Whether the importer has complied with exchange regulations and/or import controls in force in his country;

(xiii) Whether freight space has been booked on a vessel sailing well in advance of the expiry date of the credit or the latest bill of lading date, if such date is stipulated.

(d) Salient Features of a Pre-Shipment Financing Scheme

The most common form of the advances granted by commercial banks to exporters at the pre-shipment stage is the packing credit, and such advances are often offered by commercial banks under the guidance of the Central Bank at concessional rates of interest. The salient features of a pre-shipment financing scheme are summarized below:

(i) The exporters, including merchant exporters, are to be provided with the necessary finance to enable them to import raw materials from external sources or procure locally, to process, manufacture goods and ship them eventually within the terms of the LCs or sales contracts with the overseas buyers;

(ii) The exporters of all goods and commodities should be eligible for the credit;

(iii) The advances may be sanctioned by way of overdrafts, packing credits or pre-shipment loans depending upon the items/goods to be exported and the nature of the sales contracts;

(iv) There should be no insistence on LCs for export. Credit should be available for all export orders whether against LC, D/P, D/A basis or on open account;

(v) The proposals should be considered on the basis of the integrity and capability of exporters, rather than upon the tangible securities they can offer to banks. The credits should be available against the security of lodgement of confirmed orders or contracts of sale under LCs, or otherwise. Export credit guarantees/insurance policies will be regarded as collateral;

(vi) The extent of finance should be need-based. It may not normally exceed the f.o.b. value of goods to be exported or the domestic cost of production of such goods, whichever is the lesser;

(vii) Remittances received by exporters by way of advance payment will be credited to the pre-shipment account. Alternatively, the pre-shipment credit sanctioned by the bank may be reduced to that extent;

(viii) The pre-shipment credit is liquidated by the purchase, negotiation or discounting of the export bills. It may also be adjusted by the advances granted against export bills;

(ix) The rate of interest should be preferential and as low as possible;

(x) The repayment period of credit depends on the time required for procuring, manufacturing or processing, packing and shipping the goods. In no case should it exceed six months or such time period as may be prescribed by the Central Banking authority of the country.

(e) Assessment of Working Capital Requirements

In the case of manufacturers-exporters having both domestic operations and an export business, it is the practice of the banks to assess the aggregate working capital requirements of each customer and to sanction the advances limit on the basis of the requirements so computed, with an appropriate allocation for the export packing credit.

Packing credit advances may be granted up to the full value of export orders, but in stages corresponding to the actual requirements of finance for the execution of the orders. In cases where the domestic cost of the goods exceeds the f.o.b. price contracted for, banks my grant at the pre-shipment stage packing credit advances up to a stipulated maximum amount over and above the f.o.b. value of the goods. In such cases post-shipment credit limits may be sanctioned so as to cover receivables and take account of cash assistance. After the proceeds of the relative export bills are credited to the packing credit account, the balance outstanding in the account should be transferred to the relevant post-shipment credit account. The method of assessment of over-all working capital requirements and fixation of export credit limits is outlined in annex I to this chapter.

(f) Procedures for Granting Advances

The following considerations are usually featured in the procedures for granting advances:

(i) An advance is generally granted only to *bona fide* exporters of good standing who maintain an account with the Bank. Generally, their export performance for the last two to three year is taken into consideration before granting the advance.

(ii) Credit limits are established in favour of regular exporters. Packing credit limits are considered together with the limits for post-shipment finance, as the pre-shipment finance is normally liquidated from the proceeds of the post-shipment advance or export bills.

(iii) The exporter must be reasonably sure of fulfilling his export obligations. He should also satisfy the bank that he will be in a position to procure/manufacture the goods required under the Export Order/LC, and that he would be in a position to effect the shipment of goods on time.

(iv) The application for packing credit should usually be accompanied by the following documents:

A written undertaking that the advance will be utilized for the specific purpose of procuring/manufacturing/shipping, etc. the goods meant for export only as stated in the relative Export Confirmed Order/LC;

The original Export Confirmed Order/Contract or LC;

A written undertaking—if the customer wants to have a packing credit advance against preliminary information by cable or telex, whereby at a later stage the Contract or LC, as the case may be, will be received by him—that the same will be made available to the bank within reasonable time for verification and endorsement;

A written undertaking—if the customer asking for packing credit is a sub-supplier and wants to supply the goods to the Export House or Merchant Exporter—from the Export House/Merchant Exporter stating that they have not/will not use a packing credit facility against the same transaction for the same purpose until the original packing credit is liquidated. However, the two parties may share the credit extended within the credit period on an agreed basis;

Security documents, *e.g.*, demand promissory note, packing credit agreement, letter of guarantee, where there is a guarantor, or any other documents required by the bank.

(g) Scrutiny

In the matter of scrutiny, the following points are relevant:

(i) The packing credit application should be signed by an authorized person and his signature must be verified;

(ii) Since the post-shipment advances are generally liquidated by purchasing/negotiating the export documents, at the initial stage, it should be ensured that the bank will be in a position to handle the export documents drawn under the relative Export Contract/LC. Banks providing pre-shipment credit may not always negotiate such documents;

(iii) Validity of the LC/Contract should be verified;

(iv) Banks generally do not finance against a revocable LC;

(v) The terms of the contract or LC should be in conformity with the terms of limit with regard to commodity and usance;

(vi) As far as possible, the submission of a proforma invoice for the purchase of goods should be insisted upon, and the price stated in the proforma invoice should be compared with the price in the local market;

(vii) In the case of a facility to be granted against confirmed contract/cable or telex messages, the bank should have a satisfactory credit report on the buyers.

(h) Disbursement Procedures

In the disbursement of pre-shipment credit, the following procedures will usually be followed:

(i) The terms and conditions of sanction of advances must be strictly adhered to. If there is any stipulation regarding margin, proper margin should be maintained, while computing the amount of advance to be disbursed;

(ii) When disbursement is to be made in stages (depending upon the needs of the exporter), the schedule of disbursement may be called for before granting the advance;

(iii) The significance of terms like f.o.b., c.i.f., c & f, etc. should be noted while calculating the margin/granting the advance. If the actual amount of freight and insurance premium to be paid is not known, them a deduction of about 10 to 15 per cent towards freight costs (in the case of shipments by sea) depending on the destination and of 1 to 2 per cent towards the cost of the insurance premium, should be made from the c.i.f. or c & f value, as the case may be, to arrive at the f.o.b. value. In the case of air freight, the percentage of freight cost may be about 25 to 40 per cent of the invoice value, depending upon the nature of the gods. The freight amount due on shipment can be granted when it actually becomes due, by issuing a cheque in favour of the shipping company. Likewise, insurance premiums can also be paid by the bank. It certain cases, advances are given to cover the cost of labour charges and packing charges when they are actually due; however, they may not exceed the f.o.b. value of the goods;

(iv) Generally, the advance allowed is on the basis of the f.o.b. value of the goods or the actual cost of production of the goods, whichever is the lesser.

(v) As far as possible, the advance should be made in favour of the supplier of the goods to the exporter towards the value of the goods to be supplied. This is to ensure that the advance granted is utilized for the specific purpose of obtaining the goods meant for export. However, it may not always be possible to issue a cheque in favour of the supplier. In this case, the exporter's current account may be credited with the amount sanctioned and he may be requested, as far as possible, to draw a cheque through his current account favouring the supplier. The bank should ensure that the advance given has been utilized for the purpose for which it was granted;

(vi) The Export Order/Contract or LC against which the advance is granted should be retained in the bank's custody.

(i) Follow-up of the Use of Advances

Ensuring the proper end-use of the funds advanced under packing credits is a most important function, since such advances entitle the borrowers to a concessional rate of interest and priority treatment in lending. Considering the clean nature of the advance at the initial stage (when the goods are not acquired and charged to the bank) the bank should be vigilant about the use of the advance made to the exporter. When a customer enjoys credit and has also secured and overdraft against stocks, there is a possibility of *double financing* involved as packing credit advances may be used to purchase stocks to cover the overdraft. This should be carefully watched and should not be allowed under any circumstances. Cash withdrawals may be necessary for remittance to other parties and for meeting overheads for manufacturing/processing out of the advance credited to the account of the exporter. In such casses, a close watch on the conduct of the account has to be kept to ensure that money borrowed from the bank is applied for the declared purpose.

Once the goods are acquired and are in the custody of the exporter for further processing/manufacturing/packing, it is advisable to convert the clean advance into hypothecation. Even though the physical custody of the goods lies with the exporter, the bank holds a lien on the goods. The conversion of the advance from the clean to the hypothecation state may, sometimes, require the bank to call for different sets of security documents as stated in their relevant sanction advice. It may also entail the obtaining of stock statements and proof of insurance covering the stock of goods for various hazards to which they are open. When the goods are ready for shipment and do not require further treatment at the exporter's factory, the bank may prefer to take the goods under its constructive custody, thus enhancing the security. In the case of advances to companies, it may be necessary to register the charge with the Registrar of Companies or other designated authorities.

Further measures of control and supervision of pre-shipment financing embrace the following considerations:

(i) Pre-shipment advances are ordinary self-liquidating in nature since they are adjusted out of the export proceeds of the relative goods. Hence, it is necessary to ensure that the exporter hands over the export bill to the bank for purchase/discount/negotiation or collection;

(ii) The duration of the adavance must be decided by keeping in view the time taken for the manufacture, processing, packing and forwarding of the goods under export for shipment overseas; it varies from 15 days to 6 months;

(iii) It is necessary for the bank to relate the duration of the advance to the date of expiry of the export letter of credit and/or the latest period of delivery stipulated in the export sales contract, and to ensure that the advance does not run beyond such date expiry;

(iv) It is also necessary to ensure that the advance is liquidated from the export bill proceeds as far as possible, unless the export does not take place owing to circumstances beyond the control of the exporter, when he may be permitted to repay the advance from his other resources. It is not uncommon to find cases in which the previous pre-shipment advance taken against a letter of credit lodged with the bank is repaid by using a fresh pre-shipment advance by means of lodging another export letter of credit in collusion with an overseas buyer. Hence, the importance of ensuring that the pre-shipment advance is repaid out of the export bill proceeds. When the export does not take place, any credit extended ceases to be eligible at a preferential rate of interest, and suitable measures must be taken to ensure compliance with this requirement;

(v) To have effective control over the pre-shipment advance it is desirable to grant it by way of a demand loan/fixed short-term loan repayable within a certain period depending on the time needed for the manufacture/processing/packing and forwarding of the goods for shipment, but not beyond the expiry date of the relative export credit/delivery date under the export sales contract;

(vi) A suitable limit/line of credit commensurate with the exporter's requirements and turnover should be fixed under which these pre-shipment loans should be granted for servicing individual export contracts. Appropriate diary notes should be taken to ensure the liquidation of these loans before the stipulated dates.

(j) Precautions Against Misuse of Funds

Pre-shipment credit facilities may be abused by unscrupulous exporters who obtain such a facility from one bank, either as a clean facility or as an advance against hypothecation of the goods or against a trust receipt covering the goods under export, and pledging them to another bank. As a result, double finance is obtained against one and the same export transaction and goods. With a view to preventing such misuse, the bank will normally insist upon the lodgement of the relative export LC with it so that the export bill to be drawn thereunder is negotiated through the advancing bank and its proceeds appropriated to liquidate the pre-shipment advance. Instances are not uncommon when exporters have diverted the funds in their hands, received by them by way of pre-shipment advances from their bankers, for some purpose other than exporting. The exporter should therefore be required to give a proper and periodical accounting of the pre-shipment advance made available to him, and this should be verified by the advancing banks to ensure the utilization of the funds for the purposes of export.

Banks often advise exporters to cover their exports invoiced in a foreign currency by taking up a suitable forward exchange cover. This will protect the exporter against wide fluctuations in local currency realizations under the export contracts in times of devaluation or revaluation of the foreign currency or local currency respectively. otherwise, the exporter may lose substantially in the amounts realized, resulting in erosion of the narrow profit margins in the export transactions. The advances granted to an exporter under packing credit loans are generally covered by packing credit guarantees issued by export credit insurance and guaranttee organizations in various countries. As these polices provide a good security to bankers against the packing credit advances, they generally stipulate the cover as a condition of the sanction of advances.

The central banks in dveloping countries can play a positive role in the ensuring that exporters have liberal access to adequate finance at reasonable cost. The commercial banks can be motivated by the Central Bank through the usual and well-established technique of providing liberal refinancing facilities to them. Such a scheme should be simple to operate and attractive to the banks. A broad outline of the pre-shipment credit refinance scheme of Central Banks, together with operational guidelines for the commercial banks, is given in annex II to this chapter.

2. Post Shipment Financing

Exporters who sell goods abroad usually have to wait for some time before payment is received from overseas buyers. The period of waiting will depend upon the terms of payment, and the need for post-shipment finance to strengthen the financial position of the exporter varies accordingly. Based on different terms of payment, the banks have devised various methods of financing. The Central Banks in many developing countries have laid down exchange control regulations relating to the export of goods, and some of the important regulations generally stipulated for exports are given below.

(a) All exports must be declared on a prescribed form by the exporter;

(b) Banks handling export documents should receive remittances from importing countries or obtain reimbursement from their brances or correspondents in the countries appropriate to the final place of destination of goods:

(c) The amount representing the full value of the goods exported must be realized by the exporter within the prescribed time limit—generally within six months from the date of export;

(d) It is obligatory for banks to maintain certain books, such as an export bill register, indicating the full details of the export bills handled by them;

(e) It is generally stipulated that any reduction in the value of the the export bill amount after the bill has been negotiated or sent for collection requires the prior approval of exchange control;

(f) Banks should normally watch the realization of bills and, in cases where they remain outstanding, they should be followed up promptly with the exporter concerned. If the exporter fails to arrange for receipt of the proceeds within a reasonable period after the expiry dates, the necessary permission for extension of time should be obtained by the exporter from the exchange control authorities.

There is no universally acceptable definition of post-shipment credit. However, for a developing country, it may be defined as any loan or advance granted or any other credit provided by a bank to an exporter of goods from a country from the date of extending the credit after shipment of the goods to the date of realization of the export proceeds within 180 days, which is usually the maximum permissible period including the grace period. Any loan or advance granted to an exporter on the security of export incentives, if any, accruing to the exporter may also be considered as post-shipment credit.

While there are various forms in which the post-shipment advances are granted by banks all over the world, the major types of such advances are:

Negotiation of export documents under LCs;

Purchase of export bills drawn under confirmed export contracts or orders;

Advances against export bills under collection;

Advances against export incentives;

Advances against goods exported on consignment;

Advances against duty drawback entitlements;

Advances against undrawn balances;

Advances against retention money.

Before considering the operational aspects of the above-mentioned forms of pre-shipment finance, it is necessary to bring out some salient aspects of the advances against export bills.

(a) Common Features of Advances Against Export Bills

Advances to exporters against documentary export bills are essentially to be considered as advances against documents of title to goods. While making such advances, the lending bank mainly relies upon the standing of the exporter against whom it has recourse in the bill remains unpaid. It is the general practice of banks to advance against, or purchase, only those bills drawn on overseas buyers on whom satisfactory reports are available. In the case of any reasonable doubt as to the integrity or standing of the drawee, or if difficulties are anticipated in the realization of the export proceeds, banks prefer to accept such bills on a collection basis *i.e.* the exporter's account is credited only after the realization of the bill amounts.

The following features are common in respect of advances to exporters against export bills:

(i) When the export documents are suumitted under LCs for negotiation, or have been purchased under the Contract or are for obtaining any type of advance against the documents at the post-shipment level, the first step is to scrutinize them with reference to relative limits sanctioned. Stipulations regarding commodity character, margin and value should also be ascertained.

(ii) When the bills are presented for negotiation under LC, the bank generally has clear-out instructions as regards the terms and conditions to be followed. However, in the case of bills drawn under contract order, no such guidance may be available. In this case, since the bank acts on behalf of the drawer of the bill and as his agent, clear instructions must be obtained from the drawer of the bill regarding the course of action which the bank should take with regard to all important issues relating to the handling of the bill. The drawer should give definite instructions as regards protesting of the bill in case of dishonour by non-payment or non-acceptance.

(iii) Instructions regarding the fate of the bill are also important, particularly in the case of perishable goods when prompt clearance, storage and sale are important factors. To protect the interest of the customer as well as the bank, the bank may be interested in knowing the fate of the bill by cable.

(iv) Instructions as regards payment of charges should be obtained.

(v) In the case of export documents drawn under LCs, however, instructions contradictory to the terms mentioned in the LC are not acceptable, since the bank has to act as per the instructions of the documentary LC.

(vi) A full set of 'on Board' Bill of Lading documents must be submitted to the bank. The insurance policy for an adequate amount must be in the negotiable from and should cover the necessary risks. All documents called for, as per the terms of contract, should also be submitted. In the case of documents drawn under LC, the terms and conditions of the LC, which from the underlying contract, should be complied with.

(vii) In the case of usance bills, the bank should that they are adequately stamped as per the requirements of the prevailing Stamp Act.

(viii) The bank should take into consideration the Forward Exchange contract, if any, made by the exporter.

(b) Negotiation of export documents under letters of credit

Trading under LCs involves many parties from different countries subject to different national laws and ways of interperting the same terms. It therefore become imperative to adopt the same terminology and the same interpretation of the terms used in the LC in order to avoid disputes and to safeguard the interests of the parties involved. With this intention, the International Chamber of commerce has recently published a revised version of its *Uniform Customs and Practices for Documentary Credits* (UCPDC). The banks in many developing countries have adopted these and therefore negotiate the export documents drawn under LC only if the LC bears a cluse stating that the same is being issued subject to the UCPDC. However, when there is a contradiction between the terms of the LC and the prevailing exchange control regulations the bank handling exports documents should ask the exporter to have the LC amended so that the conditions stated therein do not violate these regulations.

When the export documents are presented to the bank for negotiation, the bank should make a rapid check of the LC and the documents submitted thereunder. LCs are basically of two types, *viz*. revocable and irrevocable. By virtue of the drawback attached to the revocable LC that it can be cancelled/amended at any moment without obtaining the concurrence from the exporter, banks seldom finance or undertake negotiation of export documents drawn under this type of LC. Since irrevocable LCs cannot be cancelled or amended without the agreement of the parties thereto, these types of LCs offer better security, provided all the terms and conditions of the LCs are complied with. Negotiation of documents under such LCs and financing thereunder is, therefore, undertaken by commercial banks.

(c) Scrutiny of Documents

Discrepancies, even though of a purely formal nature should not be ignored. Even a slight deviation of the documents from these specified in the LC and interpreted as per the current version of the UCPDC can cause the issusing bank to refuse reimbursement of the payment already may be the negotiating bank. A bank negotiating defective documents without prior and specific authority from the issuing bank carries a risk of non-payment. The careful examination of export documents when presented for negotiation is therefore very important and the following observations are pertinent:

(i) In the first instance, the bank should ascertain the genuieness of the LC. Banks do come across fraudulent LCs purported to have been issued by institutions that do not exist.

(ii) It has also been observed that even though some LCs are genuine, they contain an onerous type of clause, *e.g.*, an LC made available for negotiation at the counters of the credit-opening bank in a foreign location. It clearly means that, to establish the liability of the issuing bank, it is necessary that the documents in conformity with the credit terms reach the counters of the credit-opening bank before the time limit stipulated, which the negotiating bank cannot guarantee.

(iii) Some LCs are made operative only when an Import Licence is granted in the country of import.

(iv) Sometimes, it is conveyed by the credit-opening bank to the beneficiary that the credit is opened under finance made availalable by multilateral agencies, that it is provisional in nature, and that it becomes valid only after the receipt of a Letter of commitment from the financial instiution concerned. In other words, such types of credit are inoperative until the receipt of further intimation to make the credit effective.

(v) Incidents are not unknown when payment under LC is to be made available after the occurrence of an uncertain event, *e.g.*, drafts are to be drawn on the credit at 30 days from the date the carrying ship arrives at the port of destination, and the negotiating bank is to be notified about the maturity date of the draft by the credit-opening bank as soon as the ship reaches the destination. The effect of the clause normally indicates that the liability of the credit-opening bank and that of the opener to pay under LC would arise only if and after the carrying ship has reached the destination.

In scrutinizing export documents the banks would be expected to review the various documents with the following considerations uppermost:

(*i*) *Letter of credit*

Whether the credit is revocable or irrevocable;

Whether the credit is 'restricted' or 'open'. If the credit is restricted for negotiation to some other bank, the bank should not negotiate the bill;

Whether the credit is valid for negotiation or has expired. If it has expired, the validity of the credit should be extended;

Whether the credit contains certain 'offending clauses'.

(*ii*) *Bill of exchange*

It must be drawn by the beneficiary only;

The drawee should be as per the terms of the credit;

It should be made payable to or endorsed in favour of the negotiating bank. Sometimes the letter of credit may authorize payment against documents only in such cases, it is not necessary to call for a bill of exchange;

The bill amount must be within the credit amount and should bear the same relation to the invoice value as given in the credit.

(*iii*) *Invoice*

The type of invoice—whether commercial or consular—required, and the number of copies needed;

The invoice should be prepared in the name of the opener unless the credit requires otherwise;

The description of the goods must correspond with the description in the credit;

The quantity of goods, if given in the credit, should be checked from the invoice.

(*iv*) *Marine insurance policy*

It should be checked whether the insurance policy or the certificate is required. If the policy is required, the certificate cannot be accepted;

The insurance document must be issued by an insurance company or an underwriter;

A policy convering the risk as required by L/C should be accepted. When the credit stipulates insurance against all risks, the bank may accept an insurance document containing any 'all risks' notation or clause;

If the insurance policy bears a date later than the date of the bill of lading, the bank may refuse to accept it;

The amount of insurance policy should be as given in the credit and must be in the currency as the credit;

The policy should be endorsed in blank or in favour of the negotiating bank;

The description of the goods in the policy may be in general terms but should not conflict with the description in the other documents;

The insurance policy should/cover the shipment during the entire voyage and should be a current and valid policy.

(v) *Bill of lading*

It should be submitted in all its negotiable copies (*i.e.*, a full set) unless the credit stipulates otherwise;

It should be seen whether the credit requires an 'on board' or 'received for shipment' bill of lading. If the former, the latter should not be accepted;

The date of the bill of lading should be no later than the latest date of shipment given in the credit. If the bill of lading is submitted with undue delay after its issuance, it should be considered as stale and not accepted;

The bill of Lading should be clean. 'Claused' bills of lading should not be accepted, unless the credit permits them;

The port of shipment and port of destination should be as given in the credit. If trans-shipment is permitted, a "through bill" of lading should be accepted;

A general description of the goods in the bill of lading, which does not conflict with the description as given in the credit, may be accepted. The quantity should not be less than that given in the invoice. If the credit does not provide for part shipments, the bill of lading should show the shipment of the entire quantity;

If the credit is opened on a c.i.f. or c & f basis, the bill of lading should show that freight has been paid;

The name of the beneficiary should appear in the bill of leading as either shipper or endorser. Its should be drawn and endorsed as required by the credit. The bill of lading made out in favour of the consignee (importer) should not be accepted unless permitted by the credit. Normally, a bill of lading made out to order (of the shipper) and blank endorsed (by him) is required.

Some of the major discrepanies observed in export documents are:

Documents presented after expiry of the credit;

Merchandise shipped after expiry of the shipping date;

Drawing in excess of the credit amount;

Weight in invoice differs from weight in wieght list and deductions shown in the invoice not authorized by L/C;

Stale bill of lading;

Bill of lading "claused" shipped on deck;

Bill of lading marked 'Freight paid' instead of 'payable at destination' (and *vice versa*);

'Received for shipment' bill of lading presented;

Description of goods differs;

Port of destination differs;

Original L/C reported lost;

Name of the beneficiary differs;

Insufficient insurance coverage.

If the documents are found to be irregular or contain discrepancies, the bank has the following courses open to it:

(i) It may ask the beneficiary to rectify the discrepancies, if possible, and to resubmit the documents for negotiation;

(ii) It may negotiate the bill under reserve or against the indemnity of the beneficiary, in the case of minor discrepancies.

(iii) It may, in the case of major discrepancies:

Seek instructions from the opening bank by cable for its authority to negotiate the bill despite the discrepancies;

Ask the beneficiary to give his bank's indemnity or to pay his bank under reserve. If the beneficiary is its customer, negotiate the bill and hold the amount in reserve, or credit his account and earmark the amount until the reserve is lifted or payment of the bill is made by the opening bank/ opener;

Send the bill for collection and pay only after realization of the bill.

From the above alternatives, it is clear that the choice depends on several factors such as the financial standing of the customer, and market and political conditions in the drawee's country. If the bill is in order, the bank would negotiate the bill as per the negotiation clause of the credit, dispatch the documents and obtain reimbursement from the opening bank.

In the case of bills negotiated under LC, the negotiating bank holds recourse to the customer in case of refusal of payment by issuing bank on account of discrepancies. It is therefore immaterial whether the drafts drawn thereunder are without recourse. However, this is not the case when the LC is confirmed by the negotiating bank and the bill is negotiated clean. Therefore, if the finance is made available by negotiation of a confirmed LC without pointing out any discrepancy, the confirming bank loses the recourse to the beneficiary. Also, in the case where the bank specifically acts as an accepting or paying banker, as per the request of the issuing bank, and makes the payment clean or accepts a draft drawn on the bills (without pointing out any discrepancy), it loses the recourse against the beneficiary/exporter.

(d) Bills Purchased Under Confirmed Export Contracts or Orders

Export bills not drawn under letters or credit are usually referred to as 'non-credit' bills, *i.e.*, bills not supported by letters of credit. As the exporter does not wish to block his funds in the export transaction, he raise finance on his documentary bill from the bank which 'purchases' it (if it is a demand/sight bill) or 'discounts' it (if it is a usance bill). The exporter is immediately paid the bill amount (less margin, if any) on submission of the documents to the bank, which charges a commission or discount on the bill transaction. The bank forwards the documents to its overseas branch or correspondent in the importing country and arranges for the realization of the bill.

The facility of purchasing or discounting foreign (export) bills is granted by the bank if it is satisfied about the customer's financial standing, his reputation and business integrity and his capacity to repay the bill amount in case of non-payment. The other factors taken into account by the bank are the buyer's (drawee's) standing, market conditions in the importing country, the nature of the goods covered by the bill (s), and the export/import trade control/exchange control regulations in the drawer's/drawee's countries respectively. The bank may be unwilling to purchase/discount bills from an exporter-customer, because the amount may be in excess of the facilities which it is prepared to offer to the drawer, or it may be considered high for a particular drawee. In such cases, the exporter may cover the transaction under an export credit insurance policy, and the bank would grant the credit facility required by the exporter against it.

The exporter continues to be liable on the bill as its drawer until such time as the importer on whom it is drawn pays the bill according to its tenor. If the bill is dishonoured, the exporter has to repay the amount of the bill to the bank together with interest and charges. The bank also has the security of documents in documentary bills (legally speaking, it has the constructive pledge of goods covered by the documents). But, in the case of usance bills drawn on D/A (documents against acceptance) terms, the bank losses control over this additional security on delivery of documents to the drawee after acceptance of the bill by him. Therefore, it may tighten its margin requirements when discounting such bills, treating them on a par with clean bills.

Before purchasing or discounting documentary bills, the bank varifies the documents in order to ensure that are valid, in negotiable form and compete in all respects. This is essential to establish that the bank's legal/security rights are not jeopardized in any way, and that it is in a position to pass a valid title to the subsequent parties, and ultimately to the drawee of the bill.

(e) Advances Against Bills Under Collention

Sometimes there may be no accommodation to cover the entire amount of the bill by purchasing under the available limits sanctioned to the exporters, or the document drawn under LC may have discrepancies, which may not be acceptable to the overseas buyer. The bank, therefore, will not want to take a risk. In such a situation, considering the immediate need and financial requirements of the exporter, the bank may finance to some extent out of the total bill an amount by way of "Advance against Bills under Collection." The amount advanced will be adjusted out of the proceeds of the export bill and the balance paid to the exporter.

If the bank agrees to purchase/discount/negotiate a bill, it becomes, in effect, the purchaser of the bill and, in most cases, achieves the status of a 'holder in due course.' When the bank advances against bills sent in by the customer for collection, it does not become a party to the bill of exchange, but simply collects the proceeds as agent of its customer; it has only the hypothecation charge on the proceeds of bills collected. As mentioned earlier, the bank may advance the full amount of the bills, or only an agreed percentage of the total, retaining some security margin. What it does will depend mainly upon the exporter's financial standing, his capacity to repay the amount advanced and, wherever possible, on the drawee's standing and the conditions obtaining in the importing country.

(f) Adanvces Against Export Incentives

Several export incentives are provided to exporters under

Export Promotion Schemes instituted by a number of governments to compensate exporters for some of the losses incurred in their export business. Such losses arise mainly because the domestic cost of production and prices of some export items are much higher than their international prices. Cash Compensatory Support is one of the important incentives given by governments to the eligible exporters. Advance against this Cash Compensatory support are made available to exporters by commercial banks as loans, generally at the post-shipment stage. These advances are treated as clean advances.

Since the full amount of cash incentives claimed by the exporter may not be received, advances are generally made within a 10 to 20 per cent margin. An irrevocable Power of Attorney has to be receive direct payment from the government authorities against export incentive advances financed by the bank. The bank shall request the authorities to pay the claim in the name of the bank by cheque and after receipt of the cheque, the advance allowed will be liquidated out of the proceeds of the cheque and the balance paid to the exporter customer. In the case of a shortfall in the amount received, the same will be recovered from the exporter.

(g) Advances Against Goods Exported on Consignment

Where exports are made on a consignment basis, and particularly where no regular order has been obtained or contract entered into, and the arrangement envisages the sale of goods abroad by the exporter's agent on the basis of available demand, there could not be an export bill. Correspondingly, there would be no negotiation of an export bill, or a grant or advance against the export bill for collection. In such cases, the banks may make post-shipment advances to the exporter on the basis of consignment value after retaining an appropriate margin to provide for any likely erosion in the amount of receivables.

(h) Advances Against Duty Drawback Entitlements

Where a commodity for export has an import content on which has been paid at the time of import, the Government may allow an appropriate duty drawback payment. Against such an entitlement, a bank may give post-shipment credit for a suitable period until the release of the amount from the designated agency within the country.

(i) Advances Against Undrawn Balances

In the case of certain products, it is the practice of overseas importers to stipulate the drawing of an export bill for an amount less than 100 per cent of the balance assessed for release, on the basis either of the purity of the commodity or the weight as assessed by the importer. Even against the amount remaining so undrawn, banks may grant post-shipment credit to the exporter for a period of 90 days after retaining a suitable margin, depending upon the past experience in the realization of the undrawn amount in the case of such products.

((j) Advances Against Retention Money

In the case of overseas construction contracts, where the contractual terms include the retention of a certain percentage of the payment to be released at a later date, banks may advance to the project exporters and construction contractors when it is not possible for them to obtain the release of such an amount against bank guarantee. Bank credit could be at the stipulated rate of interest applicable to post-shipment credit, for a period of 90 days, when the retention money is in respect of supplies and the amount is to be received within a period of one year.

(k) Salient Features of a Post-shipment Financing Scheme

The common forms of advances to exporters granted by commercial banks at the post-shipment stage have been discussed above. Post-shipment financing schemes are often introduced by commercial banks under the guidance of the Central Bank at concessional rates of interest. The salient features of such schemes are given below, and they are applicable to all forms of post-shipment advances mentioned earlier.

(i) Post-shipment financing refers to any loan or advance granted, or to any type of credit provided by a bank, to an exporter of goods from the date of extending the credit, (after the goods are exported by any means of transport) to the realization of the sale proceeds.

(ii) The credit may be extended either by purchase of foreign demand bills, by discounting of foreign usance bills, by negotiation of export bills or by making advances against foreign bills sent for collection, whether backed by a letter of credit or not.

(iii) The rate of interest on post-shipment credit should be concessional as in the case of the pre-shipment credit scheme.

(iv) The period of credit depends on the tenure of the export bill. As exchange control regulations generally require the export proceeds to be repatriated within 180 days from the date of shipment, the maximum period allowed for post-shipment credit should not normally exceed 180 days.

(v) The credit limit should be flexible and determined in proportion to the exporter's past performance and anticipated export turn-over.

(vi) Demand for collateral should be minimal and may be confined to deposit of shipping documents and an unconditional guarantee to repay the loan.

(vii) An appropriate policy of export credit insurance may be obtained by the exporter and assigned to the bank.

1. Refinancing by Central Banks

A broad outline of a post-shipment credit refinance scheme of central banks along with operational guidelines to commercial banks are given in annex III to this chapter.

E. MERCHANT EXPORTERS AND EXPORT HOUSES

Developing countries establishing an export financing mechanism should ensure that liberal financing facilities are made available not only to manufacturer-exporters, but also to merchant exporters and export houses who have specialized in the export business. The merchant exporters and export houses have the necessary expertise and skills and also possess a through knowledge of international requirements in respect of prices, quality, delivery schedules, packing and shipping arrangements for export products. They are familiar with the payment procedures and problems, if any, of importing countries and are thoroughly conversant with exchange control formalities and regulations.

In many developing countries the contribution of export houses and merchant export development has been remarkable. They secure orders for various types of commodities and export them after concluding suitable manufacturing arrrangements with domestic manufacturers. During the initial stages of launching export promotion programmes in developing countries, it may be desirable to channel a greater volume of export products through the export houses, where they exist, particularly in the case of goods manufactured by small and medium-sized industrial units scattered throughout the country. The merchant exporters and export houses perform the important function of acting as intermediary between the local manufacturers of goods and the overseas buyers, and are interested only in their commission on the export contracts secured by them.

Since the merchant exporters or export houses are not the manufacturers of the goods to be exported, they do not require finance for the manufacture, processing or packing of goods. However, they do require funds to buy the goods from the various manufacturing sources and export them. They generally operate on a low capital base, and therefore need pre-shipment finance for procurement of goods and the execution of export orders. It often happens that, although an export house has secured the export order, it may prefer not to obtain the pre-shipment finance. Instead, the manufacturer will be requested to obtain the pre-shipment finance from the bank on the strength of the export order secured by the export house.

This disinclination on their part to secure bank finance may be because of a desire not to assume the liability themselves because of their other liabilities and commitments. In some countries, they are unable to obtain export credit facilities on the same terms as the manufacturers, because the bankers generally feel that their interests are better secured by supporting the manufacturer rather than by providing finance to intermediaries whose credibility and financial standing may not always be satisfactory.

As already mentioned, the financial assistance available to manufacturer exporters should normally be provided also to the merchant exporters and export houses under the pre-shipment and post-shipment financing schemes implemented by the commercial banks, in which case the procedures for the schemes in question will be followed in these cases as well. However, these intermediaries can also raise funds to meet their special requirements by way of:

Transferable credits
Back-to-back letters of credit
Export trust receipts.
Various aspects of these mechanisms are described below.

(*i*) *Transferable credits*

The merchant exporters or export houses are not the manufacturers of the goods to be exported. They act as intermediaries between the local manufacturer of the goods and the overseas buyer, and are interested only in their commission on the transaction. They may not wish to use their own funds, or funds made available to them for financing the export transaction. In such cases, they can obtain a transferable letter of credit from the bank of the overseas buyer. The transferable letter of credit is defined as a credit under which the beneficiary has the right to give instructions to the bank called upon to effect payment or acceptance, or to any bank entitled to effect negotiation, and to make the credit available in whole or in part to one or more third parties (second beneficiaries).

The credit is one of the methods adopted by the opening bank, at the instance of the opener, to facilitate the completion of an export transaction by an exporter-intermediary (first beneficiary without blocking his own funds. The exporter transfers the foreign letter of credit to the manufacturer of the goods to be exported, for a lesser amount, the difference being his commission, or he may transfer the credit in full, if his commission is paid separately. In the former case, he substitutes his own name for that of the opener and tenders his bill of exchange and invoice for that of the second beneficiary (manufacturer) who may approach his own bank for the export packing credit. In this manner, the exporter-intermediary finances his side of the export transaction, at the pre-shipment stage, without blocking his own funds or for that matter without crediting any liability for himself. A transferable credit thus serves as an alternative to an export packing credit.

(*ii*) *Back-to-back letter of credit*

Pre-shipment facility is granted at times in the form of packing credit in inland LC on a back-to-back basis. Here the merchant exporter, the beneficiary of an irrevocable export LC, uses the same as security with the banker for opening another credit in favour of the supplier calling for identical documents to enable him to execute the export LC. A true back-to-back LC must be issued against the foreign bank's irrevocable LC and its terms and conditions must be similar to the export LC except for the following differences:

The credit amount will be less than that of the export LC;

The name of the beneficiary will be that of the supplier;

The period of validity will expire a few days earlier than the expiry date of the export LC.

A special feature of this type of LC is that it is based on the original credit and calls for documents evidencing the dispatch of goods mentioned in that credit. Such documents are utilized by the exporter for negotiation under the original credit after substituting his invoice and drafts.

(*iii*) *Export trust receipts*

In some of the banks, export packing credits are granted immediately as 'export trust receipt advances'. In this type of advance, the pledge of goods does not precede the trust receipt facility. A merchant-exporter approaches the bank for an export packing credit, and his bank grants it as an export trust receipt advance, as per its practice, against the exporter executing the export trust receipt (besides any other required documents such as a promissory note, etc), in which the exporter undertakes to use the amount of the advance for the purchase of goods to be exported, to hold these goods in trust for the bank as its agent, and to insure them, and agrees that they will form the bank's security for the advance. The exporter further undertakes to tender the shipping documents covering these goods after shipment for negotiation/purchase, and agrees that the bill proceeds are to be appropriated by the bank for liquidating the export trust receipt advance. The effect of such an export trust receipt will be that the goods or the bill/sale proceeds will be held by the exporter-customer as trustee for the bank in respect of its pre-shipment advances to the customer. As the bank may not have any valid charge over the goods, the advance may have to be treated as a 'clean' or 'unsecured' advance. To avoid this situation, some banks take a letter or hypothecation, in addition to an export trust receipt, covering the goods under export. This type of facility is granted by bank selectively to reliable and sound exporter-customers.

F. MEDIUM AND LONG-TERM FINANCE

With the growth of exports of engineering and capital goods from some of the more industrialized developing countries, it has become increasingly necessary for exporters of these goods to offer deferred payment credit facilities to overseas importers. Machinery and other engineering goods are generally exported under medium-term credit, which extends up to a period of five years, whereas capital goods of high value and turnkey projects are normally sold on long-term credit for a period exceeding five years and sometimes extending to ten years. The non-traditional exports on medium and long-term arrangements may be classified as under:

Machinery and equipment

Turnkey projects.

Besides the above, developing countries also export civil construction projects and undertake service contracts such as the provision of consultancy services. These tasks do not usually involve an offer of term credits unless the amount involved is very large. However, they require certain essential financial services from the commercial banks, and, according to the various types of projects, exporters' needs arise at two distinct stages:

The pre-tender stage

The post-tender stage.

In the case of high value contracts, the exporter may secure a contract by participation in a global tender open to all contractors in various countries, by participation in a limited tender made available to selected suppliers on the basis of past experience and qualifications, or through direct negotiations between the buyer and the tendering authority.

At the pre-tender stage, no financial assistance is required by the exporter, but certain services may be necessary, such as the collection of essential information regarding the credit standing of the buyer, exchange regulations, the balance-of-payments position of the importing countries, and the infrastructure available for execution of a contract in those countries. While submitting the tender, the exporter may be required to furnish a bid bond to the overseas buyer up to a specified percentage of the estimated value of the contract. At the post-tender stage, the exporter needs certain bonding facilities, which are in the nature of non-financing facilities. These bonding/guarantee facilities are generally required by the exporters of both turnkey projects and construction contracts. According to the normal practice, the extent of the guarantees required is quite substantial as indicated below.

Bid bond	Normally up to 5 per cent of the value of the project, valid for 3 to 6 months, to be furnished at the time of submission of the tender.
Performance bond	Normally at 5 to 10 per cent of the value of the project, to be given at the time of signature of the contract. Validity extends over the full contract period, including the maintenance period.
Advance Payment guarantee	At 10 to 20 per cent of the value of the project after the contract has been signed. Valid until such time as the advance payment has been fully recovered from progress bills.
Retention money guarantee	5 to 10 per cent of the value of the contract, valid up to the end of the maintenance period.

Besides these non-financing facilities by way of guarantee at the post-tender stage, exporters need financing facilities by way of pre-shipment financing and post-shipment loans. The salient features of bonds/guarantees, pre-shipment loans are broadly described below.

(a) Bond/Guarantees

(*i*) *Bid bonds*

While tendering for supply contracts or projects, exporters are required to furnish bid bonds in lieu of earnest money along with their tenders in favour of the overseas body or project authorities who have invited the global tender. The bid bonds become effective if the exporter is awarded the tender but refuses to sign the contract and proceed with the execution of the work. Normally, these bid bonds are substituted by performance bonds at the time of signing the contract by the exporter. The bonds may be issued by the banks on behalf of the exporter directly in favour of the overseas importer (beneficiary) or may be furnished by them through their foreign correspondents in the country concerned. The liability of the banks issuing bid bonds arises only when the bid having been accepted, the exporter refuses to sign the contractual document. Furthermore, the issuing bank should be prepared to furnish performance bonds at the time of the signing of the contract on behalf of the exporter. The important points to be taken care of while issuing the bid bonds are:

The expiry date, which is of primary importance, should be specified in the guarantee. After that date, if no claim has been received by the bank, its liability to the beneficiary ceases;

The name and address of the guarantor and also of the beneficiary should be clearly mentioned;

The description of the tender to which the guarantee is applicable should be clearly stated in the guarantee;

The guarantee should indicate the maximum liability.

(*ii*) *Performance guarantees*

As soon as the exporter's bid is accepted and the contract is to be signed by him, the tendering authority needs a performance guarantee from the exporter's bank guaranteeing due performance of the contract. The guarantee will be to the effect that the delivery will be as per schedule, and that the other contract terms, such as the quality of the product and the operational efficiency of the machinery, will be properly carried out. The guarantee period will cover the period of erection and commissioning of the project and also the warranty period under the contract. The guarantee will be invoked and the issuing bank will be called upon to pay the amount if the exporter's performance is not in accordance with the contract requirements. In the case of performance guarantees, it will be necessary to specify in the guarantee the *pro rate* reduction in the guarantee amount on the basis of the progress achieved in the execution of the contract. This will reduce the liability of the issuing bank from time to time.

(iii) Advance payment guarantees

In the case of orders secured by exporters for the supply of machinery and equipment, it is usual to receive 10 to 20 per cent of the contract value by way of advance payment. The overseas importer making such an advance payment normally needs a security in his favour to protect himself if the exporter fails to provide the supplies under the contract, after receiving the advance payment. The security is generally furnished by way of an advance payment guarantee by the exporter's bank to the buyer, up to the amount of the advance payment made and for the period of the contract. As in the case of performance guarantees, it is also necessary to ensure that the liability is reduced *pro rate* on the basis of the progress made in the contract execution.

(iv) Retention money guarantees

In the case of high value equipment/turnkey projects/construction contracts, progressive payments are made by the overseas employer in respect of the work executed under the contract, a small percentage of the progressive payments being retained as retention money, which is payable after the expiry of the stipulated period from the date of completion of the contract, subject to the obtaining of a certificate from the specified authority. It is normal practice for the contractors to furnish a bank guarantee in favour of the overseas buyer, against which the retention money will be released by the overseas buyer. These guarantees are usually 5 to 10 per cent of the value of the contract. Their validity extends until the end of the maintenance period in terms of the contract provisions.

(b) Pre-shipment financing

The pre-shipment credit requirements of exporters depend upon the type of equipment exported and the contractual obligations devolving upon them. The position in the case of suppliers of high value capital equipment, turnkey projects, construction projects and consultancy services is briefly indicated below.

(*i*) *Suppliers of capital equipment and turnkey projects*

Pre-shipment credit is provided by specialized institutions, like Export-Import banks in participation with commercial banks, to exporters for executing large value export contracts. The assistance is provided by way of term loans for periods beyond six months. The duration of the loan depends on the manufacturing cycle, which will usually be quite long. The operational guide lines laid down for pre-shipment financing on a short-term basis are also applicable to the pre-shipment credits granted to exporters of capital equipment, and to turnkey projects. In the case of turnkey projects, the responsibility of the exporter involves the rendering of services like design, civil construction, erection and commissioning of plant or supervision thereof along with the supply of equipment. In cases where the equipment is to be procured from various domestic sources, suitable inland letters of credit limits will also be needed by the exporters in addition to the pre-shipment facilities.

(*ii*) *Overseas construction contracts*

Construction contracts, *viz.* contracts involving erection, civil works and commissioning, apart from the supply of equipment, also need financial assistance at the pre-shipment stage. Banks generally grant pre-shipment advances for financing the preliminary expenses in connection with the execution of the contract, *i.e.*, for transporting the necessary manpower and materials and for the purchase of consumer goods required for construction. The advances are generally sanctioned at concessional rates on the basis of firm contracts secured from abroad, which should be adjusted by the negotiation of bills relating to the contract or by remittances received from abroad under the contract. The normal period for such advances is for a maximum of six months, which could be extended in justifiable cases. Where the contractor is also exporting supplies like cement, steel and building materials, advances may be granted for their procurement.

(*iii*) *Consultancy services*

Banks may grant consultancy firms suitable pre-shipment credit facilities against consultancy agreements for meeting the expenses of the technical and other staff employed for the project, and for the purchase of any materials required for it. Wherever necessary, the computer system and programmes produced for export purposes by the management consultancy firms may be considered as cover for the pre-shipment advances. The period and the extent of credit may be decided on the basis of the nature and scope of the consultany contract and the terms thereof.

(c) **Post-shipment Loans**

Exporters of engineering and capital goods and turnkey projects will be required to offer deferred payment credit facilities to overseas buyers. For such exports, the overseas buyers will furnish suitable securities for the deferred payment instalments in favour of the exporters. The exporters make arrangements with their own bankers or specialized institutions for term export credit in their favour. The offer of the credit can be in two was-supplier's credit and buyer's credit.

(*i*) *Supplier's credit*

Under supplier's credit, the exporter of the goods and equipment gives credit to his buyer generally exceeding the period of six months/one year up to five or ten years, depending on the nature of the equipment. In turn, the supplier will be financed by his bank. The credit is generally covered by a bank guarantee from the importer.

(*ii*) *Buyer's credit*

If, on the other hand, the foreign buyer is afforded credit by a bank or financial institution, and the exporter is paid the export value in cash for goods by the bank or institution concerned, the relative export contract is specified under buyer's credit.

The post-shipment loans granted to exporters by a bank or a financial institution will be subject to their compliance with certain guidelines formulated by the bank or institution. Some of the important considerations in the sanction of term credits are given below.

Period of deferred credit

Four major factors—anticipated life-span of the goods to be exported, the nature of the goods to be exported, the extent of foreign competition, the nature of the foreign market and the contract value—form the basis determining the period of credit. In the case of capital and producer goods, the maximum credit period may be five years, and in the case of turnkey projects it may be ten years or more.

Advance/down payment

Generally, the importer is required to pay 15 to 20 per cent of the contract value and the credit component will be the remaining 80 to 85 per cent. This will depend on the features of each particular case.

Period of moratorium

In the case of turnkey projects, a period of moratorium or a grace period may be allowed depending on the nature of the project.

Security

The security for the deferred receivables, *i.e.*, the credit component allowed by banks to the foreign importer, will be a letter of credit or a guarantee from a bank in the country of import or in a third country acceptable to the financing institution.

Forward exchange cover

Where the contracts are invoiced in foreign currency, the exporter will be required to cover the deferred receivables under a forward exchange contract for the total credit period, when a long-term exchange cover scheme is operated in the exporting country by the central bank or any other institution. Alternatively it may be permissible for the exporter to assess his risk in respect of each instalment that is due for receipt and obtain forward cover for that instalment alone.

Export credit guarantee and insurance arrangements

Both for the financing and non-financing facilities detailed above, it is desirable that banks/exporters cover themselves appropriately against various risks by means of export credit guarantee and insurance policies. The details of these facilities are described in chapter 5.

ANNEXURE I

Assessment of Overall Working Capital Requirements of The XYZ Company

Part A *Amount in local currency*

(i) Raw materials representing......... months' consumption

(ii) Stock in process representing......... months' production

(iii) Finished goods at cost in factory representing......months' production

(iv) Bills under collection:

(a) Export bills (normally realized in.........weeks)

(b) Inland bills (normally realized in.........weeks)

(v) Cash subsidy/excise duty draw-back* (normally realized in...... ..weeks)

(vi) One month's manufacturing and administrative expenses

TOTAL

Less

(i) Sundry creditors representing......... weeks' purchases

(ii) Advance payments, if any, received

*Where admissible

(iii) Working capital:

(Current assets less current liabilities or capital and surplus plus deferred liabilities minus fixed and miscellaneous and intangible assets or value of cash and stocks shown in the credit report on the borrower under net means

Net working capital

Part B

(*Permissible limits*) (*Amount in local currency*)

Pre-Shipment Finance

Against:

Raw materials

Less margin

Stock in process

Less margin

Finished goods in warehouse

Less margin

Finished goods in transit to port towns

Less margin

Post-Shipment Finance

Against:

(i) Export bills under collection Less margin, if any

(ii) Export bills to be purchased or discounted

(a) Credit bills under LCs

(b) Non-credit bills *i.e.*, under firm export orders

Less margin, if any, to be retained under non-credit bills

(iii) Against excise duty draw-back/cash subsidy

Less margin

Permissible limit

Part C

(i) Net working capital as in Part A

(ii) Permissible limit as in Part B

N.B. If (ii) is less than (i) please comment on how the deficit will be met.

ANNEXURE II

Pre-Shipment Credit Refinancing Scheme of a Central Bank

Operational Guidelines for Commercial Banks

1. Objectives

(a) To encourage commercial banks to grant pre-shipment advances or loans to exporters in (country) on a more liberal basis and at a reasonable rate of interest.

(b) To improve the liquidity of commercial banks so as to increase their lending to the export sector on a priority basis through the provision of refinance to them by the Central Bank.

(c) To strengthen the financial infrastructure for export promotion with special emphasis on diversification of markets and products.

2. Eligible Institutions

All commercial banks and financial institutions approved by the Central Bank.

3. (a) The pre-shipment advances should be granted to *bona fide* exporters on the basis of latters of credit (LCs) established by banks abroad in favour of the exporters of firm export orders/sale contracts.

(b) The relevant documents such as LCs of firm orders should be lodged with the banks concerned.

(c) The outstanding balances in the pre-shipment advance accounts should be adjusted by negotiation of relative export bills or in any other manner as may be specified by the Central Bank.

(d) The bank should advance to exporters at the rate of interest that may be prescribed by the Central Bank from time to time.

(e) The pre-shipment advances should normally relate to shipments expected to be made within a period of 180 days from the date of advance.

(f) Advances against import documents or goods imported for manufacture or processing of commodities meant for export will also be covered under pre-shipment credit eligible for refinance.

4. Extent of Refinance Available

(a) Up to 100 per cent of the amount of pre-shipment advances granted and outstanding in the books of the bank.

(b) Total outstanding refinance borrowing from the Central Bank should at any time be fully covered by the total amount of pre-shipment advances outstanding with the bank.

5. Rate of Interest

The rate of interest charged by the Central Bank may vary from time to time. It will generally be 2 per cent lower than the rate charged by the bank on its pre-shipment advances.

6. Refinance Procedure

(*a*) *Borrowing limits*

(i) Limits will be sanctioned for one year on the basis of average outstandings of pre-shipment advances during the preceding year, as also the level of anticipated pre-shipment advances during the year under consideration,

(ii) The renewal of the limits sanctioned to a bank will be considered at the time of expiry of the limits on receipt of an application for renewal from the bank.

(*b*) *Documentation*

The documents to be executed by a borrowing bank will include:

(i) An agreement for the refinance limit fixed by the central bank setting out the various terms and conditions of the advance.

(ii) A demand promissory note for the amount of the limit.

(*c*) *Periodical statements*

(i) A monthly declaration on the prescribed from indicating the position of the outstanding refinance borrowings under the scheme and the outstanding pre-shipment advances of the bank as on the dates prescribed by the central bank.

(ii) The central bank may varify any of the statements by deputing its officials to the bank concerned.

(*d*) *Miscellaneous*

The borrowing bank should maintain suitable records to check the position of its outstanding refinance borrowing *vis-a-vis* the pre-shipment advances.

ANNEXURE III

Post-shipment Credit Refinancing Scheme of a Central Bank

Operational guidelines for commercial banks

1. Objectives

(a) To encourage commercial banks to grant post-shipment advances to exporters in—(country) on a liberal basis and at a reasonable rate of interest;

(b) To improve the liquidity of commercial banks so as to increase their lending to the export sector on a priority basis through the provision of refinance to them by the central bank; and

(c) To strengthen the financial infrastructure for export promotion with special emphasis on diversification of markets and products.

2. Eligible Institutions

All commercial banks approved by the central bank.

3. Eligible Advances

(a) All sight bills (other than these under LCs) and usance export bills having usance not exceeding 180 days under LCs or otherwise, which are drawn in—(country) or any place in any other country notified by the central bank and purchased/negotiated/discounted by the banks, or advances made against export bills by them.

(b) Export bills will cease to be eligible in the following circumstances:

(i) On receipt of their realization advance;

(ii) On their being rediscounted;

(iii) On dishonour by non-acceptance or non-payment;

(iv) In a case of usance bills negotiated under LCs, on receipt of their reimbursement.

(c) The export bills are to be handled by the banks in compliance with the Exchange Control Regulations.

4. Extent of Refinance Available

(a) Up to 100 per cent of the amount of the eligible export bills negotiated/purchased/discounted or advances made against the bills outstanding in the books of the bank.

(b) Total outstanding refinance borrowings from the central bank should at any time be covered fully by the total amount of eligible post-shipment advances outstanding with the bank.

5. Rate of Interest

The rate of interest may vary from time to time. It will generally be 2 per cent lower than the rate charged by the borrowing bank on its post-shipment advances.

6. Refinance Procedure

(*a*) *Borrowing limits*

(i) Limits will be sanctioned for one year on the basis of average outstanding eligible post-shipment advances during the preceding year as also the level of anticipated post-shipment advances during the year under consideration.

(ii) The reneval of the limits sanctioned to a bank will be considered at the time of the expiry of the limits on receipt of an application for renewal from the bank.

(*b*) *Documentation*

(i) As advances under this scheme will be separate from those under the Pre-shipment Credit Refinancing Scheme, it will be necessary for a borrowing bank to execute a fresh set of documents.

(ii) The documents to be executed by a borrowing bank will include:

An agreement for the refinance limit fixed by the central bank setting out the various terms and conditions of the advance;
A demand promissory note for the limit.

(*c*) *Periodical statements*

(i) A monthly declaration on the prescribed form indicating the position of the outstanding refinance borrowings under the scheme and the standing eligible post-shipment advances of the bank as on the dates prescribed by the central bank.

(ii) The central bank may verify any of the statements by deputing its officials to the bank concerned.

(*d*) *Miscellaneous*

The borrowing bank should maintain suitable records to check the position of its outstanding refinance borrowings *vis-a-vis* its post-shipment advances.

4

EXPORT DOCUMENTATION

An important part of export practice is a good comprehesion of the various documents involved to process the export consignment. Moreover, the need to understand the role of such documents and their limitations together with likely problems which they may encountér is likewise important. If an exporter has any doubt over the role of, or query over, a particular document the best course to follow is to contact his bank or freight forwarder.

In processing an export consignment involving extensive documentation, one must bear in mind there can be up to four contracts to execute. These include:

> The export sales contract, the contract of carriage, the financial cantract, and finally the contract of cargo insurance. All these have to be reconciled with the processing of the export consignment. The need to have the relevant documentation correctly completed and the checklists found in this and Chapter 13 closely adhered to; cannot be stressed too strongly. Failure to do so results in delay in payment for goods, loss of goodwill between buyer/seller, late delivery of the merchandise, and so on.

This chapter, in the main, excludes documentation relating to Customs, insurance and finance, which is covered respectively in Chapters 7, 8 and 9. A study of the various documents now follows.

AIR WAYBILL

The air waybill is the consignment note used for the carriage of goods by air. It is often called an air consignment note and is not a document of title or transferable/negotiable instrument. It is basically a receipt for the goods for despatch and is prima face evidence of the conditions of carriage. Overall, there are usually twelve copies of each air waybill for distribution to the shipper, sales agent, issuing carrier (airline operator), consignee, delivery receipt, airport of destination, third carrier (if applicable), second carrier (if applicable), first carrier, extra copy for carrier (when required), invoice and airport of departure. Copies 1, 2 and 3 are the originals. Each copy is not always used, but merely as circumstances demand. For example, the second carrier's copy would be used only if the consignment was conveyed on another airline to complete the transit—such as British Airways conveying it for the first leg of the journey and Air Canada the remainder. The conditions of carriage are found on the reverse of the air waybill document and are subject to the Carriage by Air Act 1961. This is based on the Warsaw rules and a number of other conventions. Overall, it is subject to the supplementary provisions in the Carriage by Air Act, 1962. Actual liability to the IATA airline carrier is based at 250 Gold Francs per kg.

The standard IATA air waybill (AWB), used worldwide, is the most important feature of the simplified system of documentation for air freight moving internationally. It is the basic airline document covering the movement of shipments on international air freight services. A single air waybill covers carriage over any distance, by as many airlines as may be required to complete the transporation. When goods carried by one airline for part of the journey are transferred to another airline, the original air waybill is sent forward with the consignment from point of original departure to the final destination.

The new 'universal' air waybill (UAWB) was introduced from 1st January 1984 and its use is mandatory. It is compatible with United Nations (UN) layout key and can be used for both domestics and international transits.

The new universal air waybill contains the following information:

1. The place and date of its execution.
2. Names of the departure and destination air ports.
3. The names and addresses of the consignor, consignee and the first carrier (airline).
4. A description of the goods.
5. The number of packages with marks, weights, quantity and dimensions.
6. The total freight amount prepaid and/or to pay is precisely defined, and the rate.
7. The declared value for Customs purposes, likewise for carriage and the currency.
8. The date of the flight.
9. Details of any special route to be taken.
10. The signature of the shipper or his agent.
11. The signature of the issuing carrier (airline operator) or his agent.
12. Details of the booked flight and actual flight.

Efficient service depends on the accuracy and completeness of the air waybill. Hence shippers themselves must give clear and complete forwarding instructions to the airline or agent. To facilitate this procedure they may use the 'Shipper's Letter of Instruction', a standardized form which may be obtained from any airline, approved IATA Cargo Agent or forwarder. The main functions of the standard air waybill are as follows.

At departure airports it is a contract of carriage receipt for goods, provides a unique reference for handling inventory control and documentation reference, includes description of goods and full rating information, includes special handling requirements, and provides basic details for aircraft manifest. Post-flight information includes a document source for revenue collection, interlining accounting and proration, and cargo statistics. At destination airports the air waybill provides a basic document for notification to consignee, Customs clearance and delivery to consignee. Additionally it is a source document for clearance and delivery charges accounting.

Where more than one package is involved, the carrier can require the consignor to make out separate air waybills. The air consignment note must be printed in one of the official languages of the country of departure, for example, French, German, etc. Erasures are not admissible, but alterations can be made provided they are authenticated by the consignor's signature or initials. If quantities, weights, or values are altered, they must appear in words as well as figures.

An increasing volume of air freight is now conveyed under consolidation with the freight forwarder sponsoring the overall consignment. It may involve a hundred individual consignments concerning various consignors/consignees. Under such consignments. the freight forwarder attaches to the air waybill the cargo manifest detailing the fullest information on each of the consignments despatched. In such circumstances the freight forwarder issues a house air waybill to the shipper to confirm details of despatch by air which facilitates payment for the goods.

Under a documentary letter of credit, certain specific information or instructions to be shown on the air waybill may be requested. This usually includes:

Names and addresses of the exporter, importer and the first carrier/airline, the names of the airports of departure and destination together with details of any special route, the date of the flight, the declared value of the merchandise for Customs purposes, the number of packages with marks, weights, quantity and dimensions, the freight charge per unit of weight/volume, the technical description of the goods and not the commercial description, whether the freight charge has been prepared or will be paid at the destination, the signature of the exporter (or his agent); the place and date of issue, and finally the signature of the issuing carrier (or his agent).

In the next few years further modernization of air freight documentation will take place. This includes the move from documentation into an automated information system. As computers are acquired by shippers, agents, handling companies. Customs and others, a new approach to documentation and procedures is required. Additionally required are the development of a neutral air waybill numbering system; use of bar codes for automatic verifications: automated information systems so that airlines and stations can adequately communicate with each other; standard data elements; standard message formats; and new codes and procedures.

An example of an air waybill is found in Appendix D.

BILL OF EXCHANGE

Under the terms of the Bills of Exchange Act 1882, a bill of exchange has been defined as an unconditional order in writing addressed by one person to another, signed by the person giving it, requiring the person to whom it is addressed to pay, on demand, or at a fixed or determinable future time, a certain sum in money to or to the order of a specified person or bearer. Drafts can be drawn either at sight—payment to be made on demand or on presentation, or, at a particular 'tenor' ('usance') —payment to be made at a fixed or determinable future date, usually within 180 days of sight of the bill of exchange by the drawer, or within 180 days of the date of the draft. Special Bank of England approval is needed for credit periods exceeding 180 days under an export sales contract. The general procedure for letters of credit is for drafts to be drawn on a bank, but some credit require them to be drawn on the importer. Drafts can be drawn in pairs called 'first' and 'second' bills of exchange.

The bill of exchange is a popular way of arranging payment. The most normal procedure is for the exporter (seller) to hand the bill of exchange together with the documents to the exporter's (seller's) bank who will send them to a bank overseas for 'collection'. The overseas bank will notify the buyer of the arrival of the documents and will release them to him subject to one of two conditions. Firstly, if the bill is drawn at 'sight' the buyer pays the amount of the bill in full, or secondly if the bill is drawn payable after a certain number of days, the buyer accepts the bill *i.e.* he signs accross the bill his agreement to pay the amount in full at due date.

The salient benefit of this method of payment is that the exporter (seller) can maintain control of the goods until the importer (buyer) has agreed to pay for them. However, there is still no absolute guarantee the importer (buyer) will pay, but legal procedures exist in most countries to recover money owing against bills of exchange.

The bill of exchange contains the following data:

1. The date.
2. A specific sum, which should agree with the amount on the export invoice.
3. The 'tenor', that is whether at sight or at a stated period after sight or at a fixed date.
4. The name of the drawee.
5. The name and signature of the drawer.
6. The name of the payee or order or bearer.
7. The endorsement of the payee where applicable.

Overall, the bill of exchange should be so worded to conform to what is laid down in the credit.

The following discrepancies tend to arise in processing bills of exchange and should be avoided.

(a) Document drawn incorrectly or for a sum different to the credit amount.

(b) Designation of the signature on the document not specified if required, *e.g.* director or partner.

BILL OF LADING

A bill of landing is a receipt for goods shipped on board a vessel, signed by the person (or his agent) who contracts to carry them, and stating the conditions in which the goods were delivered to (and received by) the ship. It is not the actual contract, which is inferred from the action of the shipper or shipowner in delivering or receiving the cargo' but forms excellent evidence of the terms of the contract. It is a document of title to the goods which is the subject of the contract between the buyer (importer) and seller (exporter).

Before examining the salient points, function and types of bills of landing, we will first of all consider two Act which have played an important role in the development of this document, namely the Bills of Lading Act 1855 and the Carriage of Goods by Sea Act 1924. More recently (in fact from (1977) the Carriage of Goods by Sea 1971 has emerged and succeeded the Carriage of Goods by Sea Act 1924.

The Bill of Lading Act 1855 established the following relevant to this document:

1. It preserved the right of the original shipper to 'stoppage in transitu' (in transit). Moreover, not only did it give the right of conditional endorsement and of reserving the 'jus disponendi' (law of disposal) but also

unpaid seller could resume possession of the goods by exercising the right of 'stoppage in transitu'.

2. It established the principle of transferability, permitting the transfer of a bill of landing from the holder to a person to whom the property in the goods passes, together with any rights and liabilities incorporated in the document.
3. It provided that once the bill of lading has been issued, it is prima facie evidence that the goods have been shipped.

Under the Carriage of Goods by Sea Act 1924, the carrier is under obligation to properly and crefully load, handle, stow, carry, keep, care for and discharge the goods carried. It was laid down that, in cases to which the Act applies, the carrier should be able to avoid liability in certain circumstances defined in the Act. In general, the extent of the carrier's immunity is laid down by the Act and cannot be increased by contract. Any clause or contract purporting to relieve a carrier of his liabilities under the Act is expressively declared void.

The basic object of the 1971 Act is simply to amend the Hague Rules relating to the Bills of Lading Act 1921, which it will be recalled were appended as a schedule to the Carriage of Goods by Sea Act 1924. A diplomatic conference was held in Brussels in 1967 on Maritime Law which examined the Visby Rules intended for amendment of the Hague Rules of 1921. A number of the proposed amendments were accepted at the conference with two noticeable exceptions:

The limitation of the carrier's liability, and the scope of the Application of the Rules. In the following year the Hague Rules were amended by the Brussels Protocol signed on 23rd February 1968 and known as the Hague—Visby Rules. The major reason for the amendment was that the Hague Rules under modern trading conditions were considered too favourable to the carrier, a view taken particularly by the developing countries. The Rules became operative after being ratified by ten states:

Denmark, Ecuador, France, Lebanon, Norway, Singapore, Sweden, Switzerland, Syria and UK. Some contracting states apply the Rules to both inward and outward voyages. These Rules now form the schedule to the 1971 Act under the title. 'The Hague Rules as amended by the Brussels Protocol 1968'.

The main provisions of the 1971 Carriage of Goods by Sea Act are given below:

1. It only applies to outwards bills of lading, that is, from a British port, as compared with many national enactments adopting the rules such as United States Carriage of Goods by Sea Act 1936, which applies to both inward, as well as outward bills of lading.
2. The 1971 Act covers the coasting trade—a feature not common to the 1924 Act.
3. It applies both to shipments under bills of lading and those under any similar documents of title'. Hence, a forwarder's receipt such as a house bill of lading or container receipt would be subject to the Rules if so endorsed. The bill of lading still provides *prima facie* evidence of receipt by the carrier of the goods such as identification of cargo marks, condition of cargo, number of packages and their weight. An addition, however, is that the bill provides conclusive evidence when the cargo has been transferred to a party acting in good faith.
4. It clearly defines the extent of the carrier's liability on container traffic.
5. The 1971 Act permits the carrier and the ship to be discharged from all liability in respect of goods, unless legal proceedings are started within one year of delivery of the cargo or the date when they should have been delivered. The Rules now indicate that the one year limit shall not embrace a third person provided that proceedings against him are commenced within the time—

allowed by the law of the Court seized of the case—for bringing an action against such a third person which must never be less than three months.

6. It limits the carrier's liability to the maximum amount of 10,000 Gold Francs (£401.78) per package or unit, or 30 Gold Francs (£ 1.21)/kg gross weight of the goods lost or damaged. Whichever is the higher. It also confirms the maximum limitation does not apply if the damage resulted from an act or omission of the carrier done with intent to cause damage, or recklessly and with knowledge that damage would probably result.

Before dealing with the salient points of the bill of lading, it is important to examine the Hamburg Rules.

The Hamburg Rules have been in existense since the late 1970s but until recently have not provoked great interest amongst the leading maritime nations; recently, however, Australia and New Zealand have been considering their adoption.

Under the auspices of the United Nations, a diplomatic conference took place in Hamburg in March 1978 to consider the UNCITRAL draft convention in the carriage of goods by sea which had also been approved by UNCTAD. The Conference attended by twenty-seven states adopted a 'Convention on the Carriage of Goods by Sea'—in future to be known as the 'Hamburg Rules.' These rules represent a radical departure from the tried and tested formula prescribed by the Hague Rules as refined by the Visby amendments, and they form an innovative approach to the question of carriers' liability.

The Hamburg Cules tend to benefit shippers and consignees in user countries rather than those who are providing the shipping services. Hence the cost of sea transport is expected to rise considerably when these rules are adopted and form part of the legislation of the maritime nations. In addition, the transfer to the ship of a significant part of the liability at present borne by cargo interests means that it will have an effect on the insurance market in some countries due to a reduction in cargo insurance premiums the risk is absorbed in the freight rates.

The major differences between the Hague Rules (as interpreted) and the Hamburg Rules are given below:

1. Period of responsibility. The carrier is no longer able to restrict his liability to the period from the time the goods were received on the ship's tackle to the time when they were unloaded from the ship at the port of discharge. Instead he is liable from the time he takes over the goods at the port of loading until delivery at the port of discharge.
2. The catalogue of exceptions in Article 4.2 of the Hague Rules is no longer available to the carrier. In particular he is no longer exonerated from liability arising from error in navigation. Instead the carrier is subject to a general rule of presumed fault under which he is liable unless he can show that 'he, his servants or agents took all measures that could reasonably be required.' W respect to liability for fire the burden of proof rests on the claimant.
3. The dual system for calculating the limits of liability has been retained, that is to say liability is limited by reference to pacakge or weight, whichever is the higher. Generally, with the exception of liability for delay, the liability of the carrier for loss resulting from loss or damage to goods is limited to an amount equivalent to 835 units of account per package, or 2.5 units of account per kilogramme of gross weight. The unit of account referred to is the Special Drawing Right (SRD) as defined by the International Monetary Fund. Special units of account exist where states are not members of the IMF. (See also pp. 173-81 of *Economics of Shipping Practice and Management.*)
4. The time bar period during which a claim may be lodged has been extended from one year to two years.

5. Provisions have been introduced which impose liability on the carrier for delay in delivery of the merchandise.

The Hamburg Rules will come into force twelve months after they have been adopted by twenty countries. By early 1985 some nine countries had adopted the Convention, including Barbados, Chile, Egypt, Lebanon, Morocco, Romania, Tanzania, Tunisia, and Uganda. Twenty-five other countries have signed the Rules subject to ratification, including the Federal Republic of Germany, France, the four Scandinavian States, the Holy See and the USA. When adopted they will displace the Hague Rules and the Hague—Visby Rules. They reflect particularly the development of combined transport operations and the need to have a common code of carrier liability throughout, coupled with the modernization of the documentation associated therewith.

The salient points incorporated in a bill of lading can be conveniently listed as follows:

1. The name of the shipper (usually the exporter).
2. The name of the carrying vessel.
3. Full description of the cargo (provided it is not bulk cargo) including any shipping marks, individual package numbers in the consignment, contents, cubic measurement, gross weight etc.
4. The marks and numbers identifying the goods.
5. Port of shipment.
6. Port of discharge.
7. Full details of freight, including when and where it is to be paid—whether freight paid or payable at destination.
8. Name of consignee or, if the shipper is anxious to withhold the consignee's name, shipper's order.
9. The terms of the contract of carriage.
10. The date the goods were received for shipment and/or loaded on the vessel.

11. The name and address of the notified party (the person to be notified on arrival of the shipment, usually the buyer).

12. Number of bills of lading signed on behalf of the Master or his agent, acknowledging receipt of the goods.

13. The signature of the ship's Master or his agent and the date.

There are several types and forms of bills of lading and these include the following:

1. *Shipped bill of lading*. Under the Carriage of Goods by Sea Act 1924, the shipper can demand that the shipowner supplies bills of lading proving that the goods have been actually shipped. For this reason, most bill of lading forms are already printed as shipped bills and commence with the wording:

   'Shipped in apparent good order and condition.' It confirms the goods are actually on board the vessel.

This is the most satisfactory type of receipt and the shipper prefers such a bill as there is no doubt about the goods being on board and, in consequence, dispute on this point will not arise with the bankers or consignee, thereby facilitating earliest financial settlement of the export sale.

2. *Received bill of lading*. This arises where the word 'shipped' does not appear on the bill of lading. It merely confirms that the goods have been handed over to the shipowner and are in his custody. The cargo may be in his dock warehouse/transit shed or even inland. The bill has, therefore, not the same meaning as a 'shipped' bill and the buyer under a CIF contract need not accept such a bill for ultimate financial settlement through the bank unless provision has been made in the contract. Forwarding agents will invariably

avoid handling 'received bills' for their clients unless special circumstances obtain.

3. *Through bills of landing.* In many cases it is necessary to employ two or more carriers to get the goods to their final destination. The on-carriage may be either by a second vessel or by a different form of transport (for example, to destinations in the interior of Canada). In such cases it would be very complicated and more expensive if the shipper had to arrange on carriage himself by employing an agent at the point of transhipment. Shipping companies, therefore, issue bills of lading which cover the whole transit and the shipper deals only with the first carrier. This type of bill enables a through rate to be quoted and is growing in popularity with the development of containerization. Special bills of lading have to be prepared for such through-consigned cargo.

4. *Stale bills of lading.* It is important that the bill of lading is available at the port of destination before the goods arrive or, failing this, at the same time. Bills presented to the consignee or his bank after the goods are due at the port are said to be stale. A cargo cannot normally be delivered by the ship owner without the bill of lading and the late arrival of this all-important document may have undesirable consequences such as warehouse rent, etc.

5. *Groupage bill of lading.* Forwarding agents are permitted to 'group' together particular compatible consignments from individual consignors to various consignees, usually situated at the same destination (country/area), and dispatch them as one consignment. The shipowner will issue a groupage bill of lading, whilst the forwarding agent, who cannot hand to his principals the shipowner's bill of lading, will issue to the individual shippers a certificate of shipment sometimes called house bill of lading.' At the destination, another agent working in close liaison with the agent forwarding the

cargo will brĕak-bulk the consignment and distribute the goods to the various consignees. This practice is on the increase, usually involving the use of containers and particularly evident in the continental trade and deep-sea container services. It will doubtless increase with containerization development and is ideal to the shipper who has small quantities of goods available for export. Advantages of groupage include:

Less packing, lower insurance premiums;

Usually quicker transits;

Less risk of damage and pilferage; and

Lower rates when compared with such cargo being dispatched as an individual parcel/consignment.

6. *Transhipment bill of lading.* This type is issued usually by shipping companies when there is no direct service between two parts, but when the shipower is prepared to tranship the cargo at an intermediate port at his expense.

7. *Clean bills of lading.* Each bill of lading states:

   In apparent good order and condition,' which of course refers to the cargo. If this statement is not modified by the shipowner, the bill of lading is regarded as 'clean' or 'unclaused'. By issuing clean bills of leading, the shipowner admits his full liability of the cargo described in the bill under the law and his contract. This type is much favoured by banks for financial settlement purposes.

8. *Claused bills of lading.* If the shipowner does not agree with any of the statements made in the bill of lading he will add a clause to this effect, thereby causing the bill of lading to be termed as 'unclean' 'foul', or 'claused.' There are many recurring types of such clauses including:

   Indequate packaging;

Unprotected machinery;
Second-hand cases;
Wet or stained cartons;
Damaged crates; and
Cartons missing etc.

The clause 'shipped on deck at owner's risk' may thus be considered to be a clause under this heading. This type of bill of lading is usually unacceptable to a bank.

9. *Negotiable bills of landing.* If the words 'or his or their assigns' are contained in the bill of lading, it is negotiably. There are, however, variations in this terminology, for example, the word 'bearer' may be inserted, or another party stated in the preamble to the phrase. Bills of lading may be negotiable by endorsement or transfer.

10. *Non-negotiable bills of lading.* When the words 'or his or their assign' are deleted from the bills of lading, the bills is regarded as non-negotiable. The efiect of this deletion is that the consignee (or other named party) cannot transfer the property or goods by transfer of the bills. This particular type is seldom found and will normally apply when goods are shipped on a non-commercial basis, such as household effects.

11. *Container bills of lading.* Containers are now playing an increasing role in international shipping and container bills of lading are becoming more common in use. They cover the goods from port to part or from inland point of departure to inland point of destination. It may be an inland clearance depot or container base. Undoubtedly, to the shipper, the most useful type of bill of lading is the clean, negotiable 'through bill,' as it enables the goods to be forwarded to the point of destination under one document, although much international trade is based on free-on-board (FOB) or cost, insurance, freight (CIF) contracts and, with regard to the latter, the seller has no further interest in the movement of the goods once they reach their port of destination.

12. With the development of combined transport operations, an increasing volume of both liner cargo trade and bulk cargo shipments will be carried involving the bill of lading being issued in association with a selected Charter Party. An example is found in the Combined Transport Bill of Lading 1971—codename 'Combiconbill' issued with selected Charter Parties.

Basically the bill of lading has four functions. Broadly, it is a receipt for the goods shipped, a transferable documents to the goods thereby enabling the holder to demand the cargo, evidence of the terms of the contract of affreightment but not the actual contract, and a quasi-negotiable instrument.

Once the shipper or his agent becomes aware of the sailing schedules of a particular trade, through the medium of sailing cards or some form of advertisement, he communicates with the shipowner with a view to booking cargo space on the vessel or container. Provided satisfactory arrangements have been concluded, the shipper forwards the cargo. At this stage, it is important to note that the shipper always makes the offer by forwarding the consignment, while the shipowner either accepts or refuses it. Furthermore, it is the shipper's duty, or that of his agent, to supply details of the consignment; normally, this is done by completing the shipping company's form of bill of lading and the shipping company then signs the number of copies requested.

When the goods have been received on board the ship the bill of lading is dated and signed by or on behalf of the carrier, usually by the Master of the ship or his agent, and stamped 'freight paid' or 'freight payable at destination' as appropriate. If the cargo is in good condition and everything is in order, no endorsement will be made on the document and it can be termed a 'clean' bill of lading. Conversely, if the goods are damaged or a portion of the consignment is missing, the document will be suitably endorsed by the Master or his agent and the bill of lading will be considered 'claused' or 'unclean'. The complete set of bills of lading is then returned to the exporter (seller) for prompt despatch to the importer (buyer). The buyer must have a negotiable bill of lading with which to clear the goods at the port of destination.

Bills of lading are made out in sets and the number varies according to the trade. Generally, it is two or three—one of which will probably be forwarded immediately—and another by a later mail in case the first is lost or delayed. In some trades, coloured bills of lading are used, to distinguish the original (signed) bills from the copies which are purely for recorded purposes. The reverse of the bill of lading bears the terms and conditions of the contract of carriage. The clauses on most bills of lading are similar in effect if not in wording.

Where the shipper has sold the goods on letter-of-credit terms established through a bank, or when he wishes to obtain payment of his invoice before the consignee obtains the goods, he will pass the full set of original bills to his bank, who will in due course arrange presentation to the consignee against payment. The financial role of the bill of lading is explained.

The shipowner or his agent at the port of destination will require one original bill of lading to be presented to him before the goods are handed over. Furthermore, he will normally require payment of any freight due, should this not have been paid at the port of shipment. When one of a set of bills of lading has been presented to the shipping company, the other bills in the set lose their value.

In the event of the bill of lading being lost or delyed in transit, the shipping company will allow delivery of the goods to the person claiming to be the consignee, if he gives a letter of indemnity. This is normally countersigned by a bank and relieves the shipping company of any liability should another person eventually come along with the actual bill of lading.

Many bills of lading are consigned 'to order' and in such situations are endorsed, normally on the reverse, by the shipper.

If the consignee is named, the goods will only be released to him, unless he transfers his right by endorsement subject to the bill of lading providing for this.

The following items are common discrepancies found in bills of lading when being processed and should be avoided:

1. Document not presented in full sets when requested.
2. Alterations not authenticated by an official of the shipping company or their agents.
3. The bill of lading is not clean when presented, such as when it is endorsed regarding damaged condition of the specified cargo or inadequate packing thereby making it unacceptable to a bank for financial settlement purposes.
4. The document is not endorsed 'on board' when so required.
5. The 'on board' endorsement is not signed or initialled by the carrier or agent and likewise not dated.
6. The bill of lading is not 'blank' endorsed if drawn to order.
7. The document fails to indicate whether 'freight paid' as stipulated in the credit arrangements *viz.* C & F or CIF contracts.
8. The bill of lading is not marked 'freight pre-paid' when freight charges are included in the invoice.
9. The bill of lading is made out 'to order' when the letter of credit stipulates 'direct to consignee' or vice versa.
10. The document is dated later than the latest shipping date specified in the credit.
11. It is not presented within twenty-one days after date of shipment or such lesser time as prescribed in the letter of credit.
12. The bill of lading details merchandise other than that prescribed.

13. The rate at which freight is calculated, and the total amount, is not shown when credit requires such data to be given.
14. Cargo has been shipped 'on deck' and not placed in the ship's hold. Basically, 'on deck' claused bills of lading are not acceptable when clean on board bills of lading are required.
15. Shipment made from a port or to a destination contrary to that stipulated.
16. Other types of bills of lading presented, although not specifically authorized. For example, bills of lading issued under a charter party, or forwarding agents' bills of lading are not accepted unless specially authorized in the letter of credit.

Our study of the bill of lading would not be complete without consideration of the national standard shipping note (NSSN), the common short-form bill of lading, and the common short-form sea waybill.

1. The NSSN has replaced the mate's receipt in most UK ports, and comprises a six-part set, copies of which are retained by these parties handling the goods until they are finally on board from which a 'shipped' bill of lading is issued. The document is complied by the supplier of the goods, or the shipper/freight forwarder giving full details of the goods similar to those found on the bill of lading, against which it is matched before issue. It accompanies the merchandise to the port or terminal. The document is unacceptable for use with dangerous-classified goods documents.

2. The General Council of British Shipping (GCBS) with the co-operation of SITPRO (Simplification of International Trade Procedures Board) introduced in 1979 a new type of bill of lading form to replace the traditional shipping company 'long-form' bills. It is called the common short-form bill of lading and in a single form is identical in legal and practical terms to the traditional bills, but is more simple and can be used with

any shipping line. The GCBS recommend their members use the document, together with as many foreign carriers as possible. A corresponding scheme introduced in other countries particularly Canada, USA and Scandinavia in the early 1970s has proved feasible from both the legal and practical viability of the concept.

The document covers shipper/forwarder and provides bills from port to port and through-transport including container bills of lading. It does not cover combined transport bills of lading which are almost always completed by computer by the combined transport operator.

The common short-form bill of lading is fully negotiable and the normal bill of lading lodgement and presentation procedures remain unchanged. However, instead of the mass of small print on the reverse, there is an approved 'short-form' clause on the face which incorporates carriers' standard conditions with full legal effect. The form has the approval of HM Customs, underwriters, ECGD and IBAP. The document is fully aligned to the SITPRO master document and offers a major opportunity to the shipper/forwarder etc. to simplify bill of lading documentation and cut down on the multiple stocks of forms which have previously been necessary. Shippers, forwarders and shipowners alike will benefit from this simplification.

The common short-form bill of lading has the following salient features:

(i) It is approved by SITPRO, GCBS, HM Customs and Excise, insurance underwriters, ECGD and IBAP. It may be used by shippers and freight forwarders and presented for signature to the carrier or his authorized agents, after a persual and acceptance of the carrier's standard terms and conditions to which the incorporation clause in the short-form bill of lading refers.

(ii) It is suitable for outward shipments from the UK involving 'through' transit, or 'port-to-port' carriage of cargo for both 'break-bulk' and 'unit loads' of all types traditionally covered by 'long-form' bills of lading.

(iii) It is based upon an internationally accepted layout adopted by the United Nations. Such widespread acceptance of its format facilitates fast and accurate recording, processing, transmission and receipt of data relating to the moment of cargo.

(iv) As confirmed by the ICC it is acceptable within the uniform customs and practice for documentary credits'. (ICC brochure no. 400 refers.)

(v) It is a document recommended by GCBS for use of all outward shipments from the UK and particularly by all UK shipper/carriers and their conference associates.

(vi) It is a document of title under which the contracting carrier undertakes to deliver the subject goods against surrender of an original document.

(vii) It is a 'received-for-carriage' bill with provision for endorsement evidencing goods shipped on board when so required.

(viii) It is suitable for conventional and through-liner services irrespective of whether the vessel is chartered or owned by the contracting carrier. (Use of the form is not currently available for goods carried by combined transport operators.)

(ix) It is described as a 'short-form' document because of the use of an abridged standard clause on the face of the document which incorporates the conditions of carriage of the contracting carrier (see Document III in Appendix D). The change eliminates the mass of small print on the reverse side of bills of lading without affecting the status of the document or rights and obligations of any interested party.

(x) It is a document fully aligned to the SITPRO 'master' document with the opportunity to complete the bill of lading from such as a document without any additional typing.

(xi) It is an aid to achieve lower stationery costs through (i) a reduced need to hold a variety of stocks of long-form bills of lading and with individual carrier's name and conditions plus (ii) the elimination of the risk of using obsolescent forms together with attendant complications.

A specimen of a common short-form bill of lading is found as document III in Appendix D.

3. The use of the negotiable bill of lading which has to be surrendered to the carrier at the destination in order to obtain delivery of the goods is traditional, but not without disadvantages. The document has to follow the goods and often, for commercial or financial reasons, passes through a variety of hands, resulting in the goods being held up at destination pending arrival of the document—and thereby expenses and additional risks are incurred and customer goodwill is probably lost.

The General Council of British Shipping with the co-operation of SITPRO has also developed the concept of a non-negotiable type of transport document—termed a common short-form see waybill—in place of the negotiable traditional bill of lading. Its basic feature is that it provides for delivery to the consignee named in it without surrender of the transport document. A specimen common short-form sea waybill. is found as document IV in Appendix D.

The common short-form sea waybill has the following salient features which are similar in many ways to the common short-form bill of lading:

(i) It is a common document upon which the shipper adds the name of the contracting carrier to be used.

(ii) It is a non-negotiable document consigned to a named consignee and not requiring production to obtain possession of the goods at destination.

(iii) It is a received-for-shipment document, with an option for use as a shipped document.

(iv) It is an aid to achieve lower stationery cost through (i) a reduced need to hold stocks of individual carriers' bills with individual carrier's name and conditions plus (ii) the elimination of the risk of using obsolescent forms together with attendant complications.

(v) It is a document fully aligned to the SITPRO 'masser' document with the opportunity to complete the sea way bill from such a document without any additional typing.

(vi) It is described as a 'short-form' document because of the use of an abridged standard clause on the face of the document which incorporates the conditions of carriage of the contracting carrier (see Document IV in Appendix D). The change eliminates the need to reprint documents to accommodate changes and conditions.

(vii) It facilitates earlier release of the goods—if received for shipment—and thereby reduces delays associated with negotiability. Moreover, it helps the speedier flow of goods tc the consignee. One must bear in mind the named consignee is not required to produce the sea waybill to obtain possession of the goods at destination.

(viii) It is approved by SITPRO, GCBS, HM Customs and Excise, insurance underwriters, ECGD and IBAP. It may be used by shippers and freight forwarders and presented for signature to the carrier of his authorized agents after a perusal and acceptance of the carrier's standard terms and conditions to which the incorporation clause in the sea waybill refers.

(ix) It is suitable for outward shipments from the UK involving 'through' transit, or 'port-to-port' carriage of cargo for both 'break-bulk' and 'unit loads' of all types. Moreover, it is suitable for conventional and through-liner services, irrespective whether the vessel is chartered or owned by the carrier.

(x) It is based upon an internationally accepted layout adopted by the United Nations. Such widespread acceptance of its format facilitates fast and accurate recording, processing, transmission and receipt of data relating to the movement of cargo.

The commercial and financial feasibility of using the waybill clearly rests with the shipper/consignee and is dependent upon the type of trade transaction involved. The waybill is the natural choice for trading between multinational companies and associated companies, and also for open account sales. However, it can be used additionally in many cases involving banking transactions, and even under letters of credit providing the credit is suitably worded.

The point at which sea waybills are released will depend upon whether the document is 'received for shipment' or 'shipped on board'. In signing waybills, the carrier on his agent is required to insert the carrier's cable address within the signature or date stamp.

If a received-for-shipment document was issued and cargo was subsequently, short-shipped or a carrier's clause required (for example, to indicate that damage was sustained whilst the goods were on the quay) then a qualification report should be issued to the shipper, consignee and those concerned within the carrier's organization; information concerning such reports should also be made available to insurers on request. Use of the 'shipped' option would, however, obviate the need for a qualification report, and, in such circumstances the normal bill-of-lading procedures would apply.

If a 'shipped-on-board' document was issued, then the provision of the 'shipped' option should be in a manner which if the document was to be presented under a documentary credit, will satisfy 'Uniform Customs and Practice for Documentary Credits' 1984 revision. This refers to a procedure whereby waybills can be endorsed to specify that the goods mentioned have been loaded on board a named vessel or shipped on a named vessel, the loading-on-board date been specified.

To conclude our study of the bill of lading, it is important to bear in mind the shipper/exporter/agent presents them correctly to the bank. This must specially indicate the bill of lading states the goods are on board the ship, an indication of the correct name and address of notify party, a full set of originals are provided as called for in the credit, and finally the bill of lading is marked 'freight paid' or 'frieght prepaid' if 'C and F' or 'CIF' shipment. The subject of bills of lading is extensively deal with in Chapter 12 of *Elements of Shipping*.

CARGO INSURANCE POLICY AND CERTIFICATE

It is most important to have insurance cover against loss or damage that may occur during shipment. The export sales contract with the buyer must clearly state who is responsible for arranging the insurance at all stages from the time the merchandise leaves the exporter's premises until the buyer takes possession. This embraces transporation of the goods to the seaport, airport, or inland clearance depot, the period during which the merchandise is stored awaiting shipment or loading, the periods whilst the goods are on board the ship, aircraft or other conveyance such as the through international road transport, the off-loading and storage on arrival, and finally transportation to the buyer. This involves primarily 'Incoterms' which are fully deal with in Chapter 8 of *Elements of Export Marketing and Management*.

The cargo insurance policy may only be issued by the insurer and is usually in a standard form covering the customary risk for any voyage or flight. The form of policy in general use today is fully explained in Chapter 8. Individual policies for single shipments are rarely used by regular exporters because a new policy would have to be obtained for each shipment. However, insurance certificates based on the overall policy may be issued and are far more common than the policy.

The insurance certificate must contain the same details as policy with the slight difference that it will carry a shortened version of the provisions of the policy under which it is issued and should be signed by the policy holder.

Overall, the insurance policy/certificate must contain the following:

1. The name and signature of the insurer.
2. The name of the assured.
3. The endorsement of the assured when applicable so that the rights to claim may be transferred.
4. A description of the risk covered.
5. A description of the consignment.
6. The sum or sums to be insured.
7. The place where claims are payable together with the name of the agent to whom claims may be directed.

Basically, the insurance policy/certificate must embrace the following relative to the processing of the international consignment:

1. Cover the risk detailed in the credit arrangments.
2. Be in a completed form.
3. Be in a transferable form.
4. Be dated on or before the date of the document evidencing despatch, for example, Bill of Lading.
5. Be expressed in the same currency as that of the credit.

The insurance policy/certificate must avoid containing the following discrepancies when presented under a letter of credit:

1. The amount of cover is insufficient or does not include the risks mentioned in the credit.
2. The insurance is not issued in the currency of the credit.

3. The insurance policy/certificate is not endorsed and/or signed.

4. The certificate or policy bear a date later than date of shipment/despatch.

5. The goods are not correctly described.

6. The alterations on the insurance policy/certificate are not authenticated.

7. The insurance policy/certificate is not in a transferable form when required.

8. The carrying vessel's name is not recorded.

2. The insurance policy/certificate does not cover transhipment when bills of leding indicate it will take place.

When a policy is called for under a letter of credit, a certificate is not acceptable. However, a policy is acceptable when a certificate is requested. Broker's cover notes are not acceptable unless specifically permitted in the credit.

It is important to bear in mind when the shipper/exporter/agent is prepared the insurance document for presentation to the bank, that it is in the currency of the documentary letter of credit; the insurance is for value specified in the credit; it covers all risks specified in the credit; the insurance document is dated prior to dispatch of goods or indicates that cover is effective from shipment date; and finally the insurance policy is presented when the credit so stipulates.

CERTIFICATE OF HEALTH

A certificate of health is usually required when agricultural/animal products are imported. The certificate is issued and signed by the health authority in the supplier's country. It states that the UK health requirements were satisfied at the time of shipment.

CERTIFICATE OF INSPECTION

Some countries insist on pre-shipment inspection of the goods by independent surveillance companies. The certificate confirms that the goods are being supplied in accordance with the contract.

CERTIFICATE OF ORIGIN

The certificate of origin specifies the nature of quantity/ value of the goods etc. together with their place of manufacture. Such a declaration stating the country of origin of the goods shipped is required by some countries often to simplify their Customs duties. It is often incorporated in the Customs invoice. In a minority of cases, the declaration has to be authenticated by a Chamber of Commerce. It could also incorporate the selling price of the goods termed the current domestic (CDV) in which case it is likely to be embraced in the invoice.

The certificate of origin is also required when the merchandise is imported to a country that allows perferential duties on British goods owing to trade agreements. In order that goods from UK may enjoy the lower schedule of duties, the Customs authorities of the importing country must be satisfied as to the value of the goods and they substantially represent British labour and British material.

Details of the two types of certificate of origin or their equivalent are given below:

1. Those issued by a Chamber of Commerce or other official body such as a Consulate. Only required when specifically called for by the creditor.
2. Exporter's own certificate or orign—may be used for any case where no special form is required by the creditor.

It is important the certificate of origin is signed and worded exactly as specified in the credit. The great majority of certificates of origin are authenticated by a Chamber of Commmerce.

CERTIFICATE OF SHIPMENT

This certificate is issued by a freight forwarder and is merely a document confirming the goods have been shipped on a specified vessel and date. It is often associated with groupage or consolidated container shipments and is also known as the 'in-house bill of lading' under groupage arrangements.

The document confirms the specific consignment has been shipped in accordance with the instruction detailed on the certificate. It contains details of the exporter, consignee, receiving dates, dork/container base, name of vessel, port of loading, port of discharge, place of delivery, shipping marks, container number, number of packages, full description of goods, gross weight of goods and cubic measurement.

CHARTER PARTY

A charter party is a contract whereby a shipowner agrees to place his ship, or part of it, at the disposal of a merchant or other person (known as the charter), for the carriage of goods from one port to another port on being paid freight, or to let his ship for a specified period, his remuneration being known as hire money. The terms, conditions and exceptions under which the goods are carried are set out in the charter party.

A very large proportion of the world's trade is carried in tramp vessels. It is quite common to find that one cargo will fill a whole ship and in these circumstances, one cargo owner or one character will enter into a special contract with the shipowner for the hire of his ship. Such a contract is known as a charter party. It is not always a full ship, although this is usually the case. There are basically two types of charter parties:

Demise and non-demise.

A demise or 'bareboat' charter party arise when the character is responsible for providing the cargo and crew, whilst the shipowner merely provides the vessel. In consequence, the charaterer appoints the crew, thus taking over full responsibility for the operation of the vessel, and pays all expenses incurred. A demise charter party is for a period of time which may vary from a few weeks to several years.

A non-demise charter arises when the shipowner provides the vessel and her crew, whilst the charterer merely supplies the cargo. It may be a voyage charter for a particular voyage, in which, the shipowner agrees to carry cargo between specified ports for a pre-arranged freight. The majority of tramp cargo shipments are made on a voyage charter basis. Alternatively, it may be a time charter for a stated period or voyage for a remuneration known as hire money. The shipowner continues to manage his own vessel, both under non-demise voyage or time charter parties under the charter's instructions. With a time charter, it is usual for the charterer to pay port dues and fuel costs, and overtime payments incurred in an endeavour to obtain faster turn-rounds. It is quite common for liner companies to supplement their services by taking tramp ships on time charter, but this practice may lessen as containerization develops.

There are several types of non-demise voyage charter and these are given below. It will be seen that they all deal with the carriage of goods from a certain port or ports to another port or ports and the differences between them arise mainly out of payment for the cost of loading and discharging and port expenses.

1. *Gross form of charter.* This is probably the most common form of charter used by tramp ships today. In this form, the shipowner—in return for a higher freight—meets the cost of employing the stevedores at either the loading port of discharge or both.

2. *Net terms.* Under those terms the cargo is loaded and discharged at no cost to the shipowner. The cost of stevedores at the loading port is borne by the shipper and, at the port of discharge, by the receiver. The term net terms is not in common use but is generally referred to as 'free-in-and-out' (FIO) with exactly the same meanning.

3. *FIO charter.* Under this charter the cargo is loaded and discharged at no cost to the shipowner. The cost of stevedores at the loading port is borne by the shipper and at the port of discharge by the receiver.

4. *Liner terms.* Under this charter usually found in the short sea trade, the shipowner is responsible for loading, stowing and discharging the cargo. Usually the shipowner selects and appoints the stevedores, but this can an area of discussion during the fixture negotiations.

5. *Lump sum charter.* In this case, the charter pays a lump sum of money for the ues of the ship and the shipowner guarantees that a certain amount of space (that is, bale cubic metres) will be available for cargo, along with the maximum weight of cargo that the vessel will be able to carry. A lump sum charter may be on either a gross basis or an FIO basis. Such a charter is very useful when the charter wishes to load a mixed cargo—the shipowner guarantees that a certain amount of space and weight will be available and it is up to the characterer to use that space to his best advantage.

The above forms of charter are all quite common today and, in each case, the ship owner pays the port charges.

There are, of course, numerous variations that may be made to the above broad divisions and this is a matter for negotiation when the vessel is being 'worked' for future business. For example, the gross and FIO charters may be modified to an FOB charter (free on board) meaning that the charterer pays for the cost of loading and the shipowner pays for the cost of discharge, or alternatively the charter may be arranged on the basis of free discharge, that is, the charterer pays for the cost of discharging. The same general terms of contract are found in all the above types of charter.

A substantial proportion of the charters in this country are negotiated through a shipbroker on the Baltie Exchange situated in London. The role of this exchange is explained in Chapter 14.

The negotiations are carried out by word-of-mouth in the exchange, not by letter, and when the contract has been concluded the vessel is said to be 'fixed'. The charter party is then prepared and signed by the two parties or their agents. In addition to the trade to and from this country, a large number of cross voyages, that is, from one foreign country to another, are fixed on the London market, quite often to a vessel owned in yet another foreign country. There is no compulsion to conduct negotiations through a shipbroker on the Baltic Exchange. Many negotiations are conducted direct between charterer and shipowner. It is a matter for the shipowner's judgement whether he engages a shipbroker to conduct his negotiations direct wiih the charterer. Obviously, when the shipbroker is negotiating a series of voyage charters for his principal, the shipowner will endeavour to reduce to an absolute minimum the number of ballast voyages. These arise between termination of one voyage charter for example at Rotterdam, and commencement of the next voyage charter, for example, at Southampton, involving a ballast voyage Rotterdam—Southampton.

It will be appreciated that the terms and conditions of a charter party will vary according to the wishes of the parties to the contract. Nevertheless, the former Chamber of Shipping of the United Kingdom—now designated General Council of British Shipping—together with the Baltic and International Maritime Conference have approved a number of charter parties (about fifty) for certain commodities in specified trades. These include primarily the tramp trades *viz.*, coal, wheat, timber, ore etc. The parties to the contract are free to make any amendments to such charter parties to meet their needs and there is no obligation to use any particular charter party for a particular trade.

The subject of chartering is dealt with extensively.

COMBINED TRANSPORT DOCUMENTS

The development of combined transport operations with its

many advantages will continue throughout the decade. This involves the container shipment, the through road haulage service, the through rail service, and so on. The documents concerned embrace the Combiconbill—combined transport bill of lading which is the carriage of goods by at least two modes of transport, the CMR (Convention relative an contrat de transport internationale des Marchandises par vois de Route) consignment note involving the conveyance of goods on a through international road haulage service or the CIM (Convention Internationale concernant le transport de Marchandises par chemin de fer) consignment note involving the conveyance of goods on a through international rail service. Moreover the FIATA (International Federation of Forwarding Agents Association) have introduced the FIATA combined transport bill of lading which is widely used by their members.

CONVENTION ON THE CONTRACT FOR THE INTERNATIONAL CARRIAGE OF GOODS BY ROAD (CMR)

The international convention concerning the carriage of goods by road (CMR) came into force in the United Kingdom in October 1967. It permits the carriage of goods by road under one consignment note under a common code of conditions applicable to twenty-six countries. These include Austria, Belgium, Bulgaria, Czechoslovakia, Denmark, Finland, France, (Federal Republic of) Germany, Greece, Hungary, Italy, Luxembourg, Netherlands, Norway, Poland, Portugal, Spain, Sweden, Switzerland, UK and Yugoslavia. Additionally, by Orders in Council, the convention has been extended to cover the Isle of Man, the Isle of Guernsey and Gibraltar. It applies to all international carriage of goods by road for reward to or from a contracting party. It does not apply to traffic between the UK and the Republic of Ireland.

The contract of carriage, found in the CMR consignment note, is established when it is completed by the sender and carrier with the appropriate signatures/stamp being recorded thereon. The senders and the carrier are entitled respectively to the first and third copies of the consignment note, and the second copy must accompany the goods. If the goods have to be loaded in different vehicles, or are of different kinds, or are divided into different lots, either party has the right to require a separate consignment note to be made out in respect of each vehicle or each kind or lot of goods. The CMR consignment note is not a negotiable/transferable document or document of title.

The consignment note must contain the following particulars: the date when and the place where it is made out; the names and address of the sender, the carrier and the consignee; the place and date of taking over the goods, and the place designated for delivery; the ordinary description of the nature of the goods and the method of packing and, in the case of dangerous goods, their generally recognized description: the number of packages and their special marks and numbers; the gross weight of the goods or their quantity otherwise expressed; charges relating to the carriage; the requisite instructions for Customs and other formalities; and a statement that the carriage is subject, notwithstanding any clause to the contrary, to the provisions of the convention.

Further, the consignment note must contain the following particulars where applicable; a statement that transhipment is not allowed; the charges which the sender undertakes to pay; the amount of 'cash on delivery' charges; a declaration of the value of the goods: a declaration of the amount representing any special interest in delivery; the sender's instructions to the carrier regarding insurance of the goods; the agreed time limit for the carriage; a list of the documents handed to the carrier; where the carrier has no reasonable means of checking the accuracy of the statements in the consignment note as to the number of packages and their marks and numbers, or as to the apparent condition of the goods and their packaging, he must enter his reservations in the consignment note specifying the grounds on which they are based; and where the sender requires the carrier to check the gross eight of the goods or their quantity otherwise expressed or the contents of the packages, the carrier must enter the results of such checks; and any agreement that open unsheeted vehicles may be used for the carriage of the goods.

The parties may enter any other useful particulars in the consignment note.

The sender is liable for all expenses, loss and damage sustained by the carrier by reason of the inaccuracy or inadequacy of certain specified particulars which the consignment note must contain, or by reason of the inaccuracy or inadequacy of any other particulars or instructions given by him.

The carrier is liable for all expenses, loss and damage sustained by the person entitled to dispose of the goods as a result of the omission of the statement that the contract is subject to the convention.

For the purposes of the convention, the carrier is responsible for the acts and omissions of his agents and servants and any other persons whose services he uses for the performance of the carriage as long as those agents, servants or other persons are acting within the scope of their employment.

There is a duty on the carrier:

1. To check the accuracy of the statements in the consignment note as to the number of packages and their marks and numbers, and the apparent condition of the goods and their packing.
2. If the sender so requires him, to check the gross weight of the goods or their quantity otherwise expressed or the contents of the packages.
3. To check that the statement that the contract is subject to the convention is properly included in the consignment note.

The sender is responsible for the accuracy and adequacy of documents and information which he must either attach to the consignment note or place at the carrier's disposal for the purposes of Customs or other formalities which have to be completed before delivery of the goods.

There is a duty on the sender:

1. To ensure that the goods are properly packed.
2. In the case of dangerous goods, to inform the carrier of the exact nature of the danger and indicate, if necessary, the precautions to be taken.
3. To ensure the accuracy and adequacy of certain specified particulars which the consignment note must contain and of any other particulars or instructions given by him to the carrier.

The statutory provisions are embodied in the Carriage of Goods by Road Act 1965. An example of a CMR consignment note is shown as Document VIII in Appendix D. The CMR consignment note must be carried on all hire-and-reward journeys involving an international transit.

DOCK RECEIPT

This may be issued by a Port Authority to confirm receipt of cargo on the quay/warehouse pending shipment. It has no legal role regarding processing financial settlement of international consignments.

EXCHANGE PERMIT

The exchange permit is particularly found in the Middle East trades and usually associated with the issue of an import licence. They are usually issued by government departments, Chambers of Commerce, or Chamber of Industry thereby authorizing import of a specific commodity. It is a means of regulating the flow of specific commodity imports and the funds associated with them.

EXPORT INVOICING

Export documents are never static—there is a continual stream of new overseas import regulations along with new developments and a constant issue of new forms etc. Accordingly, the requisite invoice for a particular market should be checked to ensure the correct one is used otherwise serious delays will be encountered in processing the export order through Customs. Moreover, the exporter's invoice should be carefully and accurately completed. Details of the various types of invoices are now examined.

1. Commercial invoice. The commercial invoice gives details of the goods and is issued by the seller (exporter). It forms the basis of the transaction between the seller and buyer, and is completed in accord with the number of prescribed copies required. Usually it bears the exporter's own headed invoice form stationery. The invoice gives a description of the goods, stating prices and terms exactly as specified in the credit, as well as shipping marks. Overall, it contains the following information:

(i) Name and address of buyer (importer) and seller (exporter).

(ii) Buyer's reference, that is, order number, indent number etc.

(iii) Number and types of packages.

(iv) Weights and measurements of the consignment.

(v) Place and date of issue.

(vi) Details of actual cost of freight and insurance if so requested.

(vii) Total amount payable, embracing price of goods, freight, insurance and so on.

(viii) The export and/or import licence number.

(ix) The contents of individual packages.

(x) The method of despatch.

(xi) Shipment terms.

(xii) Letter-of-credit number/details—if so requested.

(xiii) Country of origin of goods.

(xiv) Signature of exporter.

Basically it is a document rendered by one person to another in regard of goods which have been sold. Its primary function is a check for the purchaser against charges and delivery. With regard to insurance claims, and for packing purposes, it is useful evidence to verify the value and nature of the goods and in certain circumstances, it is evidence of the contract between the two parties, for example, packing not up to specification may give underwriters redress against the sellers. The invoice is not necessarily a contract of sale. It may form a contract of sale if it is in writing containing all the material terms. On the other hand, it may not be a complete memorandum of the contract of sale and, therefore, evidence may be given to vary the contract which is inferred therefrom.

In particular circumstances, the commercial invoice can be certified by Chambers of Commerce and/or legalized by the resident consul in the UK.

2. *Consular invoice*. Consular invoices are mandatory when shipping goods to certain ports of the world particularly to those countries which enforce *ad valorem* import duties. This applies particularly in South America. The invoices are specially printed documents which must be completed exactly in accordance with requirements and certified by the consul of the country to which the goods are consigned. This is done at the nearest convenient consular office to the port/airport ICD of departure. The invoices are issusd at the consular office and a fee is payable on certification which is often based on a percentage value of the commercial invoice value of the goods. The consul of the importing country retains one copy, returns one copy to the shipper, and forwards further copies to the Customs authorities in his own country. The consular invoice may be used in some circumstances as a certificate of origin. The forms are available from consuls or possibly through Chambers of Commerce and freight forwarders. In may countries both the consular invoice are required.

3. Customs invoices. Customs invoices may be required by the authorities of the importing country. An adequate number should be provided for the use of the Customs authorities overseas.

4. Pro forma invoice. This type of invoice is prepared by the exporter and may be required in advance for licence or letter of credit purposes. The document includes the date, name of consignee, quantity and description of the goods, marks and measurements of packages, cost of the goods, packing, carriage, freight, postage, insurance premiums, terms of sale, terms of payment, etc.

The following discrepancies relating to processing invoices under letters of credit do arise and should be avoided:

1. Value exceeds credit amount.
2. Amount differs from that of bill of exchange.
3. Prices of goods not as indicated in credit.
4. Omission of the price basts and shipment terms, for example, FOB, CIF, C & F etc.
5. Inclusion of charges not specified in the credit.
6. Invoice not certified, notarized or signed as required by credit.
7. Buyer's name differs from that mentioned in the credit.
8. Invoice not issued by the exporter.
9. Invoice does not contain declaration required under the credit.
10. Description of goods differs from that in the credit.

The following items must be borne in mind when the shipper/exporter/agent prepares the invoice and presents them to the bank under a documentary letter of credit.

1. Invoice description of the goods agrees exactly with the documentary letter of credit.

2. The invoice is addressed to the importer.
3. The invoice includes exact licence and/or certificate numbers required by the credit.
4. The invoice shows the terms of shipment mentioned in the credit.

INTERNATIONAL CONVENTION CONCERNING THE CARRIAGE OF GOODS BY RAIL (CIM)

The international convention concerning the carriage of goods by rail (CIM) has existed in some form since 1983. It permits the carriage of goods by rail under one document, a consignment note (not negotiable), under a common code of conditions applicable to twenty-nine countries mainly situated in Europe and the Mediterranean areas. It embraces the maritime portion of the transit subject to it being conveyed on shipping lines as listed under the Convention. Advantages of the CIM throughout rail consignment involving a container or train ferry wagon include through rates under a common code of conditions, simplified documentation/accountancy, flexibility of freight payment, no intermediate handling (usually) nor Customs examination in transit countries, through transists, and minimum documentation. The convention is revised from time to time to reflect modern needs and the current one is the international convention concerning the carriage of goods by rail with additional protocol, 1970.

The CIM consignment note is completed by the shipper/agent/originating rail carrier and has six copies. It embraces the original of the consignment note, the invoice, the arrival note, the duplicate of the consignment note, the duplicate of the invoice, and a supplementary copy.

The following information must be recorded on the CIM consignment note:

1. The date and originating rail station of the consignment.
2. The name and address of the sender and the consignee.

3. The originating rail station accepting consignment and the station/place designated for delivery.
4. The ordinary description of the nature of the goods and method of packing and, in the case of dangerous goods, their generally recognized description.
5. The gross weight of the goods or their quantity.
6. The charges relating to the carriage.
7. The requisite instructions for Customs and other formalities.

The foregoing may also be required under a letter of credit.

LETTERS OF HYPOTHECATION

This is a banker's document outlining conditions under which the international transactional will be executed on the exporter's behalf, the latter of whom will have given certain pledges to his banker. It may be by direct loan, acceptance, or negotiations of draft thereto.

LETTERS OF INDEMNITY

The role of the letter of indemnity is to permit cargo to be released to a consignee without production of the original endorsed bill of lading, or to permit the issue of a duplicate set of documents when the original bills of lading have been lost or mislaid in transit. It is a document of legal and commercial convenience, and should be used with care and caution. Its need arises from the risks involved in permitting delivery of cargo without an original bill of lading, or in issuing a duplicate set of bills of lading. It usually requires a counter signature of a reputable bank—but this is not necessary when submitted on behalf of a national government.

MATE'S RECEIPT

This document is sometimes issued in lieu of a bill of lading. It has no legal authority regarding processing financial settlement of international consignments but merely confirms cargo is placed on board a ship pending issue of a bill of lading. In many countries the National Standard Shipping Note has replaced the Mate's receipt.

PACING LIST

In some trades the packing list document is used. This provides a list of the contents of a package(s)/consignment(s). In particular it will include the number and kind of packages, their contents, overall net and gross weight usually in kilogrammes, the dimension(s) of the package(s) including length/width/height, and finally the cube of the package(s). The document is often referred to as a packing note and may feature the package marking.

PARCEL POST RECEIPT

This is issued by the Post Office for goods sent by parcel post. It is both a receipt and evidence of despatch. It is not a document of title and goods should be consigned to the party specified in the credit. An airmal label should be fixed to a postal receipt in respect of air parcel post despatch; alternatively the Post Office should stamp the receipt 'air parcel'. Goods sent by post should be eonsigned to the party specified in the documentary credit.

PHYTOSANITARY (PLANT HEALTH) CERTIFICATE

The importation of all planning material, forest trees and other trees and shrubs, and certain raw fruit and vegetables must be accompanied by a phytosanitary certificate in most countries. In some countries the importation of certain species of plants from certain areas of the world is prohibited. Application for such plant health certificates should be made to the agricultural agreement of the exporting country.

SHIPS DELIVERY ORDER

A delivery order is written authority to deliver goods, etc. to a named party in exchange for the bill of lading usually at the port of destination. It is issued at the port of destination and is subject to all the terms and conditions of the carrier's bill of lading. It must not contain any reservations or clauses other than those appearing in the bill of lading except where increased obligations or extra cost may be incurred in giving delivery beyond the bill of lading. The document is used at the port of destination of exchange for an original bill of lading and is legally recognized as a token of an authority to receive possession.

The delivery order should be addressed to the ship's Master, and its role arises, for example, when the buyer may not wish to know the identify of the supplier abroad for trade reasons. Hence, the delivery order issue may prove a useful document. It is important the document is endorsed by the party to whom it is made out. However, if it is issued in one port for delivery in another and the freight is payable at destination, the order would then be 'consigned' to the carrier's agent to ensure that it would have to be presented and released before collection of the goods is authorized.

VETERINARY CERTIFICATE/HEALTH CERTIFICATE

This may be required when livestock/domestic animals/ agricultural products are being exported. It should be signed by the appropriate health authority in the exporter's country.

WEIGHT LIST

In some countries, a weight list document is required. The merely given details of the weight of the consignment.

5

EXPORT QUALITY CONTROL

LENNART SANDHOLM

I

QUALITY CONTROL MECHANISMS

Producing export products of the right quality for foreign buyers requires an effective policy and organizational framework in the company. The main guide lines for the quality goals of the firm must be set down in the form of a written policy on quality and made known to all those connected with export production and marketing. In addition the enterprise must be suitably structured to assure that the quality policy is followed. These managerial aspects of quality activities are a key element in achieving appropriate quality in export products.

QUALITY POLICY

Many companies do not have a written quality policy. Instead they rely for their quality-related activities upon certain unwritten principles that result from decisions taken by the top management. Such a situation is not always satisfactory, however, as the absence of a clear quality policy can hinder the process of solving quality problems. A written policy tends to be better throughtout than an unwritten one. Also a written policy can be communicated to those concerned in an authoriative and uniform manner, reducing the risk of misunderstanding. Furthermore a written policy can form the basis for management by objectives, rather than management by crisis. Finally, it is easier to evaluate quality activities against a written policy than on the basis of a vague understanding of quality goals.

The managing director of the company should be responsible for the quality policy. The initiative for setting down the policy, however, usually comes from the quality department. Key managers in the firm should participate in the preparation process. The completed policy should be announced solely in the managing director's name.

The quality policy document should include three parts:

1. Need for a quality policy—Why have a quality policy?
2. Policy statement—What quality level should be aimed at for the products?
3. Implementation of the policy statement—What tasks should the various departments (product development, manufacturing, marketing and so on) undertake in order to achieve what is stipulated in the policy statement of the company?

QUALITY OBJECTIVES

Quality objectives are the firm's specific goals regarding the quality factor, such as the quality level of the products manufactured and the costs of achieving this level. They fit within the overall quality policy drawn up for the firm. These goals should be quantified and written down. Quantifying them provides a stimulus for action, as employees see in concrete terms what is to be achieved.

The quality objectives can take different forms, such as:

(a) Absolute values, for example, inspection cost per manufacturing department (expressed in monetary terms).

(b) Indexes, for instance scrap and rework cost related to manufacturing cost or the complant rate (expressed as a percentage).

(c) Relative differences, for example reduction of the guarantee cost by 25 per cent.

The quality objectives can apply to different categories of quality data. In most cases, it is appropriate to quantify quality objectives for:

1. Quality costs—total costs, per-factory costs and costs by product.
2. Internal failure costs—by cost centre, by product.
3. Complaint costs and complaint rate—for each product.
4. Fraction of products defective in the final inspection—per product.
5. Fraction of rejected lots of products in the incoming inspection—for each type of goods.

Some of the quality objectives and the related costs are usually included in the company's budget.

QUALITY SYSTEMS

A "quality system" for a firm covers the activities in the company that affect and the procedures that employees must follow in their quality work. The quality system in an enterprise should be based on the firm's quality policy.

Quality systems can be broken down into different parts or subsystems. These vary from one company to another. An example of such a break-down (which must be adapted to the particular case) is:

Preproduction activities.

Quality specifications.

Vendor relations.

Manufacture.

Inspection.

Customer relations.

Quality auditing.

Metrology.

Quality data feedback.

Personnel.

Product safety and liability.

The quality system can be described in a quality manual produced by the company. A copy of the manual should be given to each key manager in the firm.

Some sales contracts include requirements on the quality system to be used by the supplier. This procedure was started as an alternative to the expensive practice of having the buyer's own inspectors (or even in some cases entire inspection departments) at the seller's premises to ensure product quality. The suppliers instead produce evidence of having followed a certain plan of work. This plan must fulfill the conditions set by the buyer. These conditions sometimes develop into standard quality systems or quality programmes in the company, and in some countries they are eventually published as national standards. At the international level, the international Organization their Standardization (ISO) is now producing standards or on quality management and assurance systems (ISO's 9000 series) that consist of guidelines on the appropriate organization of the quality system within the firm.

(Setting requirements on the quality system to be used by the supplier is not, however, always the decisive factor in achieving the desired quality level. Applying suitable manufacturing processes and having competent personnel including managers) is often more important than a formal quality system.)

QUALITY ORGANIZATION

The quality of the products manufactured is the result of the work of many persons in the company. The responsibilities that these staff have, regardless of their specific jobs, include quality-related tasks. To make these responsibilities clear is a a matter of organization.

The work of organizing for quality activities includes:

Identifying the activities necessary to reach the desired quality level in products.

Determining the responsibilities for carrying out these activities.

Dividing the work into fundamental parts (jobs).

For each job, defining responsibility and authority.

Establishing coordination between the different jobs.

There is no generally applicable form of organization. This must be designed to meet the needs of each company. Factors such as the type of products, type of manufacturing processes, category of customers, management philosopy and so on vary from one firm to another. Such elements affect the organization of the quality activities.

To establish an organizational set-up suitable for a company, five areas of activity should be considered:

acceptance, prevention, improvement, coordination and assurance.

The organizational aspects of these are described in more detail below.

Acceptance: By acceptance is meant the work that, in its broadest sense, concerns decisions to accept or reject the manufactured product. This activity is also commonly, called inspection. Acceptance work includes comparing materials, semi-finished products and finished items with quality requirements and, based on the result of the this comparison, deciding on acceptance or rejection. It also includes inspection planning and other inspection-related activities (such as the checking and calibration of inspection equipment).

The different stages in the production of a product (from bought-in materials and components to the finished article) lead to natural division of the inspection work in terms of organization. In addition there are supporting functions (for example inspection planning and controls in the measurement laboratory).

The traditional organizational set-up for acceptance is to have a separate unit to check that vendors and manufacturers produce items that comply with the requirements specified. This means that the inspection department is independent from production. Such a department may have sections for incoming inspection, process inspection and final inspection. A section for inspection planning usually also exists, which follows and analyzes developments in the quality work, assists in preproduction runs, carries out quality ananlyses and conducts other studies as well as plans and prepares the inspection work.

The advantage of an inspection department independent from production is that decisions on acceptance and rejection can be taken without any direct influence from the production side. A number of larger customers often require their suppliers to have this form of organization.

A disadvantage of having all of the inspectors in the inspection department, however, is the risk that the responsibility for quality in purchasing and production activities will become diluted, as the inspection deparment is not directly involved in the production process. The interest of purchasing and production staff in quality matters is often diminished in such an arrangement. A better approach is therefore for the purchasing and production departments to have at least some of the responsibility for accepting and rejecting goods. This is a practice that is becoming more common in many firms. In this situation, the staff involved in purchasing and production are entirely responsible for acceptance of the products.

A third alternative is for acceptance work to be share between the purchasing and production departments and a separate inspection department. In this case the purchasing staff can be responsible for incoming inspection, the production staff for process inspection and the inspection department for final inspection.

Prevention: Prevention work includes planning new and modified products and manufacturing processes so that an adequate quality level will be achieved when production begins. Included in prevention are activities ranging from the market study phase to the start of production:

> feasibility studies, prototype testing, tolerancing, classification of product quality characteristics in terms of importance, design reviews, planning and so on.
>
> Various departments take part in the work:
>
> product development, design, manufacturing engineering, purchasing, production, inspection and so forth. In the organizational set-up, it is necessary to clarify the pattern of responsibilities for these activities.

Improvement: Work to reduce quailty cost includes starting with the symptop of the defect and working through to the case and the remedy. This is usually much easier for sporadie defects than for chronic defects. Correcting sporadic defects does not generally require any input of an organizational nature. It is apparent to the departments affected that such work is part of normal job. Within its area of responsibility each department can correct such defects.

CHART A

COMPANY X

QUALITY POLICY

Need for a policy

To improve the reputation and increase the competitiveness and profitability of Company X it is necessary to manufacture and sell products of high quality. To achieve this goal, all departments must tackle the factors that influence the quality of the products in a systematic and appropriate way.

Policy statement

It is the policy of Company X to market only products of appropriate quality and also to achieve entire customer satisfaction through products that perform expected functions in a reliable and safe way. The qualify level is to be of a consistently high level so that if constitutes a principal reason for purchasing the product, at the present time as well as in the future.

Implementation of the policy

The implementation of the policy requires that the activities in Company X be performed in accordance with the following principles:

1. Every employee in the company must be firmly convinced that quality is of great importance to Company X.

2. The organizational framework and responsibilities regarding all activities related to qualsty must be set down in writing.

3. Each company employee must be fully competent for his or her tasks. This requirement has to be met continuously by training and other means.

4. Orders that can put at risk the reputation of Company X must not be accepted. This means that the customer's requirements must be analyzed in each particular case.

5. Appropriate and documented methods to achieve the required qualify of product design shall be used for the product development and design stages.

6. When vendors are contracted assurance must be obtained that they can meet the stipulated quality requirements. The necessary measures should be taken to ensure that the quality requirements are complied with upon delivery.

7. Manufacturing techniques must ensure the required quality of output (conformance).

8. A system must be devised to specify quality requirements for the final product, as well as for the components and materials included.

   Specifications of this kind and essential instructions must be set down in formal documents, for which an established amendment procedure exits.

9. Procedures for checking and calibrating the equipment used must be established to verify that the quality specifications are met.

10. Quality auditing must be performed regularly.

11. Procedures must be developed for collecting processing, reporting and using quality data.

12. Annual programmes for quality improvement must be down up.

The situation is not so clear, however, when it comes to correcting chronic defects. It is necessary to direct and coordinate this part of the equality improvement work through a suitable organizational set-up. This quality improvement work should cover two aspects:

Guidance and diagnosis. The guidance activities include assigning priority to quality problems, developing a conceptual framework for studying the causes of quality problems, initiating analytical work on those problems and deciding on the introduction of proposed remedies. The diagnostic activities include carrying out analyses and experiments, finding the specific causes of the problems and proposing detailed remedies to them.

The guidance aspect of the improvement work should not be assigned to a single department, but should rather be carried out by all departments that can influence, or that in their work are dependent upon, product quality, such as product development, design, manufacture, quality control, marketing and service. It is therefore necessary to have a team that directs the quality improvement work of these departments. This team, which can take the form of a formal quality committee, must be able to take decisions. The departments concerned should therefore be represented by their heads. The quality committee should not attempt to solve the quality problems itself. Instead, it should see to it that the problems are tackled by the person or organizational units best suited for the particular task. This is the diagnostic part of the improvement work.

Coordination. Product quality is the result of the work of several departments, as discussed above. To achieve adequate quality at a reasonable cost, therefore, all of the activities that can affect quality must be coordinated. The organizational set-up for the coordination of the quality activities can take several forms:

General manager. It is natural in small firms for the general manager to have direct contact with the employees and thus to direct and follow the coordination activities.

Committees. Many quality matters can be dealt with by committees. For example, details related to product safety should be handled by a product safety committee.

CHART B

Functions of a quality department responsible for coordination and assurance

Area of responsibility

The entire company.

Organization

Reports directly to the managing director.

Responsibility

Ensure that work on product quality is carried out in an effective and appropriate manner.

Tasks

Recommend to the managing director the main features of a quality policy and the quality objectives; prepare the written policy and objectives; make the policy and objectives known throughout the company.

Ensure that an appropriate organizational set-up exists for quality activities in the firm.

In conjunction with all parties concerned, develop a quality system suited to the company's organization and product programme.

Ensure that suitable personnel are available to carry out quality activities, and organize quality training programmes for such staff, work towards a positive and active awareness of quality among the staff.

Ensure that work is carried out in accordance with the established policy and that the quality objectives are achieve

This includes carrying out quality audits, following and analyzing the development of quality and quality costs, initiating corrective measures and following up on the actions taken.

Inform the management and other interested parties of the development of quality and quality costs in the company; keep them continually up to date on any important quality-related matters that arise.

Suggest measures that will lead to reduced quality costs. Follow new developments in products and manufacturing methods from the quality viewpoint.

Chair the company's quality committee (for guiding the quality improvement work).

Take part in the management of activities concerned with quality and quality control.

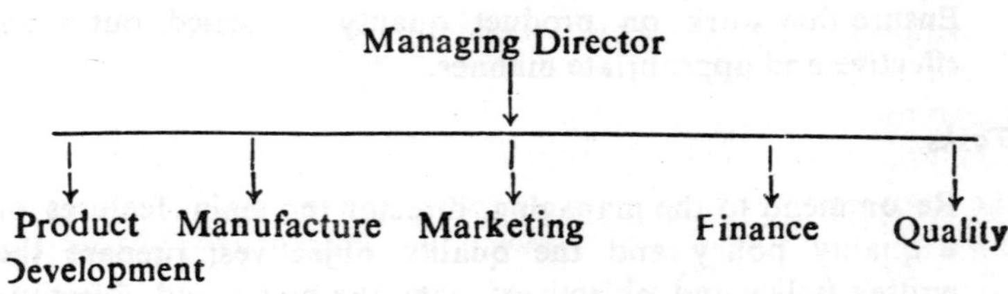

Staff specialists. In the case of the development of new products, for example, all activities need to be planned and coordinated, as well as followed up. Coordination tasks of this type can be given to staff specialists, who can be given the role of project leaders.

Department. In large and medium-size companies, it is becoming common to have a department charged with coordinating quality work, which is often called the quality department. The responsibility of ensuring that a written quality policy is available, as well as organizational plans, job descriptions, administrative procedures and training programmes related to quality, is part of this department's work. The department may also be responsible for quality assurance.

The creation of a quality department of this type should not influence the direct responsibility for product quality in the firm. This responsibility must still be assigned to the respective line functions, that is, primarily with the product development and manufacturing departments. The quality department should not, therefore, have any direct responsibility for quality but rather the responsibility for developing effective tools for quality work and assuring that they are used.

The quality department is thus the senior management's instrument for quality matters. It should be given the same status as the other major departments in the company. Responsibilities and tasks are shown in the job description at left.

Assurance. Quality assurance in this discussion refers for the activities that prove that the quality work is carried out in an adequate way, Quality assurance can include examination and supervision of work on product quality. This is done through quality audits, which can consist of a check above and beyond the ordinary inspection of finished goods (product quality audit), a check on the procedures being used and the working methods (systems quality audit), or an examination of the suitability and applicability of the manufacturing process (process quality audit).

The responsibility for quality assurance in its above form should be assigned to a department that does not have direct responsibility for product quality. It is natural to include these tasks in the work of the quality department discussed above, as shown in the figure at left.

II

EXPORT QUALITY INSPECTION

Inspection of products manufactured for export is an essential part of a firm's quality control system. Inspection activities should be carefully planned. Delivering goods of the quality specified by the importer is one of the main elements for developing a successful export business. To achieve the appropriate level of quality in its export products, a company must organize its quality control operations in an effective way. An essential part of a quality control system is the inspection process. Inspection may take place at different points throughout the manufacturing operation, using a variety of inspection techniques. A firm should establish an inspection system that is suited to the types of products that is manufactures and the nature of its production set-up. For such a system to work efficiently, it must be carefully planned and communicated to all staff concerned with inspection activities.

WHAT INSPECTION ENTAILS

Through inspection, a company evaluates a product to see if it fulfills the quality requirements and then decides whether to accept or reject the product. Inspection involves:

1. *Interpretation af the quality requirements*. These may be well defined in written specifications, drawings, instructions and so on, or they may be of a more general nature, for example by referring to good manufacturing practice. If specifications exist, they may include information on how the inspection should be carried out.
2. *Sampling*. In this process, a certain amount of the item (for number of units) is taken from the entire lot of goods for examination.
3. *Examination*. This includes testing, measurement, observation and related procedures to assess the quality of the article.
4. *Decision*. After the above measures have been taken, a a decision has to be made on whether the characteristics of the specific item conform to the quality requirements (thereby leading to acceptance). The decision is simple if the requirements are clearly stated—either the

goods conform or they do not. Otherwise, the decision may require longer study.

5. *Action.* When the decision has been made, the inspector or any other designated person such as the operator, the supervisor, the section or plant manager, and so on, has to determine what to do with the particular product or lot inspected—accept it, reject it, screen it, re-inspect it and so on. And it may be necessary to stop production. change tools or take other steps in the manufacturing process to obtain conformance with the quality requirements. At this point it is also necessary to record and report on the data obtained.

WHEN INSPECTION IS CONDUCTED

Inspection may be carried out at three different points in the production process:

Incoming inspection.
Process inspection.
Final inspection.

Incoming inspection. This consists of checking raw materials, components, sub-assemblies and the life upon delivery from suppliers. The aim is to prevent goods that do not fulfill the quality requirements from entering the production process and causing production delays or lowering the quality of the finished product. Incoming inspection therefore takes place before the materials are stored or go onto the production line.

Process inspection. This type of inspection aims to prevent products of unacceptable quality from being manufactured. It provides data for making decisions on whether to accept or reject the product as well as on whether to continue or stop the production process. Process inspection can be of several types:

First-piece inspection.
Patrol inspection.
Operator inspection.

Last-piece inspection.

Bench inspection.

First-piece inspection is carried out on the first items made after the manufacturing process has been set up or adjusted. The purpose is to detect defects of a non-random type—that is those that occur in unit after unit—after early a stage possible. The defects can result from such factors as a faulty set-up of a machine or of a measuring instrument, defective raw materials or misinterpretation of the drawings or instructions.

Patrol inspection involves periodic sampling during producttion. The inspector examines the latest items manufactured. When defects are found, all articles that have been produced after the most recent inspection are checked. Corrective measures may have to be taken.

Operator inspection means that the operator himself carries out the inspection during or immediately after manufacture. He is responsible for the decision on the item's compliance with the quality requirements. (Operator inspection is sometimes regarded as risky, the fear being that to achieve quantity in output the operator will accept items that do not meet the quality requirements. This danger is small if the work is planned and prepared carefully.

Last-piece inspection is undertaken on the last items manufactured in the entire lot of goods. When any faults exist in the equipment, these can be rectified become work is begun on the next lot. (If these faults are detected only when the next lot is started, process on may be delayed).

Bench inspection means that the control is carried out in separate inspection areas.

Final inspection. This process is undertaken after the last manufacturing stage. It often involves a trial usage of the product. The aim is to prevent defective praducts from being shipped to customers.

HOW INSPECTION IS CONDUCTED

Several methods may be used to carry out the inspection. These include:

Measurement.

"Go and no-go" checking.

Functional checking.

Visual inspection.

Measurement involves the determination of the numerical value of a particular characteristic of the product with the aid of a special instrument. "Go and no-go" checking is carried out with the use of fixed-limit gauges to find out whether a given feature of the product lies above or below a certain value (usually a specification limit). Functional checking consists of testing the working of a product, for example by simulating its use. Visual inspection is based on the appearance of a particular characteristic of product.

Inspection may be carried out on either a 100 per cent inspection basis or on a sampling basis. In 100 per cent inspection, each item in the lot is checked on one or more points. In sampling inspection, a certain number of items in the lot are examined.

Sampling inspection may be divided into spot-check inspection and statistical sampling inspection. In the spot-check method, only a few articles in the group are checked. The items inspected are not necessarily selected at random. In statistical sampling inspection, the sample size is determined by a set procedure. The sampling is done at random.

INSPECTION PLANNING

Before starting to manufacture a product, a company manager must do appropriate planning. This includes choosing manufacturing methods and machines, dividing up the operations, working out instructions for production and so forth.

All of these tasks are part of production planning. In addition, the inspection of the product must be planned. Too often a company does not plan its inspection work. Instead, it is simply left to the inspector to judge what should be inspected and the amount of inspection required. Inspection on this basis is usually not effective. The costs of planning the inspection work and of preparing written procedures for the inspection activities are more than offset by a more reliable and efficient inspection system.

Inspection planning includes:

Selecting the type of inspection for different stages in the production process.

Outlining inspection operations in detail.

Designing inspection workplaces.

Procuring inspection equipment.

Tools that can make the inspection easier and more effective are written inspection procedures; specifications such as drawings, material specifications and process specifications; standards and general procedures; tolerance tables; sampling tables: inspection equipment; visual standards and data sheets.

Factors to be considered. The inspection should be organized so that, with a mimimum of effort, it can be ensured that the quality of the products that leave the manufacturer's premises is of the appropriate level. During the planning of inspection activities, therefore, attention must be paid to all of the factors that can affect the product's quality. An inspection planner in a manufacturing firm must work closely with virtually all divisions in the company in this task.

The following factors should be taken into account in the inspection plan:

Production set-up. Before full-scale production starts, it is necessary to check that the set-up of the manufactur in process will result in a product conforming to the quality requirments. A control of the set-up should therefore be made through first-piece inspection.

Machines and tools. As the manufacturing process many change over time, it is necessary to undertake periodic checks on the equipment used and to make any necessary adjustments in it. Inspection may take the form of patrol or operator inspection.

Operator. Results are dependent upon the production operator's skill and attention. Inspection of the operator's work may be in the form of patrol inspection. Acceptance inspection (*i.e.*, classifying a lot as acceptable or rejectable, through either 100 per cent inspection or checking on a sample basis) may also be used, either directly in the production line or as a check on finished lots. Statistical sampling methods can often be applied for such inspection. In some cases it may be suitable for the inspection to the responsibility of the operator, and in other cases of the inspector.

Materials and components. The early stages in the production chain are decisive for the quality of the final product. It is therefore necessary to plan inspection activities with the suppliers of materials. This may involve, for example, joint quality planning with the supplier during his manufacturing process (through process control and acceptance inspection) and incoming inspection.

How much inspection. During the inspection planning process decisions must be taken on how much inspection is necessary. This is affected by the:

Consequences of deviations from quality requirements. If the effects of variations from these requirements are serious, it is necessary to have more inspection than when the results have only minor consequences.

Nature of the product. For a relatively homogeneous lot of items, less inspection may be applied than for a group of diverse articles.

Nature of the manufacturing process. If the variation in the manufacturing process is small compared with the degree of tolerance permitted, the risk of defects is small. Not much inspection (if any) will usually be necessary in this case. On the other hand, more inspection will be required when the variation is considerable compared with the allowed tolerances.

Previous inspection. If inspection has been carried out at an earlier stage, for example by the supplier or the operator, no more inspection may be necessaiy at the end of the production line.

Because both inspection and defects involve costs, it is often necessary in inspection planning to try to find an economical balance between the two elements. This can be obtained through a break-even analysis. It is not necessary to inspect a lot that does not contain activities. If, on the other hand, the number of defectives is large, it is often worth doing a 100 per cent inspection. Between these two extremes, there is a point at which the costs are the same for carrying out an inspection of the lot and covering the expenses connected with defectives.

WRITTEN INSPECTION GUIDELINES

The inspection system should be outlined in writing. This includes explaining where the inspection activities come into the production process and preparing instructions describing each inspection activity. Flow charts may be used for the first exercise.

Written inspection instructions should contain information such as:

Where in the production process the inspection is to take place.

Which quality features are to be inspected.

Requirements for each characteristic to be inspected.

Methods and equipment needed for inspecting each factor.

How much inspection is necessary for each quality characteristic or class of characteristics.
Action to be taken on the basis of the inspection results, for example criteria for acceptance.
Which results should be documented and how.

The inspection instructions should be written in simple terms so that they are easily understood. They should be updated regularly in the light of changing in quality levels, quality requirements, the production process inspection methods and equipment.

III

THE VITAL HUMAN ELEMENT

Producing exports of the right quality involves staff at all levels of the firm. Training can help ensure that quality requirements are met. To produce manufactured goods of the right quality for foreign buyers, exporters should not overlook the human element in their export production operations. Company staff, from the top positions on down, should be familiar with the requirements for achieving appropriate quality in output. Good quality results not only from actions taken on the assembly line but also on decisions taken at the highest management levels. Company officials should adopt appropriate measures to ensure that all those linked in one way or another to the quality of the finished product are suitably informed and skilled in their respective quality tasks.

ORIGIN OF QUALITY DEFECTS

It is commonly thought that most quality problems in manufactured export products are caused by a lack of interest and care on the part of the worker in the production process. However, it is not usually this person who is to blame for low-quality items. The conditions allowing him or her to do an adequate job often do not exist. Instructions may be insufficient, the machines may be incapable of producing goods to the quality requirements or the starting material may be defective. No tool or instrument for the inspection of the product may have been given to the worker. There are numerous different conditions over which the worker has no control, but which lead to defective work that incorrectly appears to be caused by the worker.

Defects can be separated into those that are worker-controllable and those that are management-controllable. The latter are defects that cannot possibly be influenced by workers. Whether a certain defect should be regarded as one or the other depends on the extends to which the following conditions are met:

The worker knows what he or she is supposed to do.

The worker knows the result of his or her own work.

The worker has the means of influencing the result.

If these three conditions are all met and the work is still defective, the worker can be taken as being responsible. If, however, one or more of the conditions do not exist, the worker cannot be blamed. It is then a case of a management-controllable defect.

A classification of defects in this way usually shows that most of the defects are management-controllable. Worker-controllable defects tend to be of minor importance, both in respect to their frequency and financial consequences.

CONDITIONS FOR QUALITY OUTPUT

The idea is often put forward that product quality can be improved through information and other motivational activities. This is based on the false assumption that human errors are primarily the result of lack of interest and care. Experience shows that considerably better results are achieved if, instead, the proper conditions exist for producing goods of the appro-quality. Such conditions are:

The quality requirements should be clear and unambiguous.

The technical conditions must enable the quality requirements to be met, for instance, the material must be suitable for the work and the machines must be capable of producing items of adequate quality.

Each worker should be able to judge whether the result of his or her own work complies with the quality requirements.

Each person involved must know what to do to prevent poor-quality output.

All of the staff must know the consequences of poor work for the enterprise.

TRAINING

For the firm to produce quality goods, the personnel at all levels must cooperate actively. This means a continuous development of the staff working in related areas. Training is important for staff development.

A company should investigate the need for training to improve the knowledge and motivation of its personnel, regardless of their level and function. This should lead to the development and implementation of a training programme. In an increaing number of companies this has been found to be a necessary ingradient for achieving the desired level of quality in production. The Japanese "revolution in quality" is largely the result of comprehensive education and training aimed at all functions and levels (from top management to labour). Quality education and training can take several forms:

Courses at universities and other educational institutions.

Courses and seminars offered by associations, institutes and other bodies.

Meetings and conferences organized by associations, nstitutes and so on.

Self-instruction from books and journals.

In-house training programmes.

On-the-job training.

In-house training programmes related to quality have two aims, to give the personnel knowledge within fields that affect product quality and to increase the individual's awareness of quality. Such training can be divided into three categories:

Introductory training.

Training in quality disciplines.

Other training.

Introductory training in quality is aimed primarily at shapping attitutes. Such training is relevant for everyone in the firm who has an influence on quality. It should include such subjects as the significance of quality to the company, responsibility for quality within the firm and the principles of company-wide quality control (or total quality control, which is an integrated approach for achieving quality at the company level).

Training in quality disciplines must be tailored to the needs of the different categories of personnel.

The third category concerns knowledge required in fields that do not deal purely with quality techniques. This may include, for example, information about the products, materials, manufacturing processes, drawings and tolerancing.

A plan for in-house training for different categories of personnel is shown above.

For internal training to show good results, the following points should be considered when planning:

Existing needs for training. The training should be designed to fulfill the company's training requirements. An analysis of training needs should be made for this purpose.

Instructors. The extent to which internal personnel could act as lecturers and instructors should be explored. Account should be taken of their expertise, knowledge and teaching abilities.

Course literature. The trainees should be given material to which they can refer after having completed the training.

Aids. Audiovisual tools should be used in the training.

Course content. The course should be balanced between theory and practical application. How the theory can be applied in the firm should be explained with examples.

Exercises. Trainees should be involved actively through exercises that can be done as homework or in a group during the class. The exercises should be related to the firm's activities.

Evaluation. At the end of the course, those taking part should give their views on the training, together with suggestions for improvements. This is often done through a questionnaire.

The training should be designed to improve the participants' work related to quality. The views of those taking part on the company's activities to achieve quality products should be obtained and discussed. For a more comprehensive course, the participants can be asked to judge the company's situation in the relevant aspect of quality and the importance of that aspect to the firm.

An important part of the in-house training is on-the-job training. For example, inspectors are trained primarily by a foreman, an instructor or a more experienced inspector. The results are dependent on the supervisor's technical skill and ability to instruct.

QUALITY CIRCLES

A concept that has gained great interest in recent years is workers' participation in problem-solving in quality circles

Plan for in-House Training in Quality

Subject	*Category*												*Length in hours*
				Production			*Inspection*						
	Product development	*Manufacturing engineering*	*Purchasing*	*Operator*	*Foreman*	*Engineer*	*Inspector*	*Foreman*	*Engineer*	*Marketing*	*Service*	*Top management*	
Introduction													
Quality control I				X			X						4
Quality control II	X	X	X		X	X		X	X	X	X	X	8
Quality disciplines													
Quality control Enigneering I					(X)		X						20
Quaiity control Engineering II		(X)				(X)		X	X				40
Reliability	X								(X)				20
Metrology					(X)		X	X	X				16
Materials testing								X					12
Vendor relations			X										8
Economics of quality						X			X			X	8

Other								
Products			X		X	X		8
Materials			(X)	(X)		X	X	12
Processes	X	(X)	X	X	X	X		12
Drawings		X			X			16
Tolerencing		X			X			16

X=essential. (X)=recommended.

Many managers believe that they will solve their company's quality problems by introducing quality circles into their operations. Quality circles are also considered to be a means for increasing workers' motivation to produce quality goods.

The quality circle movement started in the early 1960s in Japan. It was a result of the massive quality-related education and training programmes that many Japanese enterprises started to develop and carry out in the 1950s to promote and implement total quality control as a means for improving product quality. The education and training started with upper management and then continued down through the enterprise to the nonsupervisory level. When the workers had been trained in tools for quality improvement, it was found that their new knowledge had to be used. Quality circles were therefore set up.

The quality circle activities have obviously resulted in improved product quality. But how significant are quality circle activities when it comes to quality improvement in Japan? Discussions with Japanese experts indicate that these activities account for only a minor portion of the total result. Not more than 10 per cent of the overall improvements in product quality is due to work in quality circles.

Why is such a small fraction of the improvements attributable to the quality circles? In Japan, circles tackle almost exclusively interdepartmental problems. These usually represent the more minor problems. The major problems are difficult for the workers to deal with in quality circles because these problems are caused by an absence of management policies. inadequate quality coordination, insufficient training, design weaknesses, incapable vendors and so on.

The introduction of quality circle activities for the purpose of improving quality is therefore not to be recommended, if it envisaged as a substitute for total quality control or a company-wide quality control approach. The main impact of quality circles is probably in the field of employee relations.

6

EXPORT MARKETING: MIX AND COST-BENEFIT ANALYSIS

MARKETING MIX

The Executives Cooperating in this survey identified a wide variety of support services that must be performed in order to move a product from the end of the production line to a customer overseas. These marketing support services may be grouped loosely under ten functional headings—promotion, direct selling, selling support, pricing, inventory, product management, finance, technical, packaging, and shipping.

The importance and cost of these elements of the export marketing mix vary from company to company, and the services are performed at different points on the distribution chain. Although the survey does not permit any generalizations about their relative importance or the preferred methods of providing an individual service, a number of panelists provided specific information on their companies' practices that illustrates the variety of corporate experience.

WHERE SERVICES ARE PERFORMED

The numerous support services that make up the export marketing mix can be provided effectively at different levels in

Examples of Elements Included

A. Promotional Support

1. Local advertising
2. Umbrella advertising
3. Direct mail advertising
4. Descriptive literature
5. Trade show
6. Demonstration items
7. Printing

B. Direct Selling

8. Direct selling to customers
9. Maintaince of sales force
10. Commissions to sales agents

C. Marketing-Service and Sales-Service Support

11. Market research
12. Annual catalog of products
13. Sales budget by product
14. Prompt quote requests
15. Technical sales assistance
16. In-store service
17. Information for selling agents in advance of new products and discontinued products
18. Training agents' salesmen
19. General customer service
20. Claims and adjustments
21. Warranty service
22. Service to foreign subsidiaries arranged through U.S. parents

in the Export Marketing Mix

23. Periodic sales reports
24. General competitive intelligence

D. Pricing Support

25. Establishment of prices
26. Distribution of price lists and changes
27. Pricing information concerning competive items

E. Inventory Support

28. Maintence of inventories
29. Rotation of inventory to avoid obsolescence
30. Warehousing

F. Product Management Support

31. Development of new products for export market
32. Selecting correct products for each market
33. Determination of which producting location will provide product to which market
34. General product management

G. Financial Support

35. Planning and scheduling budget data and reports
35. Floor plan financing
37. Rental operations for heavy equipment
38. Billing and collecting invoices
39. Credit authorizations
40. Auditing
41. General financing of sales

H. Technical Support

42. Manufacturing specifications
43. Machine designs for special markets
44. Quality control
45. Product testing
46. Parts supply
47. Training service personal

I. Packaging Support

48. Export packaging
49. provision of a variety of packing and sizes in each product line to be more competitive
50. Export lables

J. Shipping Support

51. Adequate traffic and distribution support
52. Processing of orders
53. Export preparation
54. Inland freight
55. Shipping overseas
56. Landing expenses

K. Other Support

57. Data processing
58. System design
59. Insurance
60. Legal services
61. Tax analysis
62. Translations
63. Metric conversion of operating data

the distribution system, panelists say. The U.S. parent, its subsidiaries and other controlled units, and independent distributors and agents all contribute services to the transfer of products from their manufacturing sites in the United States to end-users in other countries. The responsibility for poviding particular services difiers from company to company and may differ by product, by market, and by time.

The marketing services provided by the U.S. parent, most frequently mentioned by the panelists are selling, technical, promotional, and financial services. Those provided by the independent distributions and agents are selling, inventory maintenance, promotional, and financial services. And subsidiaries most frequently provide selling, promotional, financial, technical and inventory maintenance services. The overlapping is immediately apparent. The assignment of selected marketing support services to different levels of the distribution system is shown in the accompanying table, page 163.

The provision of all export marketing services by a single level in the distribution system is reported by only five panelists in this survey. One general industrial machinery company depends entirely on a licensee. The company president says:

> "Our licensee in England markets our product internationally through a network of subsidiaries and independent agents. All services are performed by the parent [licensee] company in England".

An agricultural products company relies entirely either on licensees or on subsidiaries. An executive says:

> "We generally supply practically no services on export sales. We do give examples of our promotional materialto our licenses or subsidiary. This includes testing and all types of promotion."

A pharmaceutical company relies on its own controlled overseas units to provide all export marketing services. The president of the international division writes:

"We do not export finished products from the United States, except in rare instances. Our international sales are conducted by our overseas management centers and country managements which carry out the functions of direct selling, advertising, maintenance of inventories, technical services, and the other functions of the marketing mix. These activities are conducted only with braod policy guidance from the International Headquarters, and they can, and do, vary considerably from market to market depending on the many factors which have to be taken into account in different areas and different countries."

Executives from a machinery manufacturer and from an aircraft manufacturer report that their export marketing services are provided entirely by the U.S. parent, mainly because of the special and highly technical products sold by these companies and the fact that the purchasers are frequently governments.

For all other companies participating in this survey the services of the export marketing mix are distributed among the U.S. parent, its subsidiaries, and independent distributors or agents abroad. Frequently as the panelists report, the performance of any one service is shared among two and sometimes three levels of the distribution system. Twelve executives, for example, report that direct selling is shared by subsidiaries and independent agents; 13 divide direct selling responsibilities between distributors or agents on the one level and the parent company on the other; and 15 divide these responsibilities among all three levels. In one industrial equipment company, the vice president of its international division reports that there are four distinct levels that provide marketing services for exports—the U.S. parent, the international division, subsidiaries of the international division, and independent agents.

Typical of the companies that distribute and share responsibilities for export marketing is a manufacturer of machinery and equipment. Its vice president explains the contributions made by each link of the distribution chain:

TABLE 1

Assignment of Selected Marketing Support Services to Levels of Distribution System
(Number of Companies Reporting)

Level at Which Provided / *Marketing Supporting Services*	*Distributors and agents only (D)*	*Subsidiaries only (S)*	*Parent Company only (P)*	*D & S*	*D & P*	*S & P*	*D & S & P*	*Total including D*	*Total including S*	*Total including P*
Promotional	4	4	12	3	13	4	6	26	17	35
Selling	21	2	3	12	13	2	15	61	31	33
Financial	6	3	14	4	5	2	6	21	15	27
Inventory Maintenance	8	1	3	9	5	1	4	26	15	13
Technical	3	3	20	6	6	4	2	17	15	32
Management (e.g. training personnel, etc.)	0	0	12	0	1	3	1	2	4	17

"The U.S. parent provides certain elements of the marketing mix for exports, such as advertising (when such is in worldwide media) and certain basic themes, artwork, etc., amenable to adjustment or direct use by the marketing subsidiaries. Certain basic training materials, as well as appropriate training facilities, are also available from the parent...Product, whether made in the United States or elsewhere, is almost entirely sold via independent dealers. The exception indicated by 'almost' is in sales to the U.S. Government and to certain manufacturers who incorporate components or portions of our product in their product. Sales to foreign governments, and also some sales to certain large foreign purchasers, are by user perference billed directly by the manufacturer, but outside the United States are most generally via the marketing support of the independent dealer...The parent is generally a last resort source for inventories and for financing. The marketing subsidiary provides advertising for its particular area, provides dealer back-up on inventory and financing, and provide the manpower and field facilities for various training programmes. The independent dealer does the direct selling, employs the retail force, and advertises within its assigned territory, frequently on a cooperative basis with the marketing subsidiary. It is responsible for the first line of inventory of both machaines and replacement parts, sufficient for all normal product support. The independent dealer also provides the mechanical service and is the only source of physical service facilities. The demonstration, the training of operators, the training for maintenance, etc., is a first-line responsibility of that same dealer."

Another example of the division of responsibility for marketing services among several levels of that listed by the vice president of a chemical company—See Chart A below.

COSTS OF SUPPORT SERVICES

About half of the cooperating executives estimated the

CHART A

Distribution of the Marketing Services in Support of Export Sales by a Chemical Corporation

---

Services provided by U.S. Parent

(a) Technical sales assistance
(b) Prompt U.S. response to quote requests
(c) Adherence to delivery promise
(d) Biannual personal visits between principal and overseas subsidiaries
(e) Setting up practical perimeters of sale operation, *i.e.*, credit, service basis trials, terms
(f) Set parameters for profit
(g) Sales promotion
(h) Sale letters
(i) Advertising (partial)

Services provided by Foreign Subsidaries

(a) Technical sales assistance to representatives
(b) Warehouse location for overseas distribution and inventory
(c) Credit and terms
(d) Locate best talent as representatives
(e) Advise domestic parent of competitive market factors
(f) Advertising (partial)

Services provided by Agents

(a) Aggressive and imaginative sales effort
(b) Frequent customer and prospect contact
(c) Prompt communication of field problems
(d) Status of foreign competition
(e) Credit arrangements
(f) Maintenance of inventories overseas
(g) Advertising (partial)

---

proportion of end-user price attributable to the export marketing mix for one of their products. The range of estimates extended from 7.6 per cent (a machinery and equipment company) to 67 per cent a food products company and a household chemicals company), with the median of the sample about 30 per cent. As shown in Fig. 6.1, the proportion of

FIG. 6.1: Proportion of End-user Price Attributable to Export Marketing Mix

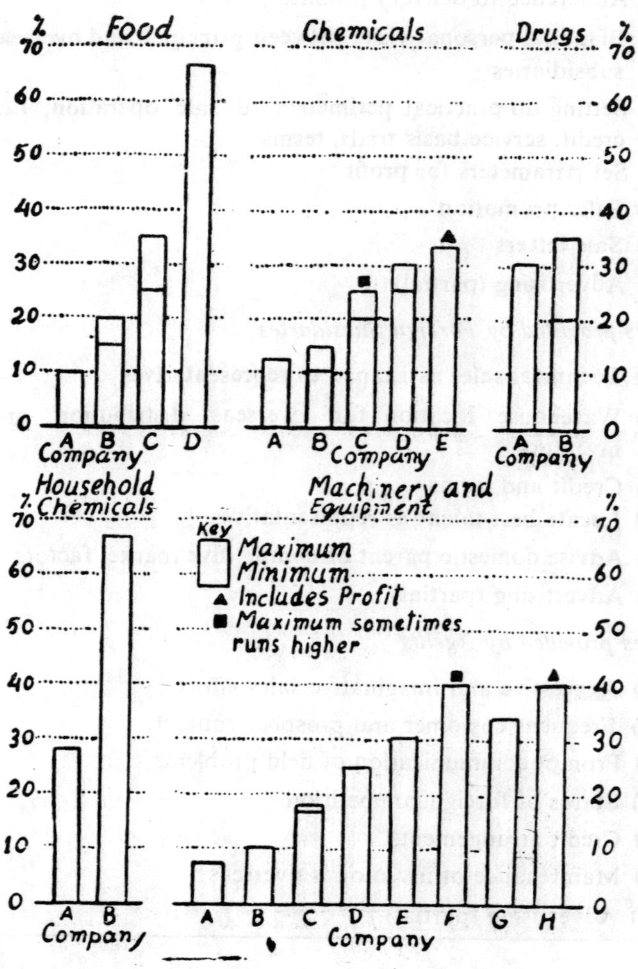

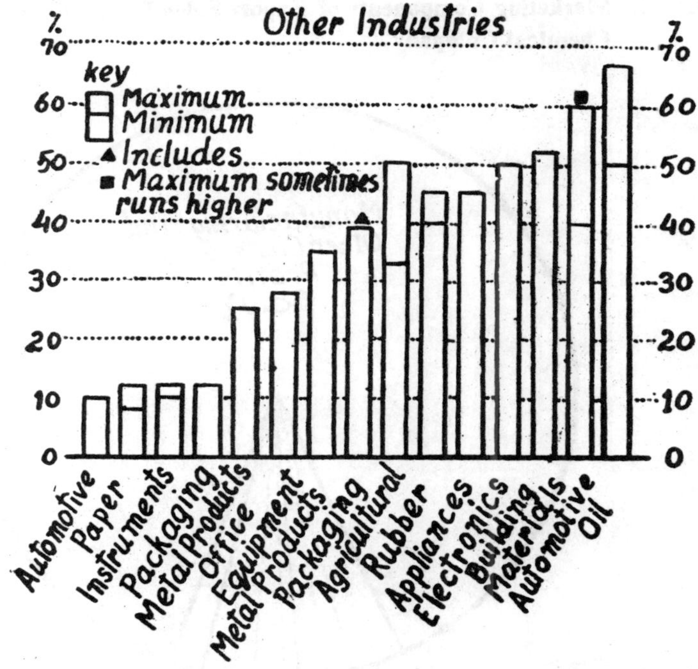

end-user price attributable to export marketing costs varies considerably even among companies in the same industry.

Several executives describe the breakdown of these costs in detail. One executive of a chemical company selected for discussion a product line for which the cost of export marketing services is approximately 12 per cent of the sales price, a cost figure which is about midway in the range for all their product lines. He then breaks down the 12 per cent cost as follows (See Fig. 6.2, page 168):

"About 15 per cent is spent by the producing division in technical service and services in support of exports, including the time of executive and marketing personnel. Another 40 per cent is charged to the international division, essentially the headquarters operation. About half of this, or 20 per cent of the total, would cover divisional overheads and

FIG. 6.2: **Marketing Components of Export Sales Dollar for a Chemical Company**

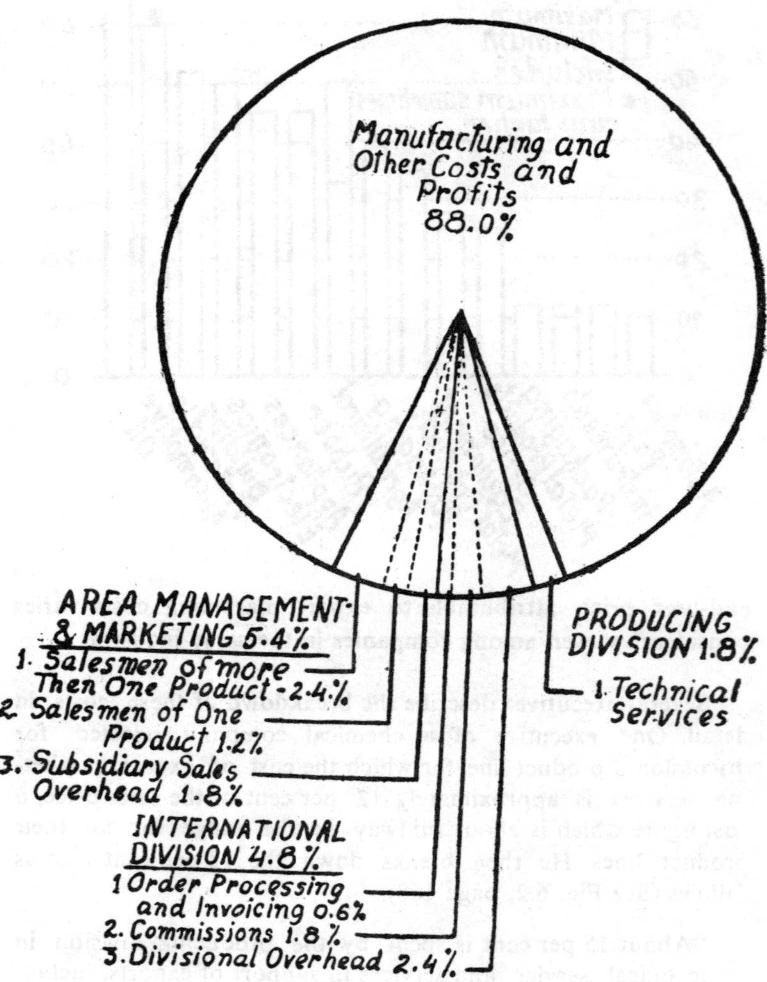

accounting and the charges to international operations made by such staff departments as Tax, Law, Treasury, etc. Five per cent of the total covers the cost of order 'processing and invoicing; 15 per cent of the total covers commissions paid either to outside agents or to certain of our member companies who, for a variety of reasons usually based on local laws, are paid on a commission rather than a flat fee basis.

"A third category accounts for 45 per cent of the total and covers area management and marketing. About one third of this (15%) covers the services and overhead associated with our field sales offices and the importing departments of our member manufacturing companies. Two third (30%) covers actual field selling effort. Of this, field selling effort, one third (10%) covers sales personnel who spend almost their full time in selling this one product line; two thirds (20%) covers the cost of people who spread their efforts over several product lines."

A sales executive in the international division of an automobile manufacturer estimates:

"Because of the heavy duties in markets, the retail price is often two or three times the f.o.b. price we charge our distributors. For Europe, for example, the rule of thumb is:

> $1.00 f.o.b. New York results in $2.50 at retail in the local market. Therefore, if duties and taxes are taken into account as cost to get the product to the customer, the proportion of retail price attributable to (the marketing) mix may reach 40-50-60 per cent or over, depending on the market."

The vice president for international operations of an industrial products firm reports:

"If we take the full inclusive appraisal of all marketing costs these costs might come out to 35 per cent of the invoice value in this extended definition. Manufacturing costs amount to about 50 per cent of the end-user price." And the manager of international operations for a machinery manufacturer says the cost of manufacturing versus marketing "is roughly on the ratio of 9 to 1."

The product manager of a firm manufacturing products for use in the construction industry prepared a diagram of the division of a dollar unit of end-user's price for the firm's export product. The diagram is reproduced in Fig. 6.3, along with specific cost data supplied by other panelists.

FIG. 6.3: Export Marketing Costs Related to Manufacturing Costs

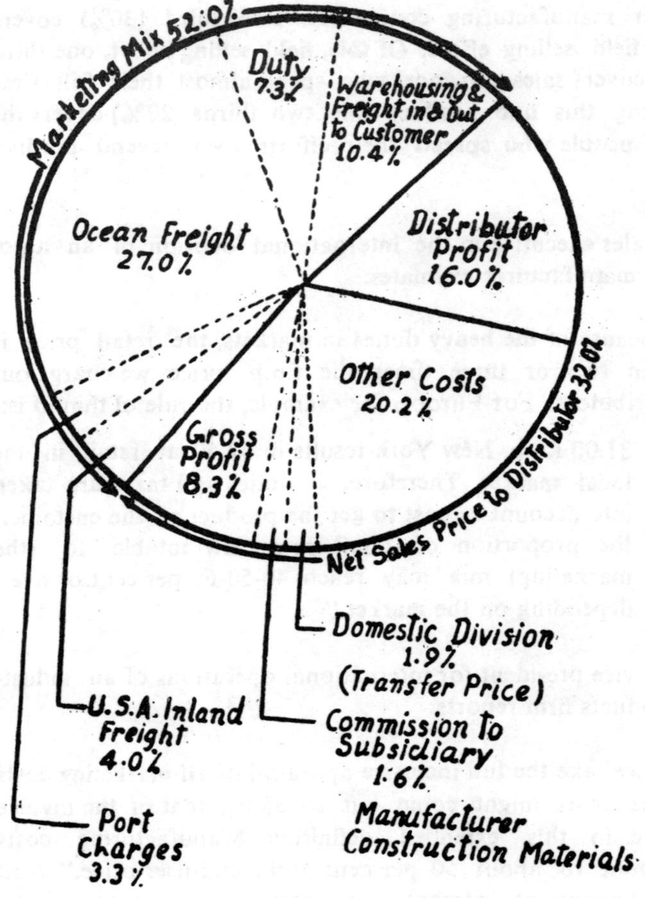

FIG. 6.3: Export Marketing Costs Related to Manufacturing Costs (Continued)

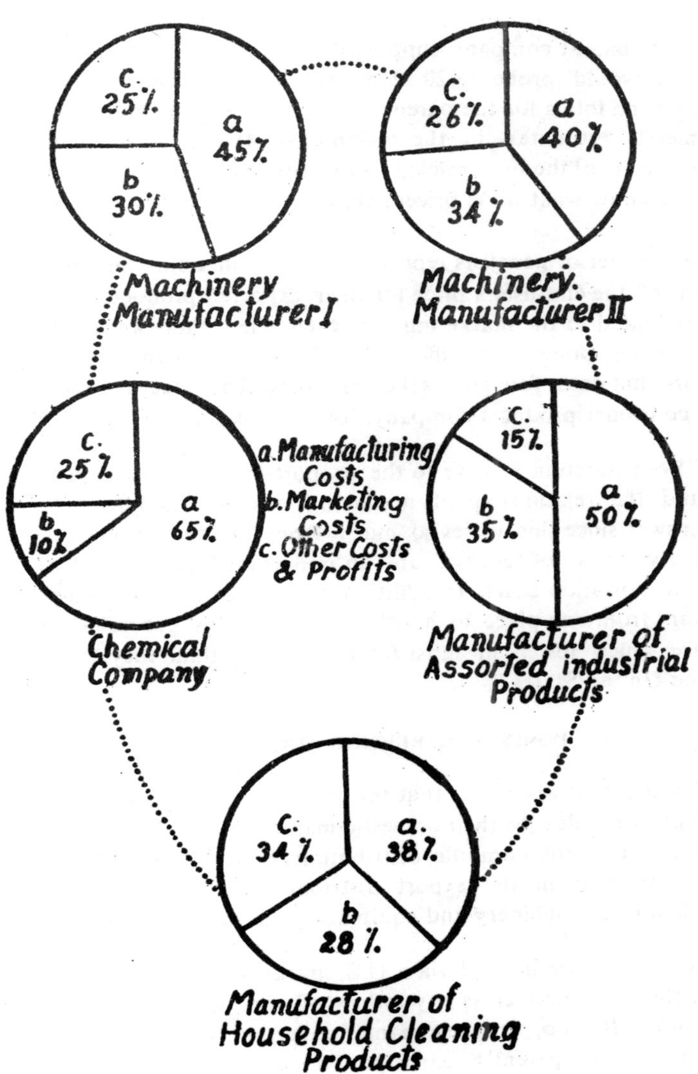

The director of marketing for a rubber company points out that the marketing portion of the end-user price is not always known precisely by the American company. He explains:

> "The parent company supported portion of the marketing mix would probably 20-25 per cent of the consumers' cost, and the totals for the parent company plus distributors are merely estimates, in the region of 40-45 per cent as we do not control the final pricing to the tiser and frequently do not know what these prices are."

A number of panelists reported difficulty in estimating how much of the end-user's price for their exported products could be attributed to the marketing mix, even when they know the final selling price. The difficulty stems from the many variable factors that enter foreign marketing costs. The vice president of a consumer products company, for example, says:

> "Your question relative to the proportion of end-user price and the relationship of marketing mix to it is difficult to answer since this varies so much from market to market. Duty costs, of course, are an important factor as well as transportation costs. In addition, traditional retail mark ups vary from one place to another, although in general they are much lower in most foreign markets than they are in the United States."

DOMESTIC MARKETING SERVICES

Seven executives report that the performance of marketing services for sales to their domestic market are divided among several units in the domestic distribution system in a manner similar to that in the export distribution system. The vice president of a machinery and equipment firm says:

> "U.S. sales are handed via a U.S. marketing group operated in the same manner as any other of the marketing subsidiaries. It, too, is a claimant for certain services. In this manner the parent's participation is quite comparable

whether the product be sold in the United States or outside." And the vice president of a consumer products firm, who lists the services provided by its overseas distributors, dealers, and agents, concludes;

> "Generally the same services are performed by domestic distributors. The only difference is that we domestically handle a greater share of the advertising,"

It contrast, a much larger group of executive (29) report that domestic marketing services in their companies are handled differently from export marketing services. In almost all instances described, the difference is that the parent company provides more of the domestic marketing services itself. The vice president for international operations of an office machine manufacturer writes:

> "In an effort to compare our international operations with our domestic (U.S. and Canada) marketing operations, the following observations will help clarify some of the differences:
>
> > There is a much higher level of centralization from corporate headquarters in sales and support prevailing between our domestic branches in the United States and the supporting headquarters' domestic marketing staff than in the international division. There is, therefore, a much greater dependency of the domestic branches on headquarters' resources than in international...Our international country, organizations have a much greater capability to be self-sufficient than the domestic branches."

These differences, he points out, have a direct effect on operations in the two areas. He says:

> "In contrast to the international division's operations, our domestic [headquarters] marketing organizations provides all financing, all technical services support, all advertising and sales promotion support, and all sales and technical

training to the domestic branches. In International, most of these activities are carried out in the individual local country organization and charged to it."

This executive effects an inportant reason for these differences:

"In the international division, our marketing group must deal with vastly different country economic environments and different individual country requirements."

Other differences between export and domestic marketing services are reported by a vice president of an electronics manufacturing company. He writes:

"About the only substantial difference between the United States and foreign distributors is the import documentation and procedural red tape required of the latter and the fact that he must deal with a longer supply pipeline. This means that he may, for the same volume of business, have more capital tied up since we normally sell f.o.b. factory both domestically and internationally. As a consequence, the foreign distributor receives a fractionally higher commission or discount than the domestic."

Otherwise, however, he concludes that "basically there is not a great deal of difference between the marketing elements provided by the various links in the distribution chain domestically as compared to offshore.

MARKETING COSTS

When the executives cooperating in this survey compared their companies' export marketing costs with the costs of marketing similar products in the United States, they came to a variety of conclusions. Among the executives who report a clear difference, the most common conclusion was that export marketing costs are higher. But a significant number say that the costs are about the same; and several say, in effect, that it all depends on the circumstances. (See Fig. 6.4).

Fig. 6.4: Export Marketing Costs Compared to Domestic Marketing Costs (No. of Companies Reporting)

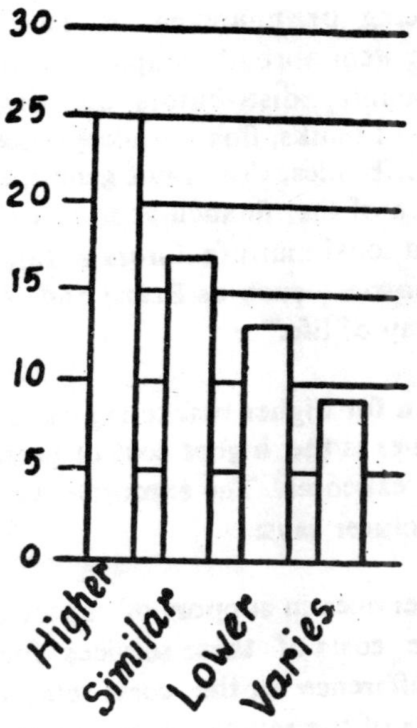

HIGHER COSTS

The largest group of panelists comparing the costs of export marketing services with costs of domestic marketing services reports higher costs for the export services. The vice president of a food products company, for example, says:

> "Our international division estimates that the cost of the services provided in export sales is about 10 per cent higher on a *unit basis*. However, it is even higher in terms of ***per cent of gross sales revenue*** due to lower average prices."

The higher costs of marketing services in support of export sales are due to several factors according to executives participating in this survey. The most frequently mentioned factor, reported by 11 executives, is the higher cost of financing export sales. The sales director of a steel products company says, "Collection periods are longer and, therefore, financing is more costly in export." And an executive of a company producing household appliances points out:

> "Dealer financing or financing of receivables exacts the highest expense item abroad compared with domestic sales. While in this country distributors and dealers have access to the facilities of banks, finance acceptance companies, and other credit possibilities, this is not generally true in foreign countries. Much of the financing has to be undertaken by distributors and local manufacturers at fantastic costs, particularly in countries—such as Brazil and Argentina—where inflation is a way of life."

A second reason for higher marketing costs in exports for a number of companies is the higher cost of promotional services and direct selling expenses. The executive vice president of a machinery manufacturer says:

> "The costs of services in support of export sales are slightly higher than the costs of these services for domestic sales. The primary difference in the costs relates directly to the general expenses of the selling organization."

The president of the international division of a manufacturer of refrigeration equipment reports:

> "In domestic sales we deal directly with large original equipment manufacturers only—supplying them with the products we manufacture which go into their complete product. We do very little or no advertising; therefore, our selling costs domestically are much less than our export selling costs."

Several other factors contribute to higher selling costs for exports, according to panelists. The vice president for sales of a company making industrial machinery points out some of them. He says that the higher costs are "due in part to the geographic dispersion of our customers (both manufacturers and end-users), the lower volume levels and product mix, and the need to provide and maintain complete market coverage on a regional basis."

Higher discounts and commissions earned by distributors and agents abroad are among the major causes of higher export selling costs, according to several panelists. An executive of a company manufacturing parts for household appliances lists among "the most important elements of our marketing mix," the "extra costs involved in commissions to our sales agents." The president of an expòrter of industrial instructions points out that "overseas agents and distributors generally charge approximately 5 per cent to 8 per cent more commission than local distributors and agents." And the director of international operations for a machinery firm credits a larger discount for the higher cost of export sales. He says:

> "For our domestic dealers, we allow 10 per cent resale discount, and give perhaps 3 per cent to 5 per cent assistance from our own technical sales people, totaling 13 per cent to 15 per cent sales cost. Fot overseas dealers, we allow 15 per cent resale discount and give perhaps 2 per cent to 3 per cent assistance, totaling 17 per cent to 18 per cent."

The high costs of ocean freight add to the higher costs of marketing services for exports, many panelists report. The export manager of a food products company points out that "a very high percentage—often as much as 25 per cent to 30 per cent of the final price to the consumer—is involved in the service of ocean freight. We have found that, due to ever increasing shipping costs, by the time we add our ocean freight charges to our f.o.b. U. S. port quotations, our final c.i.f. foreign port quotation is approximately one-third higher than our f.o.b. U.S. port price."

The high cost of international freight compared to export income on its particular product led one packaging company to discontinue its export sales altogether. An executive writes:

"Our product range is not conductive to exporting as the freight cube related to the product value is disadvantageous to us and basically we would be shipping by air. Until 1963 we ran a fairly extensive export department from our headquarters, which we found was employing most of the personnel in our international division and registering increasing losses. As we saw no prospect for profitable overseas sales at the distressed prices then prevailing, we discontinued the export sales activity completely and do not anticipate starting it again."

The expenses involved in landing products in a foreign country add substantially to the costs of export marketing, according to several panelists. The export manager of a food products company describes this cost factor as follows:

"By landing costs we mean the payments of duties and other taxes imposed by the importing country. In many export markets we are finding more and more government regulations that place protective tariffs and other taxes on imported goods such as ours that take a very big percentage of the final price to the consumer...These landing charges can amount to anywhere from 10 per cent to 100 per cent of c.i.f. value."

A related area of higher costs for export marketing is what the vice president-international operations for an instrument manufacturer calls "the excessive volumes of paper work required in an export sale." The vice president of the international division of a packaging firm cites the costs of preparing "a complete package of consular and customs documentation," while the director of marketing for a rubber company concludes:

"The complicated nature of export billing and documents makes this area a plus cost factor."

Several executives point out that export marketing costs are higher because of the language barrier. The executive vice president for international operations of an automotive equipment corporation says, "Advertising costs are relatively higher due to the need to translate promotional materials." And the vice president of a metal-working firm concludes:

> "In general, the increased cost can be laid almost entirely to the language-communications problems."

Technical services, including "the costs to maintain, train, and supervise technical personnel overseas," can add to the costs of export marketing services, a number of panelists report. A vice president of an electronics manufacturer says:

> "With regard to the costs of marketing and distribution services in total, the technical support for export sales is considerably higher than in the United States per unit or per dollar of sales because of the normally smaller volume base and the greater amount and cost of travel involved. The engineering/technical representatives, because of rapidly evolving technical changes, must come back to our factories and laboratories at frequent intervals even though they may be stationed abroad."

Several executives report that marketing costs on export sales are higher on a unit basis simply because volumes are lower. The vice president of a food products firm sees these higher marketing costs in terms of "higher fixed administrative costs per unit due to lower volumes." The manager for international sales of a manufacturer of machinery and equipment sees this problem in terms of higher servicing costs in general. He writes:

> "Cost of these [marketing] services in support of export sales is approximately twice the cost of similar services in support of domestic sales. The major reason for increased cost of these items is the very limited market for our equipment overseas and a consequent high unit cost of servicing. If we were able to increase the volume, percentage cost would come down."

In addition to those reasons for higher export marketing costs, each cited by several executives, a number of others were mentioned by at least one of the panelists. They include:

Lower advertising efficiencies abroad

Distribution system inefficiencies

Insurance costs

Heavier packaging required for exports

Package cases require special markings

Foreign language labels are needed

Complicated import and export regulations

Exchange fluctuations and controls

Greater distances to markets require larger inventories

Difficult to identify and locate overseas marketing personnel

Overhead costs must be repeated from country to country

Greater risks in foreign sales.

LOWER COSTS

In comparison with the 25 executives reporting higher marketing costs for export sales, about half as many (13) report that marketing services in support of export sales cost less than similar services for domestic sales. The most frequently cited reason by far is lower advertising and promotional costs for export sales. The second most frequently cited reason is lower direct selling costs including sales overhead. Both of these reasons are given by the vice president of the international division of a firm manufacturing labelling machinery. He writes:

"The cost of these services in support of export sales are about 2 per cent to 3 per cent less than the cost of the same services in support of domestic sales. I would attribute the difference mainly to a lower direct selling expense in the international field as compared with the domestic market. The sales promotion activities in international are less than the sales promotion activities by the domestic group."

The group vice president-international of a paper company reports:

> "Domestically, the end-user price will include marketing costs ranging from 9 per cent to 18 per cent of the sales value of the products. Marketing costs on export sales are generally less—ranging from 8 per cent to 12 per cent." He attributes this difference to lower foreign advertising and promotion costs.

The vice president of a consumer products company explains that export volume is the key to holding down export marketing costs per unit. He writes:

> "While travel costs, etc., are obviously higher [in foreign marketing.] each of our full-time sales representative accounts for three to four times as much volume as the average domestic salesman, whether this be on direct sales, sales through agents, or through distributor sales."

The third most frequently mentioned reason why costs of export marketing services fall below those for domestic marketing services is lower warehousing costs. A consumer products executive says. "In general our exports costs as a percentage of our sales are less than in domestic sales. We do not have the expense of operating regional warehouses, since all shipments are made direct from our factory. In no case do we make export shipments from regional warehouses."

Other elements of the marketing mix that contribute to lower costs in support of export sales compared with domestic sales, according to one or two panelists who reported each of them, include:

Less administrative overhead

Less technical service

Lower financing costs

Relative cost is much lower because export prices are much higher

International sales tend to be greater per transaction

International market development cost are lower than those for domestic market development.

SIMILAR COSTS

A substantial number of executives (17) report that export marketing costs are approximately, the same as domestic marketing costs. As the international operations manager of a machinery manufacturer writes. "On a general basis the cost of our services to support our international sales compares pretty much with similar costs in support of U.S. sales. There are some variations, but they are of relatively minor importance."

The president of the international division of a company manufacturing musical instruments writes:

"Concerning a comparison of costs for each of these services described as the marketing mix between export sales and domestic sales, an examination will reveal that costs are very similar. This is particularly true in Europe as opposed to some of the more remote international markets." But, he points out, the appearance of similarity may be mainly on the surface. He says the comparison of costs "is worthy of further analysis, particularly if international sales exceed domestic sales or *vice versa*," and explains his reservations as follows:

"Domestically, we are involved in a much more sophisticated and nationwide sales promotion campaign than the international company would ever think of employing. The reason for this becomes obvious when you examine the homegeneity of the domestic market as opposed to the heterogeneity of the international market. That is, one overall marketing program could never be applied over a group of international markets even within the Common Market. Contrasting cultures and consumer tastes, among other things, would preclude the effective implementation of such a program."

VARYING COSTS

Several executives point out that export marketing cost depend on many elements that vary in each export transaction. Therefore, they say, they cannot report that over-all export marketing services cost consistently more or less than over-all domestic marketing services. The group vice president for one food products company says for example:

> "Because of the various plant locations that are involved in the handling and exporting of our products, our costs and our marketing mix have too many variations." The vice president of a chemical company points out that corporate internal organization can also affect costs. In his company, which "has recently been reorganized so that each operating division is responsible for a worldwide market," costs of marketing services in support of export sales vary from division so that no single report for the firm can be given.

In a particular export sale, according to several panelists, one element of the marketing mix (*e.g.*, shipping services) may cost more while another element (*e.g.*, promotional services) may cost less than the same services for a domestic sale. The vice president of a chemical company says:

> "In general, we can state that export costs are lower on inland freight, warehousing, handling, and advertising, while financing costs are higher due to extended credit terms." An executive of a tobacco products firm says:
>
> > "Over-all, advertising costs for foreign sales of exported products are approximately equal to U.S. costs; distribution and sales force costs are somewhat less."

PROFIT RATIO

The Executives who cooperated in this survey are almost equally divided among those who expect higher, lower and similar profits on export sales compared with domestic sales. In addition, a small number of executives report that their profit expectations vary among export transactions depending on the particular circumstances. Few panelists note a direct relationship between the profits earned at various stages of the distribution chain and the export marketing support services provided at that stage; and most of them avoid pricing the products they export on less than a full-cost basis.

COMPARISON WITH DOMESTIC PROFITS

The expectations of 61 executives as to the relative profitability of export sales compared with domestic sales are shown in Fig. 6.5. Several executives explain why they expect higher, similar or lower profits on exports.

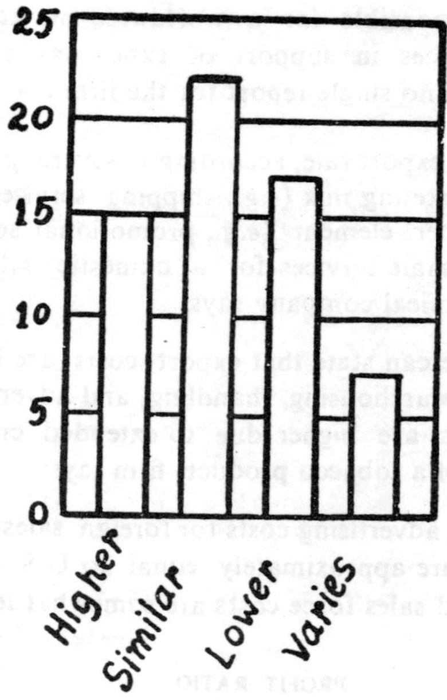

FIG. 6.5: Profits Expected on Export Sales Compared to Profits Expected on Domestic Sales (No. of Companies Reporting)

Higher Profits

Among the 15 executives expecting higher profits is the executive vice president of a household chemical firm. He writes:

"Generally a higher operating profit is expected from export sales than U.S. sales, the main reason for this being that much of the experience gained by marketing the product domestically is transferred directly to the marketing of the product in the export market. Therefore, the product goes into the export market after all the costs have been completely refined domestically."

The fact that his company's product is "a luxury product" which "cannot be sold in export markets on the basis of price" helps to account for his company's ability to earn higher profits on export sales, according to the vice president of a consumer products company. He explains:

"We expect and do earn a much higher profit margin on exports than on domestic sales. This can be attributed to the flexibility we have in end pricing and the fact that price is not as important a factor in the sale of our product in foreign markets as it is in the United States. Our product in foreign markets is sold on the basis of prestige, status, and quality, whereas in the United States important competitive factors play an important part in our pricing."

Similar Profits

A greater number of panelists (22) report that their firms anticipate earning similar profits on both export and domestic sales. The president of the international division of a food products company, for example, says:

"In general, our FAS export prices are the same as our domestic wholesale prices, and, since marketing costs are comparable, our export business represents a similar return to our company."

The senior vice president of a chemical company reports;

"Based on similar costs experienced in domestic and export activities, our firm generally expects to show equivalent profits on each segment...Our firm's export business is viewed as a long-term activity and accordingly is expected to cover total costs and generate acceptable returns on resources employed. In both domestic and export markets, competitive influences can impact the profitability of particular transactions. However, this situation is not viewed differently for export versus domestic business."

According to the vice president for international operations of a company manufacturing a variety of industrial products, over-all profits on export sales may be similar to those on domestic sales, while the profits on individual products or product lines may vary upward or downward. He writes:

"We do not specifically establish a separate profitability target on export sales versus U.S. domestic sales. We feel that the return should be generally the same. In pricing products for overseas sales, we anticipate that some product lines might require more extensive servicing and incur costs higher than domestic costs, and accordingly establish prices 10 per cent higher than domestic prices. On spare parts, we price overseas items about 20 per cent higher than domestic repair parts prices. As a balance to stronger pricing on particular products, we find that other product lines require extremely competitive prices in order to penetrate overseas market. This arises when we are competing with local manufacturing through a very high tariff wall. In those instances our profitability is lower than normal and we seek to obtain a profit from an over-all balanced transaction involving a number of items which, as a package, may contain several low and unsatisfactory prices."

Lower Profits

"We always expect lower profit on export sales than on

domestic sales," reports a chemical executive, one of 17 panelists reporting this view. An executive of and agricultural products company, who is also part of this group, says the reason for the lower profits on export sales in his firm is "the fact that we generally do not produce specifically for export, and many of our export sales are fill-in orders, which depend upon availability." The vice president of a second agricultural products firm explains its lower export profits as "due to lower average selling prices and higher per unit costs."

The president of the international division of a musical instrument manufacturer gives two reasons for lower profits on exports. He writes:

> "Because of the higher dollar value attributable to the expenses involved in the international marketing mix, the domestic company enjoy almost without exception a more favorable unit profit on each product model. Another main reason for a higher per unit profit on domestic sales is that the higher per capita income in the Unit States allows for higher pricing, particularly in the area of products used in the home."

The high cost of overseas shipping cuts down export profits, according to several executives. Prices can be raised to compensate for shipping cost, but that course is limited, they point out. If prices of supply. The vice president for marketing of a machinery and equipment manufacturer writes:

> "We expect to earn a slightly lower profit on our export sales than our U.S. domestic sales, the reason being that the transportation costs to the end-user's place of business are several times higher than for domestic sales, whereas the customer will only pay a small premium for the U.S. built product. His alternatives are usually to employ locally produced machines of similar design or tradit onal hand labour methods."

Varying Profits

A few panelists (7) report that their profit expectations on export sales compared with domestic sales vary from transaction to transaction. The most common reason given is the variation of profits by product lines. A chemical executive says of one product line. "We generally have earned a higher gross margin with lower operating costs", and of a second product line, "We believe that currently our margin on export sales will be lower than domestic sales." The president of the international division of a publishing firm also reports profit variations due to product line differences, but adds a geographical variation as well and points out that profits "will vary from country to country."

RELATION OF PROFITS TO MARKETING SERVICES

Marketing services in support of export sales are usually provided by several units in the overall distribution system. There may be little or no relation, however, between the services provided by any one unit and the profit that unit earns, according to several panelists. The vice president of a machinery company says:

"Insofar as we can see, neither the absolute profit nor the percentage profit bear any relationship to the services provided."

And the sales director of a steel company writes:

"No direct relationship exists between the services provided by a unit in the distribution chain and its profit. As the functions are interrelated and variable, it would be most difficult to assign a profit by functions performed."

The vice president for the international department of a chemical company explains unit profit in terms of the commissions paid by his company to their distributors. He writes:

"We feel there is no fixed relationship between the services provided by the units in our overseas marketing chain and the profit they earn. Some provide minimum service and therefore realize as profit most of the 15 per cent commission we grant. Others provide considerably more in the way of service and contribution to the marketing mix, and in some cases they increase the local selling price to cover the cost of these services and still realize a profit."

An executive of a firm machinery company believes that factors other than the cost of marketing services are more important in determining the allocation of export profits. He says:

"Transfer pricing policy, domestic and foreign government laws and regulations, and costs in general tend to have more influence on division of profit as compared to services provided."

In one petroleum products company the export department makes no profit on its sales of the company's product, but relies for its profit on the sales of products from other firms. An executive explains:

"The agent/distributor, etc., earns 5 per cent for his efforts, whereas the Export Department earns zero when exporting our own firm's produced material. Therefore, to survive, the Export Department buys and resells other companies' products in order to make profits and cover operating costs. In other words, most of the Export Department profits are made by selling products of other companies, and profits realized by sales of our own produced material go back to the domestic divisions, although the export Department assists in the effort."

In contrast, a number of executives find that unit profits are related closely to the marketing services provided by the unit. An executive of a pharmaceutical firm says:

"Profits earned by the units involved are commensurate with the service contribution provided."

And a vice president of a manufacturer of household appliances says:

> "The margins are allocated fairly directly in proportion to the services rendered by parent, distributor, and dealer."

The vice president of a machinery and equipment firm concludes that "the amount of profit derived by a unit in the distribution chain is attributable directly to the degree of services which it renders." He points out that units are particularly apt to earn higher profits "when they handle their own advertising, their trade show participation, and their descriptive literature in their own language, when they have demonstration units on hand for display to prospective customers, and when they are able to handle their own financing and maintain adequate inventory."

The president of the international division of a manufacturer of musical instruments believes that "virtually all the marketing aspects discussed have an indirect effect on the profit earned by the distributor unit." To illustrate, he says that "the dealer who successfuly promotes a concert is usually repaid by either the 'leads' it provides or, more directly, occasionally by on-the-spot sales. In this instance, the impact on earned profits of the parent company is, of course, indirect and realized at a later date when pipelines are filled in the case of new products and on-going products are moved out of dealer inventories."

A number of executives qualify their general belief in the direct relationship between the unit's provision of services and its profits. The vice president of a petroleum products firm concludes:

> "Almost invariably, greater contribution to the marketing mix in the distribution chain earns greater profit." Then he adds, "This is subject to variation according to the products involved."

Variations in services can affect a distributor's profits in the sense that they affect his commisions, several panelists report.

A tobacco products executive says:

> "The only relation between the distributors' services and the profit they earn might be in the area of commissions, which can vary depending on the extent of the sales services provided by the distributor."

A chemical company executive makes the same point when he says:

> "Agents, distributors, and overseas subsidiaries receive the customary commission or discount, which is adjusted in case where they are required to provide more than the normal services for the product line in question."

INCREMENTAL PRICING

Very few of the cooperating executives report that their companies "customarily" price any product for export on an incremental cost, rather than a full cost basis. About half of the executives responding to this question say, however, that under certain special circumstances they do make export sales at less than full cost. Many of them point out that similar policies apply to domestic sales.

The other half of the respondents report that their companies will not sell export at less than full cost. Several panelists are quite emphatic on this point. An executive of a tobacco products firm says:

> "We do not price any product for export on an incremental cost basis and under no circumstances do we sell to export markets at less than full cost."

Similarly, a vice president of an industrial instrument manufacturer says:

> "Under no circumstances would we ever sell in any export or domestic market at less than full cost."

An executive of a chemical company agrees, but adds:

"We may sell at a very nominal return."

And an executive of an automobile manufacturer says:

"On special cases, such as tenders or fleet sales, we grant prices below our normal distributor net price—but, we always keep a profit margin."

An executive of a machinery company points out that his firm always sells at a price to cover full costs, even though to do so it has at times had to sell at higher prices to the export market. He writes:

"In general, we find that export sales must be priced at least 10 per cent more than domestic sales on the same product in the same quantities. Unfortunately, we do not see large enough volume in this field in either Europe or Japan which would assist us in closing the gap. Therefore, we have set up our international activities on a pay-as-you-go basis and require them to pay their full costs on each order serviced. This results in higher overseas prices, but not disproportionately larger than one would expect in a limited market."

A number of executives give reasons for their company's decision to refrain from selling on an incremental basis or some other basis that does not take into account full costs. For a company making construction and mining equipment, the size of its export market is the deciding factor. Its vice president says:

"We do not treat our export market as an incremental market particularly since it represents about 50 per cent of our market opportunity."

Legal questions determine the decision of a general machinery manufacturer. Its president writes:

"We do not differentiate between export and domestic sales prices. Indeed, we consider it to be illegal to do so. We would not, under any circumstances, sell to export markets at less than full cost." And an excutive of the international division of an automobile manufacture believes his company might be faced with charges of dumping if it sold at less than full cost.

Finally, a consumer products company has decided, according to its vice president, that because its products are considered luxury goods in the export markets, "under no circumstances would we consider selling any of our finished products under cost. We don't have to."

REASONS FOR INCREMENTAL PRICING

More than half of the responding panelists report, however, that there are circumstances when their companies do sell in the export markets at less than full cost prices. A number of reasons are given.

The entry into a foreign market on a competitive level and the retention of an existing competitive position are two of the reasons most frequently reported by panelists for pricing exports on the basis of less than full costs. Thus, the vice president of a food products company reports:

> "In order to be competitive in some areas of the world, some products are priced for export on an incremental cost basis." And the vice president for finance and administration of a company manufacturing household appliances says his company would consider selling at incremental price "to allow entry into a competitive market."

The vice president of the international division of a chemical company concludes:

> "The increasing competition from Japanese and European producers is forcing U.S. companies to provide more and better services and at the same time to make increasing use of incremental costing. The marginal contribution to profits

can be substantial even though in our company no recognition of this is made in the accounting process."

For some companies, pricing on an incremental basis is limited to selected product categories. A chemical executive says:

"On certain large volume commodity products, we are sometimes forced to sell on an incremental basis to meet foreign competition. This is particularly true of products sold on a tender-bid basis and which do not call for continuing market effort."

Another frequently mentioned circumstance responsible for selling to export markets at prices based on less than full cost is idle production capacity. The director of marketing for a rubber company says:

"The traditional pricing has been on a full cost basis. However, we would be prepared to deviate somewhat from this policy if unused plant capacity became a serious problem with threatened layoffs and underabsorbed overhead costs."

The vice president of the international division of a chemical company writes:

"Export sales of international competitive commodity-type chemicals are often at less than full cost, depending on the extent of idle production capacity and competitive pressures. Except for proprietary products, we tend to view exports as a way to a way to increase the operating rate of domestic manufacturing units."

A number of market considerations are reasons for selling exports at prices based on less than full costs, according to several panelists. An executive from an agricultural products company says:

"We would only sell at less than full cost when it constituted a market introduction with programmed furure sales expectations which would return a profit." Temporary price reductions for export sale are also used at times, a petroleum executive says, "to help develop a market for a slow-moving by-product." or, according to the vice president of a food products company, for "secondary products derived in a food processing operation from producing the primary product."

Bulk orders for export might result in prices at less than full cost, some panelists say. The vice president of a machinery company reports of his firm:

"Special pricing in which incremental rather than full cost would receive consideration is limited to such special circumstanccs as very substantial orders that could result from competitive bidding on bulk purchase. In this category would be certain sales to the U.S. Government and similar circumstances outside the United States."

A petroleum executive says that his firm might sell export at less than full cost if the only choice were a more costly or less profitable alternative. He writes:

"We would only sell export at less than full cost if the product was already in tankage and the alrernative was to crack it. Then we would sell above the cracking value or, alternatively, crack it. This rarely occurs."

Several panelists point out that when a firm has planned to develop production facilities in a particular geographic area, it may first seek to develop a new market or retain an existing one there by selling exports at prices below full cost. The export manager of a food products company writes:

"The only reason we would ever sell on this basis is to preserve a market that we feel has real potential for possible later manufacture or to be supplied by a manufacturing unit in that area."

And the vice president-international for a paper company says:

> "Incremental cost prices are used occasionally, but only in assisting the development of a specific product line and only for a specific overseas unit that is planning to produce the product locally—and for a limited time only." The vice chairman of an electronics manufacturer points out that selling at lower prices under these circumstances "may mean for a period making little or no profit until the business is established, at which point we expect to establish a plant in that market and make a good profit."

Another reason for selling exports at less than full cost, according to several panelists, is to reduce excess stocks. An executive of an industrial equipment firm says, "It is always possible that we would sell to export markets (or any other market) at less than total cost on a short...as a means to reduce inventories."

This need to reduce inventories, a number of executives point out, is often the result of obsolescence of products. "If there would be a change in packaging of formula by the domestic company with stocks of the obsolete product remaning and available for export," the vice president of a household chemicals firm says, "we would in all probability market the excess of product at a reduced price." The president of the international division of another company reports:

> "We recently became involved in the dissolution of a division. Certain products sold by that division were offered for export sale at substantially reduced prices. Virtually all products sold were made obsolete by dissolution."

A number of other reasons for selling exports at less than full costs are listed by individual executives. The list includes the following:

To assist dealer organization growth

To keep a group of employees working together
To sell a special product outside the usual export line
To supply a manufacturing prototype to a subsidiary or licensee.

Other panelists report their companies might sell at less than full cost if any of the following conditions were present:

Orders are for large volumes

The product is sold in the United States at less than full cost

The export customer provides his own installation and services

Significant incremental sales would result.

In almost all these instances, selling at less than full cost would, as the vice president for international operations of a manufacturer of electrical equipment says, be "an exception to the usual practice." Or, as the vice president of a chemical company reports, such sales would be "a temporary expedient."

7

EXPORT CREDIT INSURANCE AND PRICE SETTING

AXEL WALLEN

CREDIT INSURANCE

By helping minimize risk in export transactions, export credit insurance are a major element in national trade promotion programmes. Export credit insurance agencies have the task of minimizing the risk that their country's exporters face of not getting paid for their international sales transactions. As such, these agencies have a significant trade promotion role to play, because they can help encourage the business community to overcome certain hesitations that may exist in doing business with unknown or distant buyers and markets.

To operate successfully over the long term, export credit insurance institutions must develop policies and procedures that put their underwriting activities on a viable footing. This applies equally to credit insurers that are state organizations and insurers that are private concerns. Some of the principal management aspects relate to the extent to which the insurer covers the export risks of his clients and the cost to the export of this coverage. The following discussion outlines these and other main considerations in operating an export credit insurance agency.

TYPES OF RISK COVERED

Export credit insurance agencies in the public sector usually cover both commercial and political risks in the broadest sense of these terms. This means that they are willing to insure an exporter in a "supplier credit" case (that is, when the exporter, with or without a credit from his own bank, gives the importer a time period to pay for the goods), or a bank financing the export operation in a "buyer credit" case (when the exporter's bank provides credit directly to the importer), against the risk of nonpayment on the due date specified in the sales contract.

The risk of nonpayment may arise either:

From a private buyer in the importing country, if he is not able to make the required payment (deposit) in the local currency in his central bank (a commercial risk) or,

From the importing country, when the buyer has desposited the payment in local currency but his country is not able to convert that amount into hard currency (a political or country risk).

LENGTH OF COVERAGE

When an exporter or his bank makes an application for commercial or political risk coverage, the insurer has to evaluate the risk and make his assessment before underwriting the policy, irrespective of whether the transaction is of a short-term (up to one year), medium-term (up to five years) or long-term (more than five years) nature. The problems of underwriting a risk are greater, of course, the longer the length of the insured preriod. In fact it is not possible to predict what will happen to a country or a buyer for more than a few years' time. Whenever a medium-or long term risk has to be covered, a high degree of uncertainty is involved. This is illustrated by the present debt crisis. in which many countries have payment difficulties that could not easily be foreseen in the 1970s. One must assume that long-term credits are "uninsurable" and that the governmental agencies that accept to cover these risks do so being fully aware of the fact that any coverage may lead to a total loss and that no system consisting for a large part of long-term insurance can be run on the basis of covering costs and losses. In the case of a commercial risk, however, the security provided, such as a mortage, may be satisfactory from the financial point of view to justify long-term coverage.

Commodities and other products solid under short-term contracts are usually covered by export credit insurance only from the time of shipment onwards, with post-shipment insurance. Heavy capital goods, however, such as large machinery and equipment, which are usually procured on the basis of a special order, are often covered during the production phase of the goods as well. The coverage starts at the time the order is placed, against the risk of cancellation of the contract, and then continues into the post-shipment stage. In this second situation, the preshipment coverage progressively increase in value over the production period. (A quite different kind of "insurance" in the production stage is the guarantee that some public entities offer to protect exporters' access to working capital for the production of export goods. In such circumstances the risk is on the exporter, not on the buyer or the buyer's country, and as such does not fall within the category of exports credit insurance).

INDEMNIFICATION PERIODS

Insurance against commercial risk usually covers both insolvency and protracted default of the importer. In most cases the exporter is indemnified for insolvency at once, while he is paid for protracted default only after a period of at least six months following the due date in the export contract.

The political or country risk policy generally covers inability to transfer payment because of political events and or economic or financial factors that result in a shortage of foreign exchange reserves. Insurers usually apply a waiting period of two to four months before paying implemnification in a country risk case.

EXTENT OF RISK COVERAGE

An export credit insurance underwriter can vary the extent to which he covers the risk in several ways.

Amount of premium: The most basic element for determining the degree of risk coverage is the amount of the insurance premium (or the price of the policy). Private export credit insurers tend to set the premium rate on a case-by-case basis more frequently than public agencies do. State export credit insurance institutions often use set rate schedules.

For country risk coverage, insurers often divide countries into various categories in relation to the degree of repayment risk they represent (countries with fully convertible currencies are usually in the first category). The premium for the different categories may vary considerably from one to another. For example, if a flat premium for political risk is set at between 0.05 per cent and 0.25 per cent in the first category in the fourth category of countries it may be between 1 per cent and 5 per cent depending on the length of credit. If commercial risk is also covered, it is taken into account by charging an extra amount on top of the country risk premium.

The amount of the premium may also vary according to the length of the credit period. Some insurers change much higher premiums for long credit periods than for short ones, for obvious reasons mentioned above, while others have a fixed premium over time.

Partial coverage: The insurer also limits the risk by requiring the insured partly himself to assume some of the risk Such an approach not only limits the risk to the insurance agency but also increases the insured party's own interest in the transaction and his willingness to help collect the debt, if payment problems arise later. When a public export credit insurance agency requires direct participation by the exporter and agrees to only a low percentage of cover, the agency does not usually allow the insured party (the exporter) to transfer his own risk to any other source (an exception is in buyer credit cases, when banks are entitled to transfer their risk to the exporter).

Besides the case of a general refusal of an insurer to cover a risk because of its magnitude, the underwriter may reduce the risk by deciding to cover only a part of it. Public export credit insurance agencies sometimes take this approach for large construction or engineering projects or similar transactions of a high contract value. But the same course may also be followed for risks of a smaller amount, if the buyer (in the private sector) does not appear to be sufficient credit worthy.

One possibility is for the insurer to share the amount of the risk with a third party. For instance if the cost of a project is $100 million, a public export credit insurance agency may decide to cover half of that amount. It is then up to the exporter to find the insurance cover for the rest. One solution may be through a bank syndicate.

Sometimes a risk is shared in terms of the time period covered, rather than the amount insured. In the case of a large export project, for instance, a consortium of banks may assume the entire risk during the first part of the credit period, for example for four years, after which the public export credit insurance agency takes the risk for another four years.

Often in country risk cover, in the case when the insured party is required to take on part of the risk directly, the export credit insurance underwriter will take on a maximum of 90 per cent coverage. But in certain situations this may also be lower, for example 75 per cent or 80 per cent. In commercial risk cases even lower figures may be used, if the credit rating information is insufficient or the security offered is inadequate. Otherwise in commercial risk the coverage figure is often at 80 per cent or 85 per cent.

UNDERWRITING COMMERCIAL RISK

A commercial risk concerns the possibility that a private buyer will not be able to pay on the due date. Such a risk can be covered by private credit insurers as well as public agencies. (For political risk, private insurers play a less important role than public agencies). In general, public export credit insurance agencies compete with private agencies for small and medium-size transactions of private buyers, which the credit periods go up to one or two years. Large transactions involving credit periods that are longer than one or two years are usually convered by public agencies if the security provided is not of a high quality.

Assessing creditworthiness: Public and private insurers generally take the same approach in commercial risk cases. They carefully study any available information on the buyer's creditworthiness and then base decisions concerning the premium level and any special conditions in the insurance policy on this information.

When the buyer is a company, the insurer should at least know the large shareholders, the amount of the share capital add the turnover, and have access to a company balance sheet or at least to an assessment of how much of the share capital has been paid out. This will allow the insurer to get an idea of the compauy's main objectives and its creditworthiness.

Getting information on private buyers is an even more difficult matter. To assess a private buyer's creditworthiness, insurers should try to obtain the best credit information available. Large credit bureaus are most frequently used for this kind of data. The one selected should have a record of providing reliable information. In some countries it is increasingly difficult to get details on an individual's credit standing because of the growing number of laws on confidentiality of information. Especially in the case of buyers located in distant markets, it is advisable to have a report from a bureau in the buyer's own country.

If a company status report from a credit information bureau does not provide all of the necessary background, it can be supplemented by a bank report. But bank reports are often too short and succinct to be used as a basis on their own for a credit.

A common problem with all types of credit rating information is that it is usually expensive, especially the full reports that are issued on the buyers or purchasing firms in question.

Members of the International Credit Insurance Association (ICIA), a private insurers' organization, have developed a system under which they give each other information on private buyers in their respective countries. They also reinsure the coverage of each other's policies. The International Union of Credit and Investment Insurers (Berne Union), which has around 35 members from countries throughout the world, deals with the coverage of commercial risk, credit status reports for such coverage, short-term premiums and so on. Through this forum members can inform each other of problems with buyers and related matters.

If an underwritter finds that the information provided by the exporter or through the underwriter's own efforts is not sufficient and is not up to date, he should refuse to underwrite the transaction, unless satisfactory security can be put forward. (It is not always easy, however, to refuse cover simply because the credit rating information is not sufficient, if the credit reports do not contain any negative signs.)

Securities: The question of what securities to require in connection with an insurance policy, if this course of action becomes necessary, is a complex one. For an export transaction of high-value capital goods, it may be advisable to use them as collateral, for example to have a mortgage on the goods exported. But the problems of claiming the security at a later stage are so extensive, both legally and practically, that the real value of such security is doubtful. Leasing transactions may give a better legal and practical basis for action.

If the buyer is a company that is part of a larger entity such as an industry group, it may often be advisable to get a guarantee from the head company. If the buyer is a state-owned company, a governmental guarantee may be requested, if the volume of exports is large.

Personal guarantees from shareholders or other persons connected with the purchase are sometimes offered as security. They may be a reasonably good alternative, but they do not usually greatly enhance the creditworthiness of the total transaction. Again, if payment problems arise, the legal and practical difficulties of having recourse to the guarantee can be substantial in international transactions.

INSURING AGAINST POLITICAL RISK

In the written material, documents, statistical data and so on that an underwriter examines in an appraisal of a particular country risk, there may be indications of an impending political change, which might in turn influence the country's possibilities to meet its payment obligations. Changes in the country's economic and financial position might also imply future payment problems, if remedial measures are not taken.

To distinguish between "political" and "economic" events is not always easy. For instance, in a worsening economic climate, a government may take actions to restrict imports, for example by imposing prohibitive customs duties. Although this could be seen as an economic measure, underwriters generally decline such steps as "political" events. If the risk is covered by an instance policy a distinction between both types of risk is not relevant, of course, as both "political" and "economic" events are covered by the country risk policy in contrast to wh t is covered by the commercial risk policy.

Typical signs of political risks are growing ethnic, social, cultural, religious or political tensions in a country, which might lead to an overthrow of the government or a civil war. Other indicators of possible future political change are growing strains with neighbouring countries or other foreign-policy-related problems.

Political changes can have major effects for an exporter in another country doing business in the market concerned. A change of government could have serious repercussions on the continuation of large projects or the country's ability to honour payments to foreign suppliers for major transactions, as a new government's views on the use of imported goods or services might not be the same as those of the current government.

An underwriter may foresee certain political changes without being able to predict when they will occur. He must take the risk into account when deciding on the level of the premium, but it is seldom reasonable to refuse to cover the transaction because of the risk itself (which is not necessarily the case when economic risk are involved), if major changes are not imminent.

As mentioned above, it is often difficult to foresee when political events will occur and how they will influence the payment situation. It is, however, generally easier although not simple to forecast a country's economic and financial situation over several years to come. This is especially so for countries cooperating with the World Bank and the International Monetary Fund. These international organizations can provide detailed information on their members' economic performance. Their periodic reports give a good basis for appraisals for export insurance policies. The reports may be supplemented by reports from the exporting country's own foreign ministry or from private banks or consultants.

An appraisal of a country's economic conditions should take into account a number of different factors. It is generally important to look into such elements as:

The size of the country's economy: The value of foreign trade as a percentage of gross national product (GNP).

The current level and recent trends in per capita GNP in real terms.

Population growth.

Balance of payments situation—trade balance, overall balance.

Rate of inflation.

Diversity of the country's exports; if exports are concentrated on only a few commodities, international price trends of those; general out-look for the country's terms of trade.

The country's debt burden and debt servicing situation; relation between debt servicing and export revenues; the debt-service ratio.

Foreign exchange reserves in relation to imports and debts; ability to borrow abroad.

Exchange controls; the exchange rate, including whether more than one officially exists and if any black market rates are in operation (all indicating that the economy is in difficulty); degree of capital flight (generally capital flight is evidently a negative element).

Government subsidies—frequency, dominance in certain sectors.

The country's record in handling economic crises.

A fundamental consideration in forecasting a country's level of risk is of course the length of time for which a realistic judgment can be made. It is generally not difficult to make an appraisal of a country's economic situation for the next few months. Thus short-term transactions do not generally need the same country appraisal as transactions with longer credit periods. Another reason that short-term business is usually not as risky is that short-term debt is seldom rescheduled.

In general, it is usually possible to make reasonable forecasts on countries for which fairly extensive economic information is available for a period of two to three years to come. This is also the reason that private insurers are often willing to cover country risk for transactions of such periods. And banks are sometimes willing to cover even longer periods.

Long-term cover, however, for periods of more than five years, is usually handled only by export credit insurance agencies in the public sector. As in other cases of coverage, the insurer has the responsibility to assess the relevant information and draw the conclusions concerning the extent and type of coverage applicable. As stated above, public agencies often have to presume that the economic and political situation in the importing country will not change drastically for the worse during the latter part of a long credit period, which they have to cover to promote exports.

Because long-term assessment involves many unknowns, and because of the possibility of adverse developments over a long period, many export credit insurers charge higher premiums for the longer credit periods than for short or medium-term ones. As can be seen today, the public agencies are nevertheless running huge deficits as a consequence of the present debt crisis.

SETTING COMPETITIVE EXPORT PRICES

Pricing products for export requires an approach on two fronts—studying the market situation and analyzing the production and marketing costs. Price is one of the key variables in the export marketing mix a mix that aims to provide the right product in the right place at the right time at the right price. What is the "right" export price? This is an easy question to ask but a difficult one to answer because so many factors enter into the establishment of an export price. Some of these factors are controllable by the export company, but others are not. Export pricing is an art—it is not simply reducible to a set of rules or cost calculations. Flexibility is essential in any export pricing operation.

Many firms that are just starting to export assume that setting an export price for their products merely involves calculating production and marketing costs, and then adding on an amount for profits. Export pricing is much more complex than this. It includes, of course, an evaluation of a firm's costs of producing the product and bringing it to the market, but it also entails an assessment of the marketing situation for the product. The market, and the company's objectives in that market, should be the starting point for pricing decisions—cost information should be used only to determine whether that market can be satisfied at a profit. This dual assessment—looking at the markes as well as the costs—is central to successful export pricing.

The dual assessment of market and costs does not make it any easier to establish the "right" price for an export transaction. But it does provide the basis for laying down the appropriate approach to export pricing. This article outlines the approach step by step, discussing the kinds of factors that companies should bear in mind when working out a price for their products in foreign markets. These steps are defining pricing objectives, analyzing the market situation, calculating costs, establishing target price structures and presenting price quotations.

Step 1: Defining Pricing Objectives

The first step in determining export prices is setting overall pricing objectives for the enterprise. Companies often launch into exporting without having a clear idea of what they want to achieve through their export operations or understanding the role of pricing in this activity. Is the marketing goal to use excess production capacity? In this case, decisions about export prices can be related to the marginal costs of exporting. Is it to project a high quality image? If so, this gives a promotional purpose for pricing. Whatever the overall marketing aim, the export pricing objective is closely related to it.

Pricing objectives should not be established only when export inquires are received—instead they should be set in advance of the actual export operation. They are, therefore, essentially matters of policy, and the decision on what the pricing objectives should be taken by top management.

Step 2: Analyzing the Market Situation

When the company management has set its pricing objectives, it should assess the market to arrive at a concrete sales forecast for its products, given the pricing objective. The function of market analysis in relation to export pricing is to establish an upper limit—a ceiling—for the pricing decision, based on demand for the product and the nature of the competition. For exporters in developing countries, it is usually the market situation that will determine the range of export price possibilities.

Studying market size. The first stage in such an assessment is to obtain information about the total size of the market available to the exporter and the factors (including price) that might limit his market potential. Market research (both desk research and field research) can provide such information. In addition to a survey of the current situation, the research should give an indication of the market outlook for the future.

In an analysis of market size, the more specific the market information obtained, the more valuable it is likely to be. For example, if an enterprise wants to export mangoes and wishes to obtain information helpful in marketing pricing decisions, details on the overall demand for tropical fruit in the target market would of course be useful. Even more useful, however, would be information on the consumption and prices of mangoes of specific grades. But the most important information for the exporter would be the demand and pricing for his particular type of mangoes. It would then be of interest to find out such details as the seasonal and regional variations in this demand, and consumer or user groups for the particular product.

Assessing the competition. In addition to market size, the strength and behaviour of the company's competition in the foreign market should be assessed. In many cases the question of the type and degree of competition is the key factor in setting the export price.

CHART A

Steps in Export Pricing

1. Define pricing objectives.
2. Analyze the market situation.
3. Calculate costs.
4. Establish a target price structure.
5. Present a price quotation.

Competition can be direct or indirect—the line between them is sometimes hard to draw. A direct competitor sells a product that is similar, while an indirect competitor sells one that is substantially different but that competes for the same buyers and usage. For example, in the case of a coffee exporter, other coffee suppliers would be direct competitors; tea suppliers would be indirect competitors. In terms of pricing decisions. both direct and indirect competitors should be taken into account.

The amount of pricing discretion available to an exporter depends on the nature of his competition. For example, if the market is dominated by only a few large competitors, an exporter will probably have little pricing flexibility and will be forced to adopt a "price follower strategy." Emphasis will then have to be put on other marketing variables to differentiate the product from that of the competition, such as design, style, quality, distribution and promotional services.

Similarly, if the market is characterized by many sellers of highly substitutable products, competition is likely to be vigorous' with the result that no one seller can influence price to any large extent. Price changes will be difficult to institute. If one company introduces a price increase, buyers will switch to other products. In this situation competitive forces set a market determined rate, and ricing strategy is referred to as "going-rate pricing."

Researching pricing data. In setting his export price, an exporter will also need detailed information on prevailing prices for his product line, in addition to information on the market size and the nature of the competition. A product price is usually composed of a number of elements that are related to the marketing package. These include such factors as terms of payment, discounts and distribution margins. It is important for an exporter to gather as much data on these factors as possible. He should also get information on laws and regulations that can influence pricing decisions such as price control legislation, internal tax systems, customary conditions of sale and so on.

One obvious difficulty about market analysis is that the data required may not be readily available. This is particularly the case with pricing information. Exact prices and discounts offered by the competition are sometimes difficult to ascertain. But some sources of information can usually be found by a persistent exporter.

Step 3: Calculating Costs

In parallel with a market analysis, a firm must conduct a study of its production and marketing costs to provide the background for setting its export prices. The costing side of the exercise should be carried out separately from the costing undertaken for sales on the domestic market, as the elements to be considered will sometimes be different.

Calculating export costs calls for a sound knowledge of cost accounting techniques and a thorough understanding of the company's production and marketing operations. (Given the somewhat complex nature of costing techniques, they will not be discussed here.)

The main elements that should be covered in a calculation of export costs are:

1. Direct production costs—materials, labour and other expenses required to produce the goods.
2. Production overheads—materials, labour and other expenses that are indirectly involved in producing the goods.
3. Marketing and distribution costs—materials, labour and other expenses necessary for getting orders, handling orders, packing the goods and shipping them to customers.

All of these costs should be carefully determined and analyzed into fixed and variable elements. The ascertainment of relevant costs for exporting is an important process in pricing. However, the role of cost analysis is not to determine export prices but rather to help establish target price structures in the light of market conditions. Many exporters will use a form of "cost plus" pricing, *i.e.* adding a national profit margin to product costs to obtain a price. This kind of pricing policy can lead to uncompetitive price quotations and does not take account of the prevailing market conditions for the product.

There are of course particular cost elements that must be considered in relation to establishing export prices, the most important of which relate to the various possible terms of delivery or trade terms under which an export transaction may be concluded. Many of the terms of delivery used in international trade have been defined by the International Chamber of Commerce (ICC) and are referred to as "Incoterms." (They are available in published form from the ICC, 38 Courts Albert Her, 75008 Paris.) Incoterms indicate the division of costs and administrative responsibility between the exporter and his customer. Different markets, products, marketing channelsand customs of the trade all influence decisions on terms of delivery and thus on export price structures.

Each Incoterm provides a different set of advantages and disadvantages for the exporter and the importer. For instance,

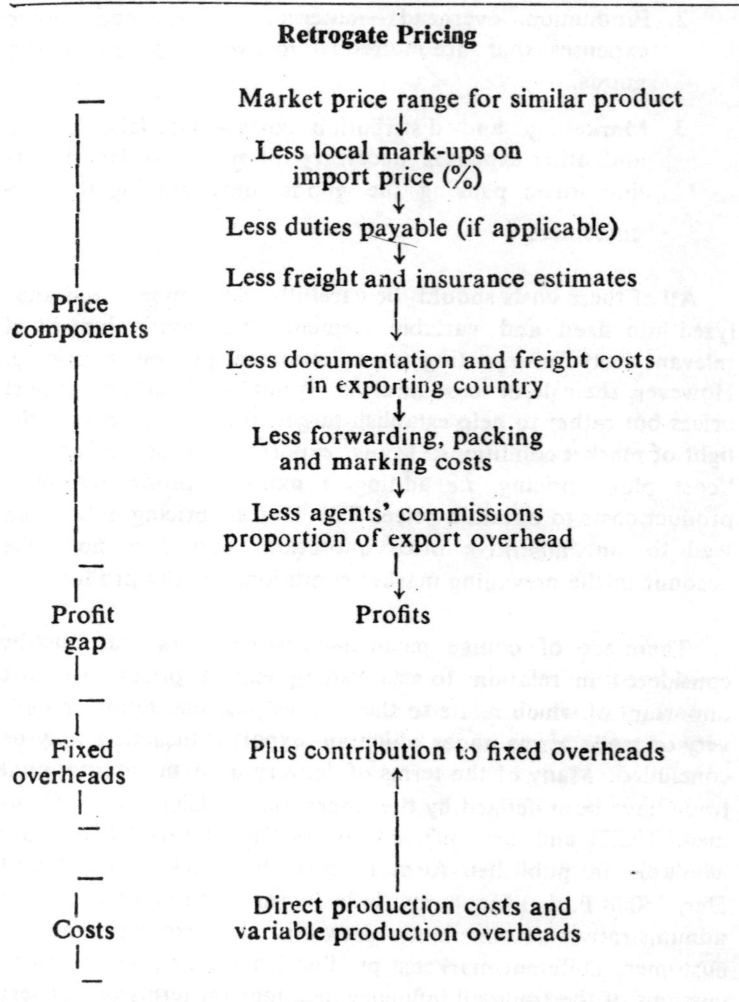

an importer might prefer FOB (free on board) terms for an export transaction, if he is a major buyer or is located near shipping centres and may be able to negotiate advantageous freight and marine insurance rates. Or an importer might request CIF (cost, insurance and freight) terms, so that he can easily compare price quotations from various countries or to guard against losses from fluctuations in freight and insurance rates. When an exporter has worked out an export price structure, he can negotiate with the buyer on the particular trade terms that will form the basis for the specific price quotation.

Other factors to be taken into account in establishing the export pricing structure include:

Agents commissions. Depending on the target market, the product and the marketing channel used, these must be accounted for in the export pricing structure. They are usually calculated as a percentage of the ex-works price of the goods, packed for export, even though a CIF or an FOB price may actually be used as the basis for the eventual price quotation.

Drawback. If imported goods are used in any articles that are produced for export, the exporter may be allowed a duty drawback at a predetermined level. Such a drawback should be taken into account in the export pricing structure.

Interest costs. One important cost that is often not taken into consideration by exporters in drawing up a target price structure is the loss of interest earned on export revenues because the exporter receives his money from the buyer a considerable time after the goods have been solid. This cost should also be calculated.

Step 4 : Establishing Target Price Structures

After a cost and market analysis, the next step in determining export prices is to establish a target price structure for the firm's products. In doing this, the exporter should attempt to determine the effect of a market opportunity on his profits by working backward from the established or accepted range of market prices (obtained through market research) and simultaneously working forward from the cost side. Working backward from established market prices in this way is known as "retrograde pricing." The gap that remains between the costs and the price presents the exporter with his profit and/or contribution to overheads. (*See box on page 214.*) If the gap is large, the exporter has some pricing discretion. He might consider setting a target price somewhat lower than the current market price. Before doing so, however, he should ask himself:

How might the competition react?

Is the market price artificially high?

Might a lower price suggest lower quality to buyers?

If the price were kept at the current market price level, would this help support the development of other export markets?

Have all of the relevant costs been taken into consideration?

How difficult might it be to raise the price far?

Alternatively. If the gap between the market price and costs is very small or even negative, the exporter will have to consider such questions as:

Will the market bear a slightly higher price?

Can the mark-ups in the importing country be negotiated?

Are there ways to reduce the impact of customs duties?

What alternatives exist for transportation?

Can packing costs be lowered?

How far could production costs be cut?

Of course, in this second situation one alternative might be to reject that particular export market and examine the possibility of selling to other.

The establishment of a target price structure in this way does not determine what any individual export price to a customer is going to be, nor is it a price list. It is simply an internal calculation process that can be used to establish the effect on enterprise profits of market conditions and enterprise costs.

Step 5: Presenting Price Quotations

Based on the price structure that he has drawn up, an export can make price quotations to prospective importers in foreign markets in response to their specific inquiries. With a price quotation, an exporter provides a potential customer with a precise and the exact conditions under which he is willing to supply his goods.

An export quotation should contain the following:

Some expression of thanks for an inquiry.

A clear and concise description of the goods.

A statement of the terms of delivery and what the prices cover (such as packing).

Details of prices, discounts, payment terms.

An indication of the date of delivery.

Period for which the quotation is valid.

Minimum and maximum quantities of the product that can be ordered.

The nature of the quotation can very greatly. Many export quotations are now made by telex, but there are still many others that involve sending a form and a covering latter to the potential buyer. Some exporters send quotations on special forms that include an acceptance slip, which a prospective buyer can fill in and return if he wishes to accept the price and to place an order. Such a price quotation is a definite offer to supply. Another approach often used is to send a proforma invoice as a form of quotation. This looks like a normal commercial invoice, but it does not go through the normal bookkeeping system until an order is forthcoming. (Proforma invoices are often required by customers governments when issuing import licenses or currency permits).

In all of these cases an exporter must present his quotation to the potential customer clearly and professionally. All too often export orders are lost because the exporter has not taken enough care in this area. Equally, it is important to provide a quick response to an export inquiry, as this shows an importer that the exporter is interested in the business and has an efficient operation.

The buyer may well have sent inquiries to other potential suppliers, and speed is essential if the order is to be obtained. If the importer is not able to send a price quotation rapidly, he should send an immediate acknowledgement in the meantime while the quotation is being prepared:

The quotation as a selling document. The price quotation, besides containing information about price, terms of delivery and so on, is also a selling document. In the case of written quotations, and when it is possible, an appropriate set of publicity materials should accompany the quotation, perhaps all within an attractive binder. Such a binder could include pages from the company's current catalogue. The exporter should provide information that reflects the particular customer's needs.

The covering letter could include such information as the specific product advantages, compared with those of competing products; a breaknown of the price to show the unit price of the product; any reasons that the terms of payment or delivery are especially advantageous; and any other particular benefits in the offer for the prospective consumer.

An example of a price quotation is given in Chart C.

CHART C

Example : A Price Quotation

Alpha Garments Co. Ltd.
35, Beta Road,
Zeta City, Zeta
22 August 1988

Your ref : HOB/462 Your date: 10 August 1988
Our ref : ABC/491

To : Smith Clothing Store
1209 Main Street
London EC4 5BX

For the attention of Mr. Brown, Purchasing Manager

Dear Sirs,

Quotation for Cotton Shirts

Many thanks for four inquiry of 10 August 1988 about our range of white cotton shirts.

Enclosed please find a page of our new catalogue which provides full details of sizes, colour and designs. As you will know, our shirts sell well in Europe and we regularly supply these and other garments to a variety of department stores, including several of the largest in London and Paris. Our cotton shirt range, we feel sure, will be an excellent complement to your current product lines.

We have pleasure in quoting as follow:

White 50/50 polyester/cotton mixture men's shirts as per sample, label No. 203, in assorted sizes between 35 and 44, individually packed in plastic bags and boxed in 100s, no less than 50 of each size, packed in export crates of 1,000 shirt:

£5.00 per shirt CIF SOUTHAMPTON, INCOTERMS 1980.

For an order of 2,000 or more shirts we allow a quantity discount of 5%.

General terms:	As specified on back of this sheet
Quantity:	Minimum order 1,000 shirts
Terms of payment:	Letter of credit, irrevocable and confirmed
Delivery:	Shipment from Zeta City within 2 weeks from receipt of order
Validity:	This quotation is firm for orders received before 5 October 1988

We hope that this meets with your approval and we look forward to hearing from you soon. Please let us know if you require any further information.

Yours faithfully,
John Coulter
Export Manager
Alpha Garments Co. Ltd.

Encl: Catalogue sheet

8

TRAINING FOR EXPORT MANAGEMENT

CLAUDE CELLICH

Organizing training for business executives differs greatly from that for business students. Suggestions for conducting such programmes. Planning and presenting training programmes for senior export executives differs significantly from organizing training for students of international business. Because of their professional level, degree of business experience, management responsibilities and time constraints, senior business officials have special requirements that must be taken into consideration when training is arranged for them. Care is called for in setting the training objectives, deciding on subjects to the covered, determining the target audience, selecting training methods, identifying training specialists, arranging for training materials, setting the dates and duration, making the physical arrangements, promoting the event to the target audience and choosing the group of participants. These factors are essential for running training events successfully for this highly select business audience.

TYPE OF SPONSORING INSTITUTION

Several types of institutions in developing countries provide specialized international marketing programmes for export executives, namely foreign trade institutes, trade promotion organizations, chambers of commerce, exporters' associations, business schools, marketing and management institutes, and productivity development centres. Although some of these have regular programmes for export executives, most provide such training on an ad hoc basis only. An institution wishing to be considered in its own country as a centre of excellence for executive export training should offer specialized workshops and seminars on a regular basis.

Depending on the subject being covered, it may be advisable to invite another organization to co-sponsor a particular workshop or seminar. For example, if the theme is exporting ready made garments to a specific market, the country's association of ready-made garment exporters could serve as a co-sponsor. Experience shows that such joint ventures in organizing training programmes can have a greater impact than those arranged by the training institution alone.

CORE STAFF

One of the basic requirements for organizing training programmes for senior export executives is the existence of a core staff in the training institution that is well versed in international marketing techniques and practices, experienced in organizing short programmes for executives and competent in applying the latest training techniques, or, in other words, persons who function as training managers. The core staff should be in constant contact with the export community, including follow-up with former participants; to assess the impact that the training programmes have had on the export performance of the companies concerned. It is therefore essential that the core staff responsible for organizing seminars occupy senior positions in the training institution, and that they be given a high degree of autonomy and flexibility in managing such programmes. Furthermore, this training unit should be allowed to operate like a business enterprise, rather than a traditional institution, in arranging and running the training programmes.

The core staff should be responsible for ensuring that the requirements for senior executive training are complied with, from selection of the training programme through follow-up after the event. The various tasks of the core staff organizing the training are discussed in the following sections.

IDENTIFYING OBJECTIVES AND BENEFITS

Determining the objectives of the training event and the benefits that the participants can expect should be one of the first tasks of the organizers. A common problem in staging such training is the lack of precision in specifying the objectives of the training programme and in defining benefits (skills) that the business executives can expect to acquire. Too often the benefits described in the seminar announcement are so vague that prospective participants have little idea of the advantages in taking part in the programme.

Many terms that are frequently used by training institutions to describe seminar of course benefits either are too vague, are subject to several interpretations or fail to reflect the expected outcome. For instance, describing course benefits in relation to "analyzing" a particular subject, "examining" a certain situation, "developing" a given technique, "planning" a specific operation or "solving" a stated problem are more precise than referring to benefits in terms of "considering," "reviewing," "studying," "learning," "understanding," "becoming informed," "becoming familiar with," or "becoming presented with."

SELECTING TRAINING TOPICS

The subjects covered by training programmes for senior export executives must be determined from a training needs survey and must meet the priority requirements of the exporters concerned.

In developing the programme, the course organizer should bear in mind that an export executive is more concerned with the management of a particular export marketing function than with its technical aspects. The training programme should therefore stress the decision making or problem-solving aspects of the subject instead of the acquisition of extensive technical knowledge related to that subject. This is a point that is often not followed in organizing such training, thereby diminishing the event's success.

For example, a workshop on export market research for senior executives should not give an in depth treatment of desk and field research techniques, statistical analysis methods, sampling techniques or approaches for questionnaire development (these subjects would instead be of interest to junior staff or business students). Rather it should concentrate on the design of a research plan and its cost estimation; the benefits to be derived from such research: and the development of strategic plans on the basis of the findings.

(See the box on page 226 showing these and other differences in training organized for senior executives and business students. Some of the more dynamic training institutions are, however, increasingly using selected training methods relevant to executive development in their senior or graduate programmes).

Another problem that often arises in organizing such training is that too many subjects are covered in the course or seminar. Only the key topics should be included in the programme. Selecting fewer subjects will allow more time for effective coverage each of them.

THE TARGET GROUP

A major task is identifying the target group for the training. Too often organizers mix senior executives and junior company staff in the same training event. From a teaching point of view, it is difficult to organize a short practical programme for both levels at the same time. Moreover, senior executives may not be willing to participate in programmes that are attended by lower ranking staff.

In a few cases company officials at different levels could beneficially attend the same event, particularly programmes of an informative nature (rather than those aimed at acquiring problem-solving skills), but this is an exception.

The selection of an appropriate group of senior executives can be greatly facilitated by establishing specific objectives for the training, as discussed above, and defining the target audience at the outset. The type of participant expected to attend (the participant profile) should be clearly spelled out in the early planning stages. The profile can describe the kind of tasks the participants should be responsible for in their own companies. When applications are examined later, they can be compared with features of the profile.

The size of the training group should not be any larger than 40 persons, with 30 being a more suitable maximum figure. If the number is greater than this, the executives will not be able to express their views and share experiences in a constructive and effective manner.

TEACHING METHODS

The programme organizers should be selective in developing the appropriate teaching mix. For senior export managers the lecture method should be used sparingly. (A common weakness of many such training programmes is that lectures are relied on too extensively.) Emphasis should instead be given to "participative" methods of teaching (*i.e.* with the active involvement of the participants). An appropriate teaching mix for a group of senior executives would be presentations, business games, group discussions and case studies. Audiovisual aids and computer-based applications (for instance of decision making games) can be used to help reinforce the acquisition of skills. The exact combination of techniques for a particular event depends on the specific objectives of the training programme. (This contrasts with the methods that should be employed for other types of business training. For junior company staff, for instance, lectures, case studies and group projects should be used

CHART A

Major Differences in Training Programmes for in-and Pre-career Business Personnel

Programme features	*Export executives*	*Students of international business*
Justification	Based on identified needs	Institutional requirements
Title	Specific or technical	General or global
Objectives	Job-oriented	Curricula oriented
Benefits	Acquiring problem-solving skills	Learning about trade
Content	Highly practical	Mostly theoretical
Learning methods	Participative	Mainly lectures
Testing	Self-assessment	Standard examinations
Expected outputs	Increased exporting skills	Acquired knowledge
Speakers	Practitioners	Academics
Programme materials	Made to order	Textbooks
Training technologies	Innovative	Standard

Participants' motivation	Seeking professional development	Fulfilling academic requirements
Participants' profile	Management experience	Limited export experience
Duration	Short	Long
Timing	Flexible	Pre-arranged
Location	Most convenient site	Academic facilities
Programme	Tailor-made	Standaralized
Brochure	Essential	Not relevant
Publicity	Must	Unnecessary
Validation	Enhanced job performance	Academic degree
Registration fee	High	Low

more extensively. Training of students of international business, on the other hand, should focus on lectures, computer exercises, simulation games and field study visits.)

A chart illustrating the most—and least—effective teaching methods for developing export marketing management skills for different target groups is given on page 230.

PROGRAMME SPEAKERS

The selection of the programme resource staff and speakers is one of the most important tasks in organizing a training programme for senior export executives. Generally, a team of subject and product experts, training specialists, representatives from related export services and senior government trade officials should be recruited for this purpose. This selection is handled by the core staff referred to above. Each team member should bring to the programme particular expertise related to the subjects covered in the programme. Besides their knowledge of products, markets and or marketing techniques, the programme speakers should be effective communicators and willing to share their experiences with the participants. The right blend of experiences, personalities and delivery styles is essential for a successful team.

The number of speakers should be kept small for the programme to be effective. Generally, two speakers each day (one in the morning and one in the afternoon) are recommended. This will allow each speaker to present the subject, have discussions with participants and in the process get to know the executives in the group (and *vice versa*). If feasible, some of the speakers could be scheduled for more than one presentation in the programme. Experience shows that having a few high-calibre speakers who are active throughout the event is more effective than relying on a large number, each handling only one session. The composition of the lecturing team is therefore crucial and should be decided upon in the early stages of the planning.

The organizer of the event should be responsible for selecting the most suitable teaching techniques and audiovisual aids for each speaker. He should also be in charge of choosing and producing training materials, organizing programme logistics, renting training equipment and so on.

TRAINING MATERIALS

Programme organizers should try to obtain relevant, up-to-date training materials for their executive training events. A common problem, however, is that the training materials used for such seminars are often outdated or simply extracted from textbooks. It is important to use high-quality materials on selected topics. Training materials of a general nature are of little benefit to such a group and should not be used.

An instructor who regularly conducts executive training is in an ideal position to develop original training materials derived from his training experience—each training programme is a source of raw material (copies of presentations, list of questions raised, problems solved and discussions) from which practical training documents may be developed for the future.

DATES AND LENGTH OF TRAINING

Selecting training dates that do not conflict with any major commercial events in the country is important, as is avoiding the time of the year when the exporters travel to foreign markets (for instance for major trade fairs abroad) or importers from abroad come to visit suppliers in the country. Local holidays and vacation periods should also be checked when the seminor or workshop dates are being fixed.

The duration of a training programme for senior export executives should be short, ranging from a few days to one or two weeks at most. If the training even completes for more than one week, it may be necessary to offer morning sessions only, leaving the afternoons free for the participants to manage their businesses. Programmes longer than two weeks should be

CHART B

Effectiveness of different teaching methods for two different target groups— export executives and business students

Teaching methods | Effectiveness: least — marginally — most

Technical presentations
Group discussions
Business games
Case studies
Brainstorming
Lectures
Distance teaching
Group projects
Role playing
Programmed learning
Field studies
On-the-job training

Export executives
Business students

considered only if they are held in a location that is away from the executives' business operations and are preferably on a residential basis (*i.e.*, participants reside on the premises of the school or nearby).

WHERE TO HOLD THE EVENT

Selecting the location of the training event, including the physical facilities, is a key factor in ensuring success and particularly in attracting the desired target group. Attempting to reduce expenditures by holding seminars in secood-rate facilities is not advisable.

The organizing institution may use its own facilities for reasons of convenience or cost, provided that the set-up is suitable for the level of the group. If the institution has no such facilities, it should consider renting a conference room in a hotel. In most major cities the better hotels have appropriate conference facilities and are experienced in servicing events of this type.

To astract export executives to the training event, the organizers should assure that the conference room is air-conditioned (in the case of hot climates), is sound-proof, is sufficiently large and has comfortable seating arrangements. It should also have appropriate etectrical plugs for audiovisual aids, adequate lighting and curtains thal can be closed during video presentations. Participants should have access to nearby telephones, food services, small working rooms and parking.

PUBLICIZING THE ACTIVITY

An effective brochure announcing the seminar or workshop is a key element in any successful training programme. The brochure should be sent to a selective, up-to-date mailing list, sufficiently ahead of the event. The malling should be limited to the export firms most likely to benefit from the training.

The brochure should be of a high quality (in terms of design, printing and paper) and should be produced professionally. A one-page leaflet folded in thirds (the same size as a business letter (21×28 cm) is the least expensive format to produce and fits easily into a normal business envelope. Colour should be used on the brochure if the budget permise. The front cover should display the title and dates of the programme in bold letters, together with the name and logo of the sponsoring organization. The back cover could list future training activities. On the inside, the details of the training event should be given under the following headings:

Reason for organizing the training.

Objectives of the event.

Benefits for participants.

Content of the programme.

Who should attend, along with the participant profile.

Professional background of the workshop leaders.

Location of the event.

Dates of the event.

Dates for the receipt of applications.

Attendance fee.

Examples of brochures from several different training institutions are shown on page 229.

A brief application form and a letter (preferably of one page) from the head of the training institution, welcoming export executives to apply, should accompany the brochure. The application form should request prospective participants to give details on their professional position. This information is useful in assuring that the desired composition of the training group will be achieved, *i.e.*, executives who are qualified, who will benefit from the training and who can contribute to the programme. An example of a brief application form for executive training is given in the box on page 236. It should be adopted to the training institution's own requirements and be tested with a select group of executives before it is used on a regular basis.

Advertisements of the training programme should be placed in appropriate trade journals, business magazines, news bulletins and so on to attract executives who may not have been included in the original mailing.

SELECTING PARTICIPANTS

The applications received should be evaluated by a selection committee that includes persons from the export community, co-sponsors of the training programme (if applicable) and members of the training institution. The candidates should be assessed on the basis of the participant profile. Those who are

CHART C

Suggested Seminar Budget Sheet: Direct Costs

Staff hired for the seminar

Speaker's fees

Secretarial support

Subtotal

Facilities

Rental of conference room

Rental of audiovisual equipment

Conference services (reception, etc.)

Subtotal

Promotion

Printing of seminar brochures

Printing of invitation letters

Mailing charges

Placing advertisements

Public relations expenses

Subtotal

Documentation

Purchase of publications

Reproduction of handouts

Participants' folders name cards, etc.

Supplies (flip charts, pens, notepads, photocopier paper, etc.)

Transport of staff and participants

Communication charges

Miscellaneous

Subtotal

TOTAL

---

not selected should be informed officially and encouraged to re-apply for other programmes in which their interests and experience would be more relevant. If an export firm has nominated a junior staff member for the programme instead of a senior executive, the organizers should contact the firm's management and invite it to nominate a more senior member. Careful and personal attention to the selection of candidates is essential to maintain a healthy and permanent working relationship between the training institution and the export community.

EVALUATING THE TRAINING PROGRAMME

Training events should be evaluated to assess the impact of the programme upon the participants. The evaluation should assist the programme organizers to:

Determine whether or not the programme objectives were met.
Measure to what extent the investment made resulted in an efficient use of resources.
Obtain ideas that may increase the effectiveness of similar future training programmes.

Evaluation may be carried out by having the participants complete a one or two-page questionaire. The questionnaires should be given to the group the day before the end of the programme. This will allow them sufficient time to complete the forms. On the last day, at the closing session, the organizers should analyze and discuss the results with the participants. Such a procedure will provide an opportunity for both the export executives and the organizers to share views and clarify any misunderstandings.

A longer evalution questionnaire may be used later to obtain more comprehensive information on the full impact of the programme on the participants' jobs and on each company's export performance. Such follow-up evaluations may be carried out anywhere from three months to a year after the training ends, depending on the training programme objectives.

Other informal, yet effective, evaluation procedures may also be applied. One key indicator of the programme's success is the interest of participating firms in sending other staff to take part in similar future programmes. The organizers can also obtain useful feedback on the effectiveness of a particular event through, for example, the extent to which the attendance level is maintained throughout the sessions and the coverage given to the event in the local press.

(Such evaluation methods differ significantly from training programmes for business students. In their case, the results relate to grades on examinations and other written assignments.)

FINANCING REQUIRED

Successful training programmes should be self financing and contribute to the training organization's fixed costs. Before being developed, each training programme should be budgeted, including the estimated income from registration fees. When the budget has been prepared, listing all of the direct costs, it is possible to determine the cost per participant and the fee to be charged. Some of the best known business schools are able to finance many of their regular activities through income earned from executive training programmes.

The fee should be neither exorbitant (representing a serious handicap to potential participants) nor too low. The tendency to increase significantly the number of participants (for example from 30 to 100) to lower the unit cost should be discouraged, as it may be detrimental to the effectiveness of the programme. If the cost per participant appears to be high, the overall costs should be thoroughly reviewed. Alternative inputs could perhaps be proposed or the programme objectives and expected outputs revised. A major cost might be the international travel expenses and fees of a well known consultant located in another country. An alternative would be to replace that person with a national authority on the subject or obtain funds from other sources to cover such expenses. The main cost elements in organizing executive training programmes are the lecturers' fees,

CHART D

Application form for Executive Training Programme

Family name:	Company name:
First name:	Company address:
Title of present position:	
Description of duties:	Nature of business:

How long has your firm been exporting?...years

What percentage of revenue is accounted for by exports?.. %

Why do you want to attend this programme?

What are your expectations from attending this programme?

Would you recommend other staff members from your organization to participate in future training programmes?

Yes No

If yes, please indicate title of person(s) and for what type of seminar:

Please send to:

The Programme Organizer
Name of Training Institution
Full address
Telephone:
Telex:

---

rental of conference facilities, printing or acquisition of training materials, printing of the seminar brochures, mailing charges, secretarial services and rental of audiovisual equipment. In addition, a certain amount should be set aside for promotion and follow-up activities. Each seminar should have a separate accounting system so that it can be determined if the seminar is covering its costs. An example of a seminar budget sheet covering direct costs is given in the box on page 233. If the organizing institution wishes to recover its indirect costs, it can charge a percentage of the regular staff costs and fixed charges to the seminar budget. For example, if it offers 12 seminars a year (each one of a similar duration), it should charge 1/12th of the institute's stationaries plus a similar percentage of regular expenses (administration, library and so on) to each seminar.

GAINING RECOGNITION BY THE BUSINESS SECTOR

A large number of training institutions, trade promotion organizations and other bodies in developing countries apply the approach mentioned above to varying degrees. The most successful make special efforts to integrate these procedures in a systematic and comprehensive manner to ensure that the programmes meet the needs of the target group. Only institutions offering practical training programmes based on real needs and proven training techniques will gain recognition by the business community as a centre for excellence in executive skill training.

9

PROCESSING THE EXPORT ORDER

An important activity of export practice is the processing of the export consignment through all its numerous procedures. It is an area which must be fully understood by the exporter. However, before examining the procedures involved, we must first consider the contract of affreightment embraced in the terms of delivery which now follows

CONTRACT OF AFFREIGHTMENT: TERMS OF DELIVERY

The basis of a price quotation depends on the correct interpretation of the delivery trade terms. The export marketing manager will through experience accumulate information which will enable him to quote accurately. It is important to bear in mind each delivery trade term quoted embraces three basic elements:

The stage at which title to the merchandise passes from the exporter (seller) to the importer (buyer), a clear definition of the charges and expenses to be borne by the exporter and importer, and finally, the stage and location where the goods are to be passsed over to the importer.

The international consignment delivery terms embrace many factors including particularly insurance, air or sea freight plus surface transport costs, Customs duty, port disbursements, product cost, packing costs, etc. Moreover, the importance of executing the cargo delivery in accordance with the prescribed terms can not be overstressed and this involves a disciplined process of progressing the export sales contract order dealt with elsewhere in this chapter. In the ideal situation, the sales export contract order embracing also the delivery terms should be undertaken on a critical path analysis programme devised by the report marketing mannger in consultation with department colleagues within the company and relevant outside bodies, that is, booking shipping space, processing financial aspects, obtaining export licences, etc.

There must be no ambiguity in the interpretation by either party of the delivery terms quoted particularly in the area of cost and liabilities. If such problems arise, much goodwill is lost and the exporter could lose the prospect of a repeat order in a competitive market. Moreover, costly litigation could arise. It is essential, therefore, that the exporter (seller) and the importer (buyer) agree on the terms of delivery and their interpretation. Such a situation could be overcome by quoting the provisions of Incoterms 1980 dealt with in the latter part of this section. It must be borne in mind that special provisions in individual export sales contracts will override anything provided in Incoterms 1980. Also items such as breaches of contract, and their consequences, together with ownership of the goods are outside the influence of Incoterms 1980.

The most important and popular quotations in exporting are FOB and CIF. In regard to the CIF quotation, this encourages the UK exporter to obtain the maximum income to the UK balance of payments account, as it includes not only income from the export sale of the merchandise, but also revenue from the cargo insurance and freight (assuming of course the latter two are provided by UK-based companies). Nowadays, however, an increasing number of importers are insisting the goods are carried by their national shipping or airline.

An examination of the most important and common delivery terms follows:-

(1) *CIF.* Undoubtedly the most popular quotation is cost, insurance and freight. Under a CIF contract of sale, the exporter provides the goods, books cargo space on a ship, pays freight to the named port of destination, and insures the goods on behalf of the buyer against normal marine and fire risks to the destination port. The exporter provides the importer with the invoice, a clean bill of lading and cargo insurance policy or certificate. The seller's liability ceases when the goods pass over the ship's rail at port of loading subject to the buyer's payment being forthcoming.

The seller is entitled to payment in exchange for the documents, including bill of lading or alternative document of title, and insurance policy or certificate, relative to the consignment. Hence, the CIF contract is one to deliver documents rather than goods. If any loss or damage ensues after the shipping company has received the goods and given a clean bill of lading, the buyer will take the necessary steps against the shipowner or underwriter. The seller cannot be held liable for any such loss or damage. The buyer will be responsible for the unloading costs at the port of destination to the extent they are not includen in the freight. The bill of lading must be marked 'freight paid' thereby confirming the goods have been placed on board the vessel and the requisite commercial invoice is required for this type of contract. Moreover, it is often necessary for imported goods to be accompanied by special forms, for example. Consular invoices. In such cases it is usual for the CIF seller to defray the expenses of preparation.

The CIF contract has many advantages. It permits the seller at the see port of shipment to arrange the shipment and accept such liabilities which overall is a convenient arrangement bearing in mind the exporter is situated in the country of origin. On the other hand, the buyer is responsible for arranging delivery, lighterage, cost of discharge, import duties in his own country, and lost or damage of the cargo after the clean bill of lading has been issued.

A number of variations exist relative to the CIF quotation and these are detailed below:

(i) Cost and freight (C&F). Under this term the buyer (importer) arranges his own insurance while the seller (exporter) pays the freight to the named port of destination. Basically, the exporter is responsible for all charges until the goods are discharged at the sea port except insurance. Again the buyer (importer) pays all the unloading charges at the port of destination to the extent they are not included in the freight. The buyer's (importer's) risk commences on acceptance of the goods when they pass the ship's rail at the departure port.

(ii) CIF and E. The quotation—cost, insurance, freight and exchange—is used to safeguard the buyer against any loss due to fluctuations in exchange. It is sometimes lossely employed to indicate payment of banker's charges. It does not feature in Incoterms 1980.

(iii) CIFCI. The quotation—cost, insurance, freight, commission and interest—is quoted by an agent in the country of export to the buyer. The agent in his quotation would include his commission and interest on the value of the shipment until he receives payment. If commission is not included, the quotation would be CIFI—cost, insurancc, freight and interest. It does feature in Incoterms 1980.

(iv) A franco, 'franco domicile' or 'delivered' quotation is an extended form of CIF contract. It includes all charges incurred on delivery to the buyer's warehouse. Such prices are difficult to quote unless the seller has wide experience of costs of the overseas market. The term franco means free, whilst the term domicile confirms free delivery will be effected to the importer's warehouse at the exporter's expense. 'Franco' quotations and 'ex-ship' are most suitable for the buyer and eminently ideal for the manufacturer who sellsd irect via his branches or agencies abroad. It does not feature in Incoterms 1980.

2. *FOB.* This quotation—free on board—implies that the duty of the seller is to produce the goods, get them to the port and see they are actually placed on board the vessel which the buyer arranges. Hence, the seller meets all charges incidental to placing the goods on the ship according to the custom of the extent they are not included in the freight. When the goods are placed on board the ship and the seller has obtained a receipt for the goods, the seller's responsibilities cease. Thereafter, the buyer pays all charges including insurance of goods from the departure sea port to destination and pays the freight.

The seller still retains some dominion over the goods in certain circumstances. For example, the right of stoppage 'in transitu' is one which accrues to an unpaid seller when the buyer is insolvent as soon as the transit commences. Hence, once the seller has placed the goods in the carrier's vessel, the carrier being the agent of the buyer (only for carriage purposes) takes possession of the goods. The seller loses the right to dispose of the goods and other rights of ownership but, in the event of the importer (buyer) becoming insolvent before the delivery of the cargo takes place, the exporter (seller) can exercise his right of stoppage in transitu. In such circumstances, the exporter (seller) can reclaim the goods following payment by him of the requisite freight.

Documents required under the FOB terms are the requisite commercial invoice and a full set of clean on-board bills of lading evidencing the goods have been shipped on the carrying vessel and stating the freight is payable at the destination.

3. *FOB airport.* Free on board airport is based on the same principle as found in the ordinary FOB term. The seller (exporter) completes his obligations by delivering the goods to

the nominated air carrier at the departure airport. The risk of damage to the goods is transferred from the seller to the buyer when the goods have been so delivered. The buyer pays the air freight and insurance and all other cost following delivery of the goods by the seller to the nominated air carrier at the specified airport.

4. *FAS.* Under the free alongside ship term, the seller pays all the costs incidental to delivering the goods alongside the ship on the quay or in lighters. The custom of the port may give FAS a special meaning such as 'goods placed in steamer's shed' instead of the more usual interpretation. There also should be provision for determining where the loss lies when goods are lost before they are actually taken onto the ship. Under such terms, the exporter accepts all charges up to delivery alongside the ship, but exclusive of loading charges. Actual delivery of the cargo by the exporter takes place when the cargo is placed alongside the specified vessel at which place title of the goods passes to the importer. The buyer bears all the cost and risk of loss or damage to the goods when the goods have been placed alongside the ship. Additionally the buyer is responsible to clear the goods for export.

5. *FOR.* Under this cargo delivery term—free on rail—the seller's (exporter's) responsibility is to deliver the goods to the railway and, in the case of a 'full loads' to obtain and load the wagon(s). The buyer (importer) accepts delivery of the goods when they have been delivered to the railway, and the invoice and transport documents have been provided by the seller. The buyer's risk and resultant cost thereafter commences when the goods have been accepted at the railway deposit. Ii may be also referred to as FOT—free on truck.

6. *Ex-works.* This quotation places the exporter's liability for cargo loss or damage and duties at a basic minimum. The seller bears all the cost and risk of the goods until such time as the buyer is obliged to take delivery of the consignment and to assist the buyer, at his request and expense, to obtain the documents issued in the country of origin which the buyer

may require to convey the goods to their ultimate destination. The buyer takes delivery as soon as the goods are placed at his disposal, pays all fees charges of exporting and accepts risk from the factory gate. Title to the goods passes at the factory gates and it is normal to place after the terms ex-works the place name, for example, 'ex-works Birmingham.' Hence, under such terms, the exporter merely submits commercial invoice for the cost of the goods. The insurance and freight expenses are borne by the importer. Similar terms liabilities relative to exporter importer apply to ex-warehouse, and ex-store. Overall the cost of cargo packing is borne by the exporter to enable the buyer to take delivery of the goods.

7. DDP. Under this term—delivered duty paid, the seller undertakes to deliver the goods at the named place of destination. Accordingly, the seller undertakes the maximum obligation. This involves payment of freight, insurance, duty and delivery charges and provision of all the documents to enable the buyer to take delivery of the goods at the named place of distination. The buyer's obligation and risk commence when accepting delivery of the goods at the named place of destination which may be the buyer's warehouse.

8. Loco. This quotation means price of the cost of goods where they lie, including usually cost of packing or carriage of any kind. For example, 'loco London', or 'free packed London' includes the cost of the goods, packing and delivery in London. It does not feature in Incoterms 1980.

It will be noted there exist some fourteen Incoterms 1980 and the foregoing are only a selection of the more popular ones. The residue are described in *Elements of Export Marketing and Management*.

It must be appreciated that, regardless of the type of contract the exporter concludes, the actual final price of the specified merchandise to the buyer will be the same. The terms of the export sales contract merely set out the responsibilities for taking certain actions between the buyer (importer) and seller (exporter). Nevertheless, it is most important to ensure that, when arranging whatever delivery terms are chosen, the exporter and importer fully understand them and their interptetation.

To overcome any difficulties in interpreting the chief delivery terms used in foreign trade contracts, a set of international rules have been agreed by the member countries of the International Chamber of Commerce (ICC). These rules, known as Incoterms 1980, are embodied in the International Chamber of Commerce booklet *Incoterms 1980 Eddition—Guide to Incoterms No. 354*. It is available from only UK Chamber of Commerce. Exporters/shippers are strongly urged to obtain a copy. Exporters/shippers are also advised to use these terms/rules and in so doing specify in the export sales contract, 'subject to the provisions of Incoterms 1980.'

The subject of Incoterms 1980 is dealt with very extensively in Chapter 8 of *Elements of Export Marketing and Management* which readers are urged to study.

It must be borne in mind that whilst Incoterms 1980 are widely used internationally, other standardized trade terms do exist, details of which are given below:

1. The American Foreign Trade Definitions emerged in USA in 1919 and were revised in 1941.
2. The Rules of Warsaw and Oxford were proposed by the International Law Association in 1932.
3. The General Conditions for Delivery of Merchandise were developed in 1968 in the Council for Mutual Economic Assistance (for the USSR and some countries in Eastern Europe). They were revised on 1st January 1976 and contain a number of clauses that define the scope of certain trade terms.
4. In 1969 Combiterms were proposed. Their objective was to simplify the division of cost and risk between the parties by introducing code numbers for the cost units contained in the trade terms.

The foregoing terms reflect, in most areas, the same rules as Incoterms 1980. Combiterms are now in process of being fully compatible with Incoterms 1980 whilst the American Foreign Trade Definitions are being phased out in favour of Incoterms 1980.

THE EXPORT SALES CONTRACT

The formulation of the export sales contract represents the conclusion of some possible difficulty negotiations and accordingly, particular care should be taken regarding the preparation of its terms. It must be borne in mind that an exporter's primary task is to shell his products at a profit and, therefore, the contract should fulfil this objective insofar as his obligations are concerned. Above all, they should be capable of being executed under reasonable circumstances and ultimately produce a modest profit. It is, of course, realized that, in the initial, stages of developing a new market overseas, a loss may be incurred, but with the long-term marketing plan objective to increase the market share it should ultimately gain a favourable profit level. A further point to bear in mind is that the export sales contract also has regard to the cargo delivery terms reflecting the contracts of carriage insurance and finance arrangements.

Details of a typical UK export contract are given below, but it must be stressed that they differ by individual country:

1. The exporter's (seller's) registered name and address.
2. The importer's (buyer's) registered name and address.
3. A short title of each party quoted in items (1) and (2).
4. Purpose of the contract. For example, it should confirm the specified merchandise is sold by the party detailed in item (1) to the addressee quoted in item (2), and that the latter has bought according to the terms and conditions laid down in the contract.

5. The number and quantity of goods precisely and fully described to avoid any later misunderstanding or dispute. In particular, one must mention details of any batches and reconcile goods description with custom tariff specification.

6. Price. This may be quoted in sterling depending on its general stability or some other currency which is not likely to vary in value significantly throughout the contract duration, such as American dollars or deutchemarks. Today over 30 per cent of UK exports are quoted on a foreign currency basis. To counter inflation particularly in a long term contract, it is usual to incorporate an escalation clause, and to reduce the risk of sterling fluctuations implications, the tendency is to invoice in foreign currencies. Readers are particularly urged to read Chapter 6 dealing with costing and pricing in *Elements of Marketing and Management*. It gives particular attention to measures available to counter currency fluctuation.

7. Terms of delivery, for example, FOB Felixstowe, ex-works Birmingham or CIF Aqaba. There is an increasing tendency for many importers, particularly those situated in Communist states or Third World countries to insist on the goods being conveyed on their own national airline or shipping company. It is important both parties to the contract fully understand their obligations as the interpretation of the terms of delivery can sometimes vary by individual country. The ideal solution is to quote Incoterms 1980 which are generally recognized worldwide.

8. Terms of payment, for example, open account, cash with order, letter of credit, open account or documents against payment or acceptance. Again this requires careful consideration, particularly the relevant aspects dealt with in Chapter 9. Many importers today require extended credit and the exporter's local banks manager

should be able to give the requiste guidance on this matter.

9. Delivery date/shipment date or period. The exporter should check with his production department the delivery date quoted is realistic and the shipping or air freight space will be available on the date or period specified. The exporter's obligations regarding the latter will depend on the terms of delivery.

10. Methods of shipment, for example, container, train ferry, Ro/Ro or air freight.

11. Method of packing. It is desirable both parties are fully aware and agree on the packing specification to ensure no dispute later arises regarding packing or any variation to it.

12. Cargo insurance policy or certificate terms.

13. Import or export licence details or other instructions. The period of their validity must be reconciled with the terms of payment and delivery date/shipment date or period.

14. Shipping/freight/documentary requirements and/or instructions. This includes marking of cargo.

15. Contract conditions, for example, sale, delivery, performance (quality) or goods, arbitration etc. With regard to arbitration, this tends to speed settlement of any disputes without costly litigation.

16. Signature. Both parties to sign the contract by a responsible person at directorial or managerial level, and the date recorded.

Obviously the terms of the export sales contract will vary by circumstance but other areas which may feature include agency involvement, after-sales activities such as availability/supply of spares, product servicing, advertising/promotion cost and so on.

A copy of the contract should be retainded by each party.

RECEIPT OF EXPORT ORDER

Before dealing with the export order acceptance, it is appropriate to give below the check points that need careful scrutiny in any price list tendered, and emphasize how important it is to ensure all the special costs which may enter into an export order are included:

1. Adequate clear description of goods indicating tariff/ trade code number.
2. Specification—use metric units.
3. Quantity to be supplied with delivery programme details.
4. *Price*: (a) amount or per unit, (b) currency, (c) delivery terms which may involve part shipments over scheduled period and/or transhipments—ex-works, FOB, CIF, etc.
5. Terms of payment including provisions for currency rate variation.
6. Terms of delivery, ex-stock, forward, etc. relevant estimate.
7. Transportation mode (s), that is, container, air freight, sea freight or road haulier.
8. Insurance.
9. Packaging and packing.
10. Offer by *pro forma* invoice.
11. Identity of country of origin of goods and country of shipment.

Prior to receipt of the indent/order, a customer may need a *pro forma* invoice, which is essential before a customer can open a bank credit in the supplier's favour. On receipt of the indent or order from the overseas client, the export marketing manager will check the specification and price in the order with the quotation together with its period of validity. Care must be taken to ensure the client is not trying to take advantage of an out-of-date quotation. For example, where the quotation was FOB, the export marketing manager must note whether the customer wishes the supplier to arrange for freight and insurance on his behalf. The method of payment will be noted and checked with quotation terms. For example, where payment is to be made under a documentary credit, the documents required by the banks must be carefully noted. The required delivery date will be particularly noted. If the delivery date is given and the client has been obliged to obtain an import licence for the particular consignment, the date ot expiry must be noted.

Given below is a receipt of order check-list:

1. Goods:
   (i) Quality.
   (ii) Quantity.
   (iii) Description.

2. Payment:
   (i) Price.
   (ii) Method, *i.e.* letter of credit, open account, or documents against payment or acceptance.
   (iii) Time scale.
   (iv) Currency variation provision.

3. Shipment:
   (i) Mode (s) of transport/route/transhipment.
   (ii) Any constraints, *i.e.* packing/weight/dimensions/statutory restrictions.
   (iii) Time scale.
   (iv) Any marks. *i.e.* special marking on cases/cartons to identify them.

4. Additional requirements:
   (i) Insurance.
   (ii) Inspection requirements.

(iii) Documentation.

(iv) Specific packing—see item 3 (ii).

(v) Commissions or discount.

5. Comparison with quotation. A *pro forma* invoice is a documont similar to a sales invoice except that it is headed '*pro forma*'. It is not a record of sales effected, but a representation of a sales invoice issued prior to the sale. As the *pro forma* invoice contains all relevant details, for example, full description of goods, packing specification, price of goods with period of validity, cost of cases and, where relevant, cost of freight and insurance, it is used for quotations to customers and for submission to various authorities. Terms of payment are also always shown but it may not be possible to give shipping marks until a firm order is received. When used as quotation the *pro forma* invoice constitutes a binding offer of the goods covered by its price and condition shown.

As soon as the exporter receives the letter of credit, he should check it againsts his *pro forma* invoice to ensure both documents agree with each other. Usually, the contract will be in a more detailed from than the letter of credit, but it is important the exporter should be able to prepare his document complying with both the contract and the credit. For general guidance the following check-list should be adopted by the exporter:

1. The terms of the letter of credit which may be revocable or irrevocable.

2. The name and address of the exporter (beneficiary).

3. The amount of the credit which may be in sterling or foreign currency.

4. The name and address of the importer (accreditor).

5. The name of the party on whom the bills of exchange are to be drawn, and whether they are to be at sight or of a particular tenor.

6. The terms of the contract and shipment (*i.e.* whether ex-works, FOB, CIF, and so on).

7. A brief description of the goods covered by the credit. Basically too much detail may give rise to errors which can cause delay.

8. Precise instructions as to the documents against which payment is to be made.

9. Details of shipment including whether any transshipments are allowed. Data on the latest shipment date and details of port of departure and destination should be recorded. Advantage is gained to permit shipment 'from any UK port' thereby premitting the shipper a choice in the event of strike action. Similar remarks apply to the port of discharge.

10. Whether the credit is available for one or more shipments.

11. The expiry date.

It is important to check the reverse side of the letter of credit and any attachments thereto, the credit as further terms, and any conditions which from an integral part of the credit. Ideally both the seller (exporter) and the buyer (importer) should endeavour to make the credit terms as simple as practical.

In situations where the seller (exporter) is uncertain of just how much of the credit he will draw, arrangements should be made with the buyer (importer) to have the value of the documentary letter of credit prefixed by the word 'about'. This will permit up to 10 per cent margin over or under the amount specified. The world 'about' preceding the quantity of goods also allows a 10 per cent margin in the quantity to be shipped. Alternatively the documentary letter of credit may specify a 'tolerance'—such as '7½ per cent to 5 per cent more or less'—by which the seller (exporter) should be guided.

Documentation will usually involve the clean on-board bill of lading or air freight, the air waybill. For international rail movement it is the CIM consignment note, and for the international road haulage transit the CMR consignment note. Particular attention should be given to pre-booking cargo space on the required sailing or fight, and for container traffic booking a container suitable for the goods.

To facilitate progresssing the consignment in transit terms, some exporters and especially freight forwarders use a forwarding operations control folder.

PROGRESS OF EXPORT ORDER AND CHECK-LIST

To ensure the complex procedure of preparing the goods, packing, forwarding, shipping, insurance, customs clearance, invoice and collecting payment do not go wrong, it is suggested a check-list or progress sheet be prepared for each export order. A suggested version is given in Table 9.1 but it must be borne in mind there are many variation in processing a given export order.

In regard to items sent by parcel post or air freight, the credit and dispatch arrangements may vary slightly insofar as the foregoing is concerned.

Most exporters today have a separate order data folder for each sales contract order. The folder has a prescribed action chart to follow through for each contract which lessens the risk of any mistakes being made or items overlooked.

Functions Procedures of Export Documentation

We will now consider the processing of export documentation and the various procedures involved. Details of the salient points follow:

10 March	Order received for delivery end-April
(extracts from	All wool tissues
original order)	(Description of goods—wool and worsted piece goods)
	Order No. B 2
	Market: Lebanon
	Port: Beirut
	Packing type: six cases wood, waterproof paper, paper lined cases
	Marking: LAS Beirut 6

Time scale of deliveries

15 March	*Pro forma*
1 April	Payment terms (L/C etc.) received
2 April	Payment terms checked
5 April	Work store promise
18—22 April	Receivingclosing date of shipment
23 April	Insurance dealt with
25 April	Sailing date
28 April	Letter of credit—shipping date
4 May	Bill of lading required by this date
7 May	Completion of documentation to bank
12 May	Proceeds received
15 May	Letter of credit expiry date

It must be recognized that the number of documents and their type vary by individual consignment, mode of transport, commodity, contract of sale, importing country, customer's country, statutory obligations, financial arrangements etc.

TABLE 9.1

Export Order Progress Check-list

Order cleared for credit worthiness; terms of payment	*Signature*	*Order cleared for exchange control purposes*	*Signature*	*Order cleared for export licensing purposes*	*Signature*

1. Customer's name and address.
2. Customer's order no. and date.
3. Date of receipt and export department's serial number.
4. Brief details of the order.
5. Import licence no. and date of expiry.
6. Export licence no. and:
   (a) Date of application.
   (b) Date received.
   (c) Date of expiry.
7. Method of packing.
8. Shipping or airline—if prescribed.
9. Type of insurance.
10. Terms of payment.
11. Details of letter of credit, including full list of documents required.
12. If FOB, who arranges and pays for freight/insurance.
13. Date order acknowledged.
14. Promised delivery date.
15. Date order put in hand.
16. *Pro forma* invoices sent (often required by customer to open credit).
17. Production department—completion date.
18. Goods inspected or tested.
19. Packing ordered.
20. Merchandise ready.
21. Shipping bill completed.
22. Consular invoices completed.
23. Certificate of origin or equivalent completed.
24. Application for shipment/air freight space booking dispatched/accepted.
25. Shipping marks.
26. Shipment etc.—instructions. received/goods called forward/ closing date/despatch department instructed.
27. Bills of lading/CMR/CIM/air waybill prepared in requisite quantity.
28. Insured value declared—giving number of certificates required freight paid.
29. Bills of lading/CMR/air waybill received—documents serial no. and date of shipment/despatch.
30. Insurance certificates received —serial no.
31. Draft and document lodged with bank.
32. Accounts copy of invoice passed through the books.
33. Payment received.

TABLE 9.2

Export Documents Required

	Bank	*Custo-mer*	*Agent*	*Customs clear-ance*	*Consu-late*	*Total*
Commercial invoices	—	3	—	—		3
Certified invoices	3	1	2	1	3	10
Certificate of origin	—	—	—	—	—	
Bill of lading	2/2	2 copies	—	—	2	2/4
Certificate of shipment	—	—	—	—	—	
Insurance policy	—	—	—	—	—	
Insurance certificate	—	—	—	—	—	
Weignt and contract note	1	1	—	—	1	3
Bank draft statement	1	—	—	—	—	1

PRESENTATION OF DOCUMENTS TO THE BANK: CHECK LIST

When preparing his documents for presentation to the bank, the exporter should bear in mind the following points which can form a 'check list':

1. All the documents are presented within expiry date.
2. Goods are shipped within the stipulated period.
3. Documents are presented to the bank within twenty-one days of the date of shipment/despatch or such shorter time as laid down in the letter of credit.
4. The aggregate amount of the drawing is within the credit amount.
5. All documents requiring endorsement are correctly endorse, for example, bills of ehchange, insurance documents.

6. Invoices contain exact credit description.
7. Invoices are addressed to the importer.
8. Invoices contain exact licence numbers and/or certifications required by credit and such certifications are signed, and must be warded exactly as specified in the credit.
9. Invoices show terms of shipment mentioned in the credit.
10. Quantity, weight both gross and nett, shipping marks, unit price, etc. agree with credit and with all the relative documents.
11. Bills of lading show goods 'on board' a specified named vessel.
12. Bills of lading show correct name and address of notify party.
13. Bills of lading are in a full set of signed originals (that is, 2/2, or 3/3) or as called for by the credit.
14. If FOB shipment, ensure bills of lading show freight payable at destination.
15. If C & F or CIF shipment, ensure bills of lading are marked 'freight paid' or freight pre-paid'.
16. Insurance document is in currency of credit.
17. Insurance is for correct value (for example, as specified in the credit).
18. Insurance covers all the risks as specified in the credit.
19. Original letter of credit accompanies the presentation.
20. The insurance document is dated prior to despatch of the goods or specifically states that cover is effective from shipment date.
21. Insurance certificate is not presented where credit stipulates insurance policy.

The foregoing check-list must not be regarded as exhaustive, but merely deals with the salient points. To the exporter dealing with a documentary letter of credit, the following data must be contained on it relative to a consignment by sea:

1. The name and address of the beneficiary.
2. The type of credit (revocable of irrevocable).
3. The amount of credit in sterling or a foreign currency.
4. Whether the credit is available for one or several drawings/shipments.
5. The expiry date.
6. The name of the party on whom the drafts are to be drawn and whether they are at sight or of a particular tenor.
7. Precise instructions as to the documents against which payment to be made.
8. A brief description of the goods covered by the credit (too much detail may give rise to errors which can cause delay).
9. Shipping details including whether transhipments are allowed. The names of the ports of shipment and discharge should also be recorded, and the least date for shipment.
10. The terms of contract and shipment (that is, whether ex-works, FOB or CIF).

Credits should further state that they are subject to the Uniform Customs and Practice for Documentory Credits (1980 UCP) International Chamber of Commerce Publication No. 400. This is a standardized code of practice formulated by the International Chamber of Commerce; it was introduced in October 1984.

The following check-list must be rigorously adopted by the exporter when handling the letter of credit.

1. It is confirmed by a British bank?
2. Is the quantity described correct?
3. Is partial shipment permitted or required?
4. Is the letter of credit irrevocable?
5. Is the name of the exporter and that of the customer complete and spelt correctly?
6. Is shipment permitted from any place in the UK, or only one named point?
7. Does the named destination quoted (port of discharge) agree with the letter of credit?
8. Are the following needed?
   - (i) Export licence.
   - (ii) Import licence.
   - (iii) Exchange licences.
9. Is the letter of credit amount sufficient to the quotation? The following aspects should be checked:
   - (i) Cost of goods plus profit element.
   - (ii) Inland transport cost to ship, including wharfage and handling charges at port of loading, or similar charges relative to air freight or air freight charges.
   - (iii) Shipping—sea freight or air freight charges.
   - (iv) Forwarding fees.
   - (v) Consular fees.
   - (vi) Insurance cost.
   - (vii) Inspection and/or miscellaneous charges.
10. If it is 'on-deck' cargo, does/the letter of credit authorize 'on-deck' shipment?
11. Compare the contract of sale with the letter of credit to ensure its compatibility.
12. If a chartered vessel is involved, does the letter of credit state charter party/bill of lading acceptable'?

13. Can the exporter comply with the insurance risk required in the letter of credit and does the credit requested a policy or certificate?
14. Does the expiration and shipping date give sufficient time to assure payment?
15. Is the letter of credit irrevocable?
16. Can the exporter obtain the following relevant executed documents to conform with the letter of credit?
    - (i) Bill of lading
    - (ii) Air waybill
    - (iii) Parcel post receipt
    - (iv) Invoice packing list
    - (v) Consular invoice
    - (vi) Certificate of origin
    - (vii) Insurance policy/certificate
    - (viii) Certificate of inspection
    - (ix) Certificate of quality
    - (x) Certificate of health.

Circumstances do arise which make it impossible for the exporter to present documents to the bank exactly as stipulated or within the prescribed time. Moreover, unforeseen circumstances can arise. In such foregoing situations, the following options exist to the exporter after presenting the documents to the bank:

1. Request the advising bank to cable the issuing bank for permission to effect payment despite discrepancies in the documents. Actual cable cost would be for the beneficiary's account.
2. Ask the advising bank to accept a guarantee order that the exporter requests payment against an undertaking to hold the bank harmless for any loss or damage incurred through making payment against presentation of irregular documents.

3. Instruct the advising bank to send draft and documents to the issuing bank on a collection basis, that is, documents to be delivered to the importer against authority to pay.

In circumstances where the documents can be corrected/amended, the exporter should arrange for this to be done ensuring that the documents are returned to the paying bank as soon as possible but within the expiry date of the credit. The exporter should remember to check the reverse of, and any attachment to, the credit; further terms and conditions may appear and form an integral part of the credit. Basically, the simpler the credit terms between exporter/importer the easier it is for trade to take place and expand between the parties and countries concerned.

Although it is often desirable for the UK exporter to ensure that the credit is opened in sterling, that is, the currency of his country, this may not be possible and a foreign currency may be used. To protect himself from any losses due to rate fluctuations in the period between the time he ships the goods and receives payment, he may wish to sell the foreign currency forward to his bank. The bank will quote him a special rate and, no matter what happens to the exchange rate in the meantime, the importer knows exactly how much he will receive. On the other hand, there may be distinct advantages in invoicing in foreign currencies.

In circumstances where extended credit is granted to the importer, the beneficiary should be contracted to pay interest and will receive an acceptance/usance credit providing for payment at a future date.

At the time of drawing up the contract, the period, rate and method of payment of interest should be agreed with the importer and can be incorporated in the price, or the importer could ask his bank to add a clause in the credit stating that the interest is for the importer's account and may he clarmed accordingly. Alternatively, the term discount charges are for buyer's account' could be incorporated in the credit terms. Interest rates fluctuate, sometimes on a daily basis.

Following presentation of documents in order, the accepted bill can be discounted (that is, sold to a discount house) usually by the bank accepting the bill, or by the beneficiary's own bankers. An interest charge is levied by the discount house which, if for buyer's account, will be paid by the importer. In effect, the beneficiary then receives settlement as if the bill had been drawn at sight.

If the credit makes no reference to settlement of the discount charge, the bill can still be discounted at any time, but the interest charge levied should be for the beneficiary's account. Unless the credit specifies that drafts are needed in duplicate, a single draft will be acceptable.

Many credits stipulate the name of the port from which shipment is to be made but in some circumstances it may be advantageous to the exporter for shipment to be allowed 'from any UK port' thereby providing a choice. This must be arranged in consultation with the importer and provides a degree of flexibility. It can be extended to include the port of discharge.

There are three features which are basic for export success in terms of documentation, *viz*. quality of management, quality of staff, and effective communication.

Exporters are not just simply selling a product, but also service and efficiency. Of vital importance is the ability to examine each problem as it arises, to obtain correct information without delay, to use it effectively and to make correct decisions.

The overseas customer has the same attitude to business detail as the good businessman in the UK. Hence, he will be impressed by clarity, accuracy and suspicious of the exporter who fails to produce correct documents in the correct sequence. Export documents must be precise and accurate. Documentation is required for the following reasons:

1. To provide a complete and specific description of the goods including values and all relevant details so that goods can be correctly assessed for Customs purposes.
2. Documents may be needed for exchange control regulations—quantitative or quota restrictions and also for statistical purposes.
3. Buyer requires the relevant documents for his own purposes, for example, in order to obtain the goods.

Delay in deliver/despatch of shipping etc. documents has reached serious proportions in recent years and has resulted in excessive delays in despatch of goods. It has arisen for many reasons and these can be summarized as follows:

1. Non-availability at time of dispatch of commercial invoices and packing lists.
2. Late submission of bills of lading by manufacturers and/ or shippers to shipping companies, etc.
3. Delay in releasing bills of lading by shipping companies.
4. Errors in compilation of bills of lading, insurance certificates, etc.
5. Delays in communication between clerical staff in seaport/airport/ICDs and shippers.
6. Delay in obtaining necessary consular invoices.
7. Inadequate scrutiny at time of receipt of letters of credit.
8. Delay by banks in processing documents due to discrepancies found in them.
9. Delay due to one or more of the following:
   - (i) Letter of credit expired or withdrawn.
   - (ii) Partial shipment *i.e.*, only part of consignment sent.
   - (iii) State or incorrectly completed bill of lading.

(iv) Insurance certificate not enclosed or dated after shipment, or cover incorrect in terms of value or currency.

(v) Incorrect invoices, consular documents or draft drawn incorrectly.

10. Documents sent by surface post when they could be delivered by air.

11. Documents sent to small local branches of banks when the main or foreign branches deal with shipping documents.

12. Wrongly completed documents including Customs invoices, delaying Customs clearance. To overcome the foregoing problem, the exporter should do the following:

(i) Employ professional services of a freight forwarder and/or

(ii) Provide an adequate trained staff of good calibre.

(iii) Study letter of credit carefully so there is time for amendments to be made if necessary and send copy to freight forwarder.

(iv) Apply the aligned documentation system. This involves use of the simplified method of documentation with standard-size forms. By engaging the aligned system and mechanization, and one-run series of production, the complete operation is speeded up. Discuss the matter with SITPRO.

(v) Maintain a record of documents flow and status reports in order to isolate consistent bottle-necks with a view to correction.

(vi) Fully use the telex and other aids for rapid transmission of information when appropriate, which is dependent on the time scale.

COMPUTERIZATION

Computerization features more and more in the processing of data/documentation relative to the export order. It is therefore desirable we examine one of the most popular schemes called SPEX (SITPRO, Export Consignment, Processing and Invoicing system.) The scheme has been developed by SITPRO and is very popular amongst export companies.

SPEX is a powerful, low-cost export software package which stores and processes information associated with export shipments, and produces a wide range of export documents. It has been designed to enhance exporting efficiency through increased speed and accuracy at a very low cost. Moreover, SPEX is extremely flexible on output, allowing users to choose between continuous stationery or cut sheets or sets. Final documents can be printed direct onto preprinted stationery or can be produced via overlays and a copier. Written in Micro-Focus COBOL, it is available on a wide variety of computers, and is sufficiently flexible to meet the needs of most companies. Single and multi-user versions are available.

It is supplied complete with a comprehensive 160-page manual. There is a direct reference from each screen in the system to the appropriate page(s) in the manual, which also contains information on links in and out of the system, file sizings, back-ups etc. The SITPRO SPEX exporter software flowchart is shown in Chart A.

Creating Consignments

The information required for each export consignment can be assembled rapidly within the SPFX system and amended at will. Consignments can be created in three different ways:

1. By calling up information from master files held on disc, then keying in variables. (In an extreme case all the information for a consignment could be keyed in. This would still be better than a manual system because of the ease of amendment).

2. By copying a previous or master consignment then alterning it as necessary.

3. By accessing a file of invoicing data transferred from an order-processing system running on the same machine or on a larger one.

CHART A: SITPRO SPEX Exporter Software Flowchart

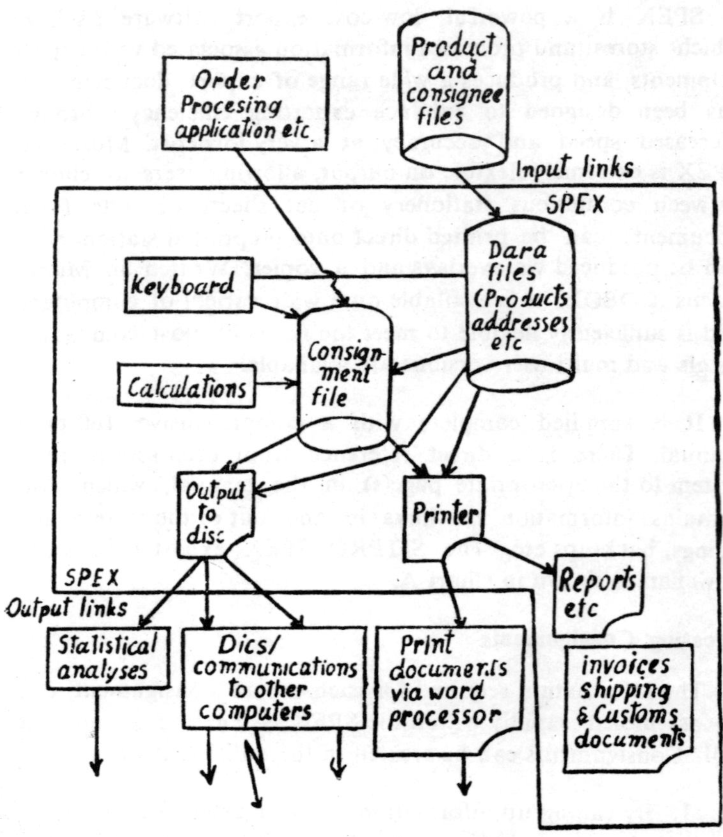

Whichever the method(s) selected by each user, SPEX will allow the information required to be assembled quickly and accurately. For example the invoicing facility allows charges to be added separately or to be included by applying a loading to recalculate each price and line total. Discounts and foreign currency conversions are also performed.

System operation is made easy through menu screens and user prompts at every stage. Many of the screens follow the familiar formats of export documents. Keying is kept to a minimum by the use of files of static data relating to consignees, products, declarations etc. Complex calculations (*e.g.*, for foreign currency conversions on the export invoice) are carried out automatically.

Printing Documents

In principle, any selection from the 'pool' of data items held against each SPEX consignment can be printed anywhere on any size or shape of document. In practice SPEX offers a wide variety of document print formats. Other documents can also be produced using overlays plus a SITRPO 'master' printed from SPEX. Document produced from SPEX can be printed on plain or pre-printed continuous stationery or on single sheets or sets. Documents (totalling forty) include 'masters', invoices, certificates of origin, Customs declarations and transport documents covering Ro/Ro, deep-sea, postal and air freight shipments.

Master Files

Indexed sequential master files are maintained within SPEX, allowing much information to be keyed in once, then re-used indefinitely. For example, details relating to a customer (name, address, routing, terms etc.) can be entered once, then used for each subsequent shipment, via the code allocated by the user. In a manual system this information would have to be re-typed at least once per consignment, making errors and delays inevitable.

Master files are also provided for products, exporters, forwarders, terms, declarations, signatories and ECSI details (forwarder instructions). The same files can also accommodate buyer details, notify parties, Customs goods descriptions, bank addresses, etc.

Users can create, amend and delete records, and can also browse through the files. This facility allows one to jump into or out of any position in a file, to step through records sequentially or to skip records forwards or backwards. No knowledge of the codes used is necessary. Prints of the master files are catered for, and any segment of the file can be selected for printing.

Files Sizes

The SPEX software totals approximately 390K, depending on the operating system, and must reside on one logical disk drive. Data files can be allocated to the same or any other drive. Consignments require a realistic minimum of 2.5K each and an average of about 5K (this assumes five invoice lines and two triff items; additional lines/items require approximately 0.25K each).

Records on master, or static, files held within SPEX have the following lengths, (in characters):

> Consignee—659, buyer—227, product—154, terms, declarations, forwarders etc—244.

Disc space must also be allocated for the order and history files by those using these facilities. The size of the order file depends on the number of invoice line items and on how much data is transferred for each, so on useful guidelines can be given. The history file requires up to 229 characters per record (*i.e.*, per consignment). In practice, most users find a 5-or 10-megabyte hard disk system ideal.

Linkages

SPEX can be used as a powerful stand-alone package. However, it has also been designed to be linked with other applications to give users the maximum scope for increased efficiency. These allow exporters running SPEX on microcomputers but with large computers in the background to exchange data between the two machines, thus eliminating re-keying of data. Outlets suitable for the telex network are also provided.

On input, SPEX incorporates an order-processing link which allows the transfer tnto SPEX of invoice line item details, references and buyer name and address. If this information is available on another computer the data can be transferred by floppy-disc ex-change or direct communication.

On output a summary record for each consignment can be written to a history file. This can then be used as input to the sales ledger or for statistical analysis. This latter by-product of SPEX can save exporters a considerable amount of time. Additionally, any report of document which can be printed from SPEX can also be writtent to disc, and then transferred to another computer or accessed by other applications software. For example, where a 'difficult' letter of credit would normally give no alternative to manual preparation of documents, in SPEX the main work of assembling data can be done within the system then a word-processing package used immedately before printing. This gives the best of both worlds:

The power of SPEX plus the flexibility of word processing.

Enhancements

SPEX is a genuine 'package', and SITPRO will not tailor it for individual users, except that additional print formats may be available. Its linkage facilities allow it to be used as a module in a comprehensive system covering order processing, accounting etc.

SITPRO continuously endeavouring to improve/develop SPEX, to offer even greater flexibility and more options internally, and also to provide further avenues for the exchange of data with other applications of software and/or other computers. Great care will be taken to ensure that future enhanced versions of SPEX are compatible with the files that users have built up. This will allow users to obtain the major benefits of using SPEX immediately and then to build up the more sophisticated linkages over time.

CONCLUSIONS

SPEX has been designed with a strong emphasis on flexibility in order to handle the complex variations typical of export operations. It can be run on hard or floppy discs with daisy-wheel or dot-matrix printers, and users can run SPEX in the way which is most appropriate for their kind of business. They can start by quickly learning to use SPEX to do what they are doing already in a far better way. Once familiar with the system they can go on to use some of its more sophisticated features.

10

SHIPPING AND TRANSPORTATION

A. ESSENTIALS OF SHIPPING IN SUPPLY MANAGEMENT

Transportation of cargo by sea, air and land, including inland waterways, as a function of supply management, is particularly important to developing countries since most of them experience difficulties in materials availability and flow because of limited shipping facilities, inexperience and lack of technical know-how, poor port operations, and lengthy customs and other import control procedures. Additional difficulties result from the lack of adequate foreign exchange resources to pay for freight and other shipping charges.

Proper transportation and logistics planning, the choice of the appropriate mode of transportation and the timely delivery of orders are paramount in this analysis. Various aspects of shipping and transportation operations are analyzed to demonstrate the potential for cost control and efficiency attainable through improved practices and procedures.

In deciding on the mode of moving goods, especially imports from foreign countries, four major factors are relevant:

(a) The degree of urgency for the needed goods;

(b) The size and weight of the items to be moved;

(c) The location and accessibility of the point of delivery; and

(d) The cost of transportation.

For example, transoceanic transportation of bulk supplies such as grain, rice, cement and steel products is obviously more economic and better suited for carriage by sea than by air; if the quantity involved can justify it, it may be even cheaper to charter a vessel to carry it than to use a regular liner sesvice. On the other hand, emergency supplies, such as spare parts to repair unexpected machinary breakdowns, and drugs to meet immediate needs in the case of the out-break of an epidemic, call for the use of airlines as the fastest mode of transportation.

The cost of transportation should be considered in terms of:

(a) Freight, or the charge for carrying the goods; in this regard, it is sometimes cheaper to carry goods by air than by sea, especially where transshipments involving the use of different modes interlinking transport services are inevitable, as in the case of goods consigned to land-locked countries;

(b) The cost of door-to-door delivery; this is usually comprised of expenses incurred in transporting goods from the site of supplier's factory to the port of embarkation, through delivery at the port of discharge and then to the warehouse of the buyer or consignee;

(c) Transfer costs arising from handling charges in the use of different modes of transportation;

(d) The cost of insurance to protect goods in transit against damage, loss or pilferage;

(e) The fee imposed for delay or failure to discharge and clear cargo at ports in time; this is usually in the form of rent charged by the port authority for warehousing the uncleared cargos;

(f) Port-handling charges including stevedoring costs for cargo handling, documentation and clerical costs connected with customs clearance procedures and customs duties: and

(g) Packaging costs, especially for delicate goods and equipment, which require special packing to prevent damage in transit.

The degree and impact of transportation costs depend upon the type of mode used and its characteristics as described below.

B. SEA TRANSPORTATION

The major characteristics of a sea transportation include:

(a) Freight charges, which are cheaper than those for other modes of transportation;

(b) Almost limitless capacity to carry all types of cargo irrespective of weight;

(c) A wider range of storage facilities for different kinds of cargo, including perishable commodities, which require preservation by refrigeration, and highly explosive items for which special security and safety measures must be provided; and

(d) built-in self-equipped cranes and other handling and lifting gear that facilitate cargo loading and discharging.

Whereas transportation of goods by sea has considerable advantages, it does present some problems to developing countries, especially those that have no shipping lines. Significant among the difficulties are:

(a) Insufficiency and irregularity of shipping space; and

(b) Delays in discharging cargo at ports of destination.

To overcome the former problem, some governments have established national shipping lines or encouraged the development of private lines. However, this has presented some problems for a number of reasons: limited financial resources to procure and operate ships; poor management; and stiff competition from well-established and better-organized shipping lines flying other national flags. In the light of these difficulties, some governments have sponsored liner conferences and others have sponsored or encouraged their national shipping lines to join established liner conferences.

Basically, a liner conference is a group of shipping lines, irrespective of the origin of their flags, operating on a given route, which merge their resources to rationalize the services they provide. The benefits generally include:

(a) frequent and regular sailings;

(b) extensive geographic coverage permitting the servicing of various ports in different countries;

(c) Acceptance of cargo, whether easy and attractive to handle or not;

(d) Ready availability of port cargo-handling gear;

(e) Quality of service; and

(f) Stability of rates that enable the shipping lines to draw up realistic plans and budgets.

The conference system can lead to monopoly and abuse, if not properly controlled. Other than that, the facilities the system provides are more comprehensive than when each shipping line operates independently.

The second major problem associated with sea transportation of cargo is the bottlenecks and delays in port operations often caused by:

(a) Congestion due to limited space;

(b) Poor port facilities;

(c) Cargo difficulties;

(d) Stowage factors;

(e) Bad weather; and

(f) Labour shortages. Frequently, ships arrive at ports to find no berths to accommodate them, forcing them either to reschedule their voyages or to pay a second visit to the port.

Frequent equipment breakdowns have also contributed to port difficulties; costly delays in discharging and loading cargo have been caused by inoperative cranes and lifts; barge shortages; and inadequate warehousing facilities. In the case of a shortage of storage facilities either cargo discharge is suspended to await available warehouse space, or cargo is dumped on open quays; in the latter case, there have been instances where valuable goods have perished or been damaged through exposure to bad weather.

Stowage difficulties arise from the size of the cargo in relation to its weight; heavier consignments, such as cement, which occupy relatively smaller space are more acceptable as freight than lighter consignments, such as bales of cotton, which require larger volumes of space. Cargo difficulties, on the other hand, are caused where consignments, such as machine parts, intended to be handled together are split and stowed in different holds of a ship. This has led to delays in assembling and installing plant and equipment needed for essential projects.

Bad weather impedes port operations, resulting in delays in discharging and loading certain types of cargo such as sugar, salt, flour and cement packed in paper bags, which are ruined in wet weather. This means that buying agents must give proper packaging instructions to enable suppliers to provide adequate precautions against weather hazards associated with port operations. Delays in port operations can also be caused by labour difficulties; for example, stevedoring or cargo-haddling services have from time to time been disrupted by labour disputes, public holidays and other factors that keep the staff away from work.

Other factors that militate against efficient port operations are poor inadequate documentation and clumsy clerical procedures. Inadequate labeling or identification of cargo, faulty preparation of bills of lading, delayed or missing shipping documents, long-winded customs entry procedures, time-consuming pursuits of import licenses and exchange control approvals are some of the difficulties characterizing port clearance procedures. The immediate effects are delays and port congestion, which generate unnecessary costs.

Supply organizations should be sufficiently aware of these problems to take appropriate measures or advise the Government on steps to be taken to prevent waste and inefficiency in public supply management. Often responsible and top-level public officials fail to recognize the serious effects of port delays and similar import-related problems. Many of them assume that costs and inconvenience that arise from such port delays are borne by the shipping companies, shippers and cargo-handling firms, not realizing that such costs are ultimately passed on to the user.

C. AIR TRANSPORTATION

Although transportation of cargo by air is generally more costly than other modes of cargo transportation, specially reduced rates for certain commodities have introduced by some international airlines to encourage use of their cargo services. These concessions, coupled with speed of flying, can make the use of air transportation attractive. Packing costs for air cargo are much lower since cartons and other lighter, cheaper forms of packaging are used rather than the expensive and heavy wooden boxes and crates needed for sea transportation. Moreover, transit insurance charges for air transportation are lower because of the shorter transit time. Incidence of pilferage is also believed to be lower than in the case of other forms of transportation—another reason for lower transit insurance charges.

High-value items of small bulk involving large cash outlays would better be moved by air. Similarly, it is better to move perishable cargo, such as food and drug items, by air than by sea or land; the risk of deterioration and the cost of refrigeration or special preservatives are considerably reduced or eliminated.

The cost factor in air cargo transportation is usually influenced by the kind of service that is utilized. There are two kinds of such services:

(a) Scheduled airline service; and

(b) Charter service.

The scheduled service is provided through either regular passenger flights on which provision is made for cargo to be carried, or all-cargo flights. The scheduled flights are usually frequent and regular and are suitable for carrying cargo in small quantities. Charter service is also provided on flights limited to the movement of cargo only, except such service is irregular, being specially arranged when needed. Charter service can be cheaper, provided larger quantities of cargo are moved. However, one major drawback of the charter system, which has a direct cost impact, is the risk of "empty" flights on return journeys. Some governments have approached the problem of return-voyage freight by encouraging part charter service, which permits several shippers to share one common service. Usually government regulations are introduced, setting a limit to both the number of shippers who can share one service and the minimum weight of freight each consignor can forward.

Major disadvantages in the use of air cargo transportation include:

(a) Limitations placed on certain goods considered not normally suitable for carriage by air; these include flammable and explosive materials, firearms and ammunition, compressed gases, radioactive materials and other dangerous cargo requiring extra safety measures;

(b) Inability of airports in certain countries, because of their limited size, to accommodate larger planes such as "jumbos";

(c) Inadequate handling equipment for lifting and moving cargo on discharge;

(d) Freight charges, which are higher (as explained earlier, the overall cost of transporting cargo by air may be cheaper for certain commodities because of their volume and the type of service utilized in carrying them); and

(e) Port clearance bottle necks and difficulties due to poor documentation, cumbersome customs and other regulatory procedures, inadequate service facilities and generally human problems similar to those at sea ports.

In regard to documentation problems, it is essential that all relevant shipping papers be moved rapidly to match the speed of air cargo. With appropriate measures to solve the problems that have been identified and others that are known to exist but not mentioned in this study, the use of air transportation for carrying cargo can help many developing countries improve their systems of supply management.

D. OVERLAND TRANSPORTATION: RAILWAY, ROAD AND WATERWAY SYSTEMS

The importance of overland transportation to carry goods is reflected by the need to move cargo as rapidly as possible from the ports of discharge to final destinations. This is even more significant in landlocked countries, which depend upon port facilities outside their territories.

The ability of modern motor trucks and other road vehicles to carry loads weighing more than 40 tons up steep gradients has made it possible and cheaper to move large quantities of goods from door to door. The railway system also continues to provide the means for heavier and long distance haulage, although it is more expensive because of higher capital, operating and maintenance costs. Waterways have been found useful and also cheaper in countries where there are navigable rivers, especially where many parts of the country are not served by the road and railway systems. The existence of river craft with capacity for loads weighing over 100 tons makes the waterways more attractive as an intermediary approach to inland transportation and distribution of goods, particularly in the absence of road and railway systems which require susbtantial capital outlays and considerable time to develop, maintain and expand.

1. Railway Transport

The advantages of using railway transportation include the following:

(a) The railways are by far the best means of hauling large quantities of heavy freight over long distances;

(b) The rail system is best suited for easy and handy distribution of bulky and heavy goods and equipment to different customers through the use of separately consigned freight cars, containers, pallets and other compact detachable vehicles, which are dropped off along the service routes to be collected on the return journeys;

(c) Door-to-door delivery of heavy equipment and goods, avoiding costly intermediary transshipment, is possible where siding and material-handling facilities are provided at discharging and loading points.

Against the benefits that the railway system provides is one major disadvantage:

The cost in comparison to other forms of transportation services. The relatively high cost of railway service arises from the substantial expenditures incurred to meet the capital and operating needs such as track laying and maintenence, the acquisition and use of railway engines and freight cars, the large supporting staff including train crews, traffic personnel, track and building maintenance personnel and administrative personnel. The cost of spare parts and fuel is also significant. Operational costs may also be high where railway cars move around half empty; this often happens as a result of poor logistics and traffic planning. Lastly, the railway system is costly because in must cases it must be supplemented by a trucking system to insure door-to-door service. This sometimes creates delays because of inadequate trucking facilities; these delays in turn create congestion and warehousing problems.

2. Road Transport

The road transport system is exteasively used in most developing countries because it is more flexible and relatively cheaper to operate. Its greatest advantage is that it enables door-to-door deliveries to be made, and there are various types of vehicles to handle diverse loads and different road conditions. There are also various types of vehicles, including trailers and containerized trucks, open trucks, tilting trucks and low-loaders that facilitate loading and unloading. Trucks can be used practically everywhere and generate little need for complex and costly loading and discharging platforms, which are critical to the other transportation systems. Furthermore, a smaller staff is required to support the road transportation system.

To maximize the use of road transportation one basic requirement is that the vehicles should operate on the shortest possible routes with, as far as practicable, maximum loads all the time. Unless this condition is met, it would be uneconomic for an organization to separately own and operate road transport vehicles, as may government departments do. Separate ownership of trucks and other road transport vehicles has been justified by different departments on the ground that it is faster, safer and more reliable to move materials and equipment around than to depend on outside facilities over which they have little control. Private ownership has been motivated also by the relative cheapness of the trucks; but very often, uneconomic operational costs, which cancel out possible savings, are ignored.

The hiring of outside services provided by well-established transportation corporations and firms or the common ownership of transport facilities are among the approaches adopted in place of total dependence on a central government transport organization. In some cases, the central gupply organization of the government operates a road transport service to meet the needs of different user departments. In other cases, department and agencies with the need for continuous movement of large quantities and heavy volumes of materials and equipment, such as public works and utility agencies, national trading corporations, health administrations and the uniformed disciplinary forces are allowed to maintain separate road transportation units.

Sound traffic planning or logistics is a prerequisite for optimizing the use of transportation facilities, whether internally operated or rented from outside. This planning is often neglected, leading to considerable waste of resources and unnecssary delays. One, way to strengthen the materials traffic planning capability is to establish a separate unit within the central supply organization to assume that responsibility. On the other hand, effective monitoring or follow-up is essential to insure better service by outside facilities. In this case, it is necessary that departments utilizing a common transportation facility create liaison offices to provide for the necessary monitoring and reporting linkage with the transportation organizations that serve them.

The benefits generally expected to result from internally operated transport services have often been negated by delays and other difficulties caused by vehicle and equipment breakdowns, generally resulting from lack of adequate maintenance facilities; this often is caused by shortages of spare parts and other repair resources. Neither the use of in-house workshops nor dependence on outside garages has proved effective in avoiding this problem. In some cases, the problem has been approached by standardizing spare parts by limiting the types of vehicles in use to a selected few; this facilitates expanded and more flexible use of spare parts. The standardization approach often lacks popular support as a result of fears that the limited supply approach could lead to monopoly and abuse.

In summary, a road transport system in support of supply management will not operate efficiently unless certain conditions are fulfilled:

(a) Vehicle scheduling should be planned realistically and proper allowances made to accommodate delays;

(b) Adequate provision should be made both for routine and properly programmed preventive maintenance, and for the prompt repair or restoration, if practicable, of vehicles that have broken down or been damaged through accidents. Maintenance and repair facilities should be decentralized as extensively as necessary to prevent problems, especially those arising from the breakdown and stranding of vehicles in remote places; and

(c) Reserve stocks of vehicles should be available to replace those that break down or are being serviced.

3. Inland Waterway Transport

An inland waterway transport system is practicable and viable where there are navigable rivers and where capital is available for dredging channels, building docks and maintaining navigational aids. To be considered feasible as a channel of transportation, an inland waterway should allow for draught clearance that will accommodate a barge or lighter with a minimum load capacity of 300 tons. Modern techniques in barge towing makes it possible for a number of barges carrying cargo weighing more than 5,000 tons to be towed by one tug. If these conditions can be fulfilled and the operation cost is low, waterway transportation will be useful.

In countries with less-developed road systems, waterway ferries are used to complement roads services as an interim solution to distribution problems. Loaded truks and lorries are ferried across rivers and lakes by pontoons and other roll-on craft to connect local feeder roads, which penetrate otherwise marooned districts and rural areas. Inland waterway systems are also useful in the case of transshipment especially where ports and other major points of cargo discharge are linked to navigable rivers, lakes or canals. Off-loading cargo directly from ships in midstream to barges and lighters for onward transportation to the interior is considered easy and economic. It is even cheaper where the cargo involved is packed in containers or on pallets.

The major disadvantage associated with the use of waterway transportation is that both the transit time and the time for loading and unloading are slow. The loading and unloading times are also directly influenced by the weather, which can cause delay. Rain and low tides are other common delaying hazards. In other works, the waterway transportation systeme is suitable for moving large quantities of bulky traffic, when the speed of transit is not a prime consideration.

INTEGRATED TRANSPORT SERVICES

Since any one mode of transportation cannot adequately satisfy all of a country's distribution needs, a combination of systems complementing one another offers the most practical and reasonable approach. Such a combination has the advantage of balancing the benefits of one system against the weaknesses of another. It is the basis for fostering a comprehensive and integreted system through which a more viable transportation system can be developed to support effective supply management in government. One significant benefit to be derived from a combined transportation system is that facilities and resources can be pulled together and shared by different departments and agencies in the interests of economy. Another benefit is that material-handling equipment can be standardized to promote flexibility and interchangeability in use. Uniform directives and procedures can be developed that will not only simplify transportation documentation processes but will also strengthen reporting and monitoring processes in the interests of accountability and security. Finally, the system is also capable of providing a good ground for integrated planning that can insure both efficient logistics, and optimum allocation and utilization of transport facilities.

11

INDIA'S PROJECT EXPORTS: CHALLENGES AND OPPORTUNITIES

T.J. MATHEW

It is no longer correct to say that the Indian economy is a closed one. Over the last one decade, there has been a steady growth in India's economic relationship with the rest of the world. Today, over 239 joint ventures are either in production or in different stages of implementation, promoted by Indian entrepreneurs and an equal number of such ventures are in the pipeline. What is more, Indian contractors have bagged nearly Rs. 4,500 crores worth of civil construction contracts in the West Asian and North African countries. The statistics are impressive enough. But what catches the eye is the success of Indian contractors in securing these contracts against lading countries competing for the billion dollar construction boom.

The picture of the country has been changing. Its image appears to be better now. The collaborative acceptability of the Indian businessmen—whether a trader, industrialist or a financier—is slowly, but surely, getting recognised. And the result:

Indian businessmen are now increasingly conscious of the external outlets. A host of export promotion councils and other agencies have been constantly monitoring the business opportunities abroad. The Government, in its turn, has risen to the occasion with a more positive outward looking policy.

Rather coincidently, the need for boosting the country's exports has come to the fore now more than any time before because of the pressing need to meet the ever increasing import bill, largely on the oil account. Export earnings were barely sufficient to meet a half of the last year's import bill. On the other hand, the outlook for external assistance—both multilateral and bilateral—is bleak. And then the only hopeful sign is the remittances of Indians employed abrod. But the growth prospects for remittances in the coming years are not all that bright, given the possibility of relative slackening economic boom in the host countries and the tightening of the regulations over immigration in some of these countries. In this context, pushing the exports to the hift has become imperative.

EXPORT TARGET

Against this backdrop, an ambitious target has been set for the export of engineering goods. By the end of the current decade, this lading export sector is expected to earn foreign exchange worth Rs. 10,000 crores per annum. On the face of it, the increase in the exports of engineering goods of this order from a level of nearly Rs. 900 crores in 1980-81 appears rather high. But it is not too unrealistic, given the potential of the growing engineering industry in the country.

The Engineering Export Promotion Council has suggested a national strategy for achieving this ambitious target. The major plank of this strategy will be the export of turnkey projects which may include supply of services such as designing, erection, commissioning and supervision, engineering contracts, consultancy services and constructions contracts. All these together are known as project exports. Such exports, which constituted 12 per cent in India's total exports of engineering goods in the 50s, now account for about 38 per cent

This share will have to be increased further to 50 per cent by the turn of the decade.

CONSTRUCTION CONTRACTS

Currently, majority of the projects being executed abroad are in the civil construction field. The total value of construction contracts secured by Indian firms at the end of 1980 was Rs. 3,520 crores. During the first eight months of 1981, contracts of the value of Rs. 884 crores were secured by Indian contractors. These contracts are mostly in West Asian and North African countries.

Large industrial projects, opportunities for which have emerged rapidly in many parts of the world, especially in the West Asia and African countries are, however, still elusive to Indian firms. Most of such projects are covered by firms from developed countries and Indian firms are able to win a few minor sub-contracts, especially relating to civil construction, supplies, technical services and management services.

Some of the construction projects bagged by Indian firms are, no doubt, of prestigious nature. Not only because they have been secured in the face of tough competition, but also on the merits of their quality and performance. These projects range from the construction of a township complex, defence camp, dams, foodgrain storage silos to power stationes.

INADEQUATE PERFORMANCE

India has also gained some experience in undertaking certain collaborative construction projects in third countries. The major projects undertaken in third countries include, among others, construction of an integrated modern township in Kuwait, (Pacific Consultants International, Japan, collaborated with Engineering Project (I) Limited), expansion of Self Palace in Kuwait (Fujta Corporation, Japan, in collaboration with Engineering Project (I) Ltd.) and erection of a 132-KWH transmission line in Nigeria (Sumitomo Kaisha, Japan, in collaboration with Best and Cormption).

Yet, Indian advances in the project exports have been modest, which cannot be said to match with their potentialities and capabilities. India is indeed the world's tenth biggest manufacturing nation (ranking in terms of gross value of production), backed by a vast pool of scientists, engineers and technologists. Despite our success in securing some construction jobs, it is no secret that India has hardly scratched the surface. Our achievements have been marginal as compared to the vast opportunities that are available.

MARKET DIVERSIFICATION

This calls for efforts to promote project exports. Market diversification is an important aspect. Project exports are concentrated mainly in the countries of West Asia and North Africa. India has made only modest success in South East Asia and African markets in the field of construction, civil engineering and turnkey projects involving multi-disciplinary technology. There is also some scope for exporting projects to the Carribean and Latin American countries.

The argument often put forward in support of project exports is the concept of "appropriate technology". India can contribute significantly to the programmes of industrialisation of the developing countries because of its accumulated experiences in this area. For instance, India has developed an intermediate technology and also considerable experience in erecting and running plants of smaller scale and sizes which would suit the needs of the limited size of domestic markets and the prevalent work culture in the developing countries. These countries may not be in a position to go in for large size plants and absorb the most advanced technology available from developed countries.

APPROPRIATE TECHNOLOGY

Truly, the concept of appropriate technology has relevance in the neighbouring South East Asian countries. But it does not hold much water in the West Asian countries, where the considerations are entirely different. They are not bothered about appropriateness of technology as they have no unemployment problem because of their sparse population. They have enough resources flowing from oil and what they want is the latest technology. The question that may be asked is whether India possesses the type of technological sophistication required by these countries. Though India has made some technological advances in a number of areas, they may not be sufficient to withstand the competition that the Indian project exporters face in the international markets. Therefore, it is worth considering the question whether the country should import advanced technical know-how for the purpose of re-exporting it.

India can still forge ahead in the West Asian market. The Financial Times of London has recently estimated that in West Asia alone, expenditure on construction, at constant prices, is expected to increase from $23.4 billion in 1978 to $26.2 billion in 1981. At present, about 50 to 60 per cent of the capital expenditure (10 to 25 per cent of GNP) in the region is earmarked for construction projects. It is expected that investment on construction projects will increased by 50 per cent during the next 10 years in Saudi Arabia, Kuwait and some Gulf countries. Simultaneously, some of the South East Asian and African countries have embarked upon massive development programmes for providing infrastructural facilities with financial assistance from the World Bank and the Asian Development Bank.

The construction boom in West Asian countries is, however, likely to abate after a few years. The emphasis in these countries is likely to be shifted to industrial projects, requiring capital goods. Indian project exporters will have to orient themselves to grab these opportunities.

CONSORTIUM APPROACH

But the question is whether Indian firms have the capacity to undertake the execution of very large industrial projects. Indian firms are relatively of a smaller size. Even India's biggest firms when compared to the multinationals are small. Usually, it is not possible for a single firm to undertake all the aspects of a contract, *viz.*, site clearance, designing, engineering, procurement, construction and commissioning. Further, the time factor is also important. The answer to these problems is a consortium arrangement. Different Indian firms in the public as well as the private sector can form both vertical and horizontal associations, which will enable them to tackle very large projects.

The consortium approach has been, indeed, experimented, Engineering project (India) Ltd., had, for instance, acted as a consortium leader by bringing together parties engaged in different lines. But the idea did not click well. Attempts made in the direction of setting up consortia by Indian companies have ended up in mutual distrust, squabbles and incriminations. It has been pointed out that individual manufacturing units have tried to project their own image and found it difficult to merge their identity.

This does not mean the consortium approach is wrong. It has the advantages of economies of scale. It helps eliminate the competition among Indian firms—both in the public and private sectors. Work distribution on a functional as well as on a territorial basis is possible. Over and above this, the consortium arrangement would be most effective in competing with the multinationals for the multi-billion construction projects in the West Asian countries.

FORGING CO-OPERATION

India' advances in project exports can be strengthened if efforts are made to bring about economic co-operation amongst the developing countries. Technology sharing, sub-contracting and joint-contracting are some of the ways through which firms from India and developing countries can co-operate for their mutual benefits. An agreement was recently reached between India and South Korea—the two leading developing countries competing for the Gulf construction programme—to avoid mutual undercutting among them. The two countries agreed to co-operate on the basis of either co-contracting or joint tendering for the massive projects in the West Asian countries.

The area of co-operation can be extended to developed countries as well. Such co-operation will be beneficial to all the participants. With India's experience in construction projects and intermediate technology, the total competitive strength of such bids made by joint constractors would increase efficiency and thus lower the cost of projects for the importing developing countries. It has been reported that tremendous enthusiasm is being shown by the European contractors in getting the Indian firms involved in third country projects.

In this direction, there is a proposal to set up an international sub-contracting exchange in New Delhi with a counterpart cell in Europe. The exchange would help in keeping a watch on the progress towards joint tendering and sub-contracting. Besides, the exchange would help in filling the communication gap in Europe about the details and the nature of sub-contracting project work which could be undertaken by the Indian firms.

MARKETING STRATEGY

A notable feature about the project exports is the low ratio of success to bids. This ratio is about 24 per cent in the number and 12 per cent in the value. There are two reasons attributed for this low success ratio. They are uncompetitive pricing and lack of an effective marketing strategy. It is quite common that many a contracting firm does the pricing in an unscientific manner. And in the result, they loose the projects. Even if there is high pricing of the bids, if the contractor can evolve a proper marketing strategy, he wil not find it difficult to get the project. As the prospects of project exports depend largely on marketing, there is an urgent need to inculcate a proper marketing spirit amongst the contracting firms.

Project management is a vital aspect in the execution of contracts. This aspect has not been taken seriously by many Indian firms. Project management, in fact, is the "achilles heel" of the Indian project exporters. Developing an expertise for managing large sized projects is, therefore, an essential pre-requisite for successful executions of projects. In project management, what is essential is the capacity to organise most efficiently the various factors involved.

GOVERNMENT'S POLICY

The Government's policy is anotner crucial variable. By and large, the Government has a very positive attitude towards project exporters. Indian firms are allowed to purchase construction equipments from third countries. Such equipments are allowed to be re-imported into India under certain conditions. This liberalisation in the import policy is done with a view to helping the project contractors to buy essential construction equipment and machinery which are not available in the country. In addition, with a view to encouraging project exports and also for compensating the extra risk undertaken by the project exporters, the Government provides an additional 10 per cent as cash assistance on the net foreign exchange earnings from technical and other sources. A high powered inter-ministerial committee—called Overseas Project Development Committee—has also been set up in the Commerce Ministry to promote project exports.

In the normal circumstances, exporters of projects require a wide range of banking/credit facilities at the pre and post bid stages. As they are operating in a highly competitive field, these facilities have to be made available to them at competitive rates. But, the projects that have come in India's way during the last 3-4 years have largely been on near cash terms. The financial requirements of these contracts in the form of deferred credit have been limited. There was, however, demand for a large amount of bank guarantees and bridging finance. However, the indications are that, in future, many of the Gulff countries may choose to finance their projects through credit. In the event, the demand for export finance will go up.

PROJECT FINANCING

Project financing is done by commercial banks in collaboration with the Industrial Development Bank of India. They provide both pre-shipment and post-shipment credit to the exporters. Medium and long-term export credits are also given. In addition, there are a number of quasi credit facilities including bid bonds, advance payment guarantees, performance guarantees, etc. Commercial banks also issue guarantees to foreign banks in respect of bridge finance, which foreign banks offer to the exporters. Export credit insurance facilities are provided by the Export Credit and Guarantee Corporation.

From the point of view of project exports, however, there is an "institutional gap" in terms of an institution that can devote full-fledged attention to export financing. The Government's step to establish the Export-Import Bank patterned on the model of such institutions in the U.S. and Japan is likely to fill this gap.

CONCLUSION

Although project exports have emerged as the most dynamic sector in India's exports in recent years, the majority of the projects executed abroad in the past are in the civil construction field. Indian firms have so far been not in a position to avail of the growing opportunities for undertaking large industrial projects. Even in the field of construction contracts, India's performance is not commensurate with the potentialities and capabilities. India's performance can be improved through market diversification, adoption of a consortium approach by Indian firms and forgoing co-operation among the firms from India and other developing countries. Since many of the Gulf countries are looking for sophisticated technology, it may be necessary to import the latest technical know-how from abroad so as to enable Indian project exporters to offer most advanced package of services to these countries. Over and above these, it is necessary to formulate an effective marketing strategy with greater emphasis on project management. The project exporters also must endeavour to create good reputation in international markets and try to establish their credentials in the field. Quality consciousness, adherence to schedules and a good liaison with the project authorities are some of the factors that will go a long way in creating a good image of the country.

12

EXPORT RESEARCH AND MARKETING

EXPORT MARKET RESEARCH (SCOPE AND OBJECTIVES)

Export market research is a study of a given market abroad to determine the needs of that market and the methods by which the products can best be supplied. It is intrinsic in this definition that the enquirer starts with a certain product or group of produsts prescribed in his terms of reference by the exporter, such as, a caravan manufacturer who naturally looks for sales opening for his company, for example, in Holland. The electrical engineer will be looking to the market for opportunities to install his type of equipment while the constructional engineer would be looking for building projects.

The total market in any given product over a prescribed period is the total sales realized in a defined geographical area, usually a region or country. Export research is concerned with a wide range of products and often tends to be less directed to the point of retail sale. It concerns itself with much more intimacy with the chain of distribution, and covers consumer semi-durable goods (radios, domestic appliances, cars, etc.) and capital goods (for example, building materials, machinery), as well as mere consumer goods.

For a manufacturer or merchant seeking markets overseas, there are numerous factors which arise that are not encountered in the home market. An examination of such features now follows:

1. *Distance.* International distribution arrangements involve many features, *viz.* Customs, marine insurance extensive documentation, specialized packing, etc. Additionally, international transport distribution costs tend to form a much higher proportion of the total product cost involved up to 15—20 per cent, reflecting the greater distances involved compared with the home market inland transport arrangements. Market research and operational research can help to determine the most ideal distribution method.

2. *Time.* The transit time is a critical factor in planning the distribution arrangements of an international consignment. Generally, international consignments tend to have a longer transit time than ones for the home market, so the production department must plan accordingly to ensure the goods arrive at destination on schedule.

3. *Language.* Complications can arise from the use of foreign languages involving labelling changes, special publicity and so on. In some overseas countries, more than one language is used. This presents marketing problems which market research may resolve. It can also give rise in many instances to difficulties in the market research process itself, since the most important part of the research must be conducted in a foreign language. In this area, one must ensure the correct words are used in their own language.

4. *Race and religion.* In many overseas countries, difference of race and religion have to be borne in mind in relation to the goods themselves, their presentation to the buying public (that is, the packaging) and the publicity approach. It is important to secure the

advantages of presentation in a favourable light by using predominantly those colours waich are traditionally and emotionally associated with happiness and goodwill.

5. *Local preferences.* Quite apart from racial and religious preferences local idiosyncrasies must be discovered by the process of market research in order to set up the most telling form of subsequent approach to the market. For example, the Australians are influenced in their outlook by American sales methods which, in practice, means a higher outlay in publicity than, for example, in Ireland or a Scandinavian country. Moreover, some countries are best approached by radio rather than by newspaper publicity. Similarly, in some places the cinema slide is regarded as part of the entertainment whilst in others it is practically ignored. So far as the products are concerned, and their trade marks and packaging, some things are to be avoided and others exploited. For example, the average han's egg in Egypt is very small so egg cups must be smaller than the UK standard size. Such information would be sought out during the process of market research.

6. *Environmental.* Export market research must embrace the study of the climate factors—heat and cold, dryness and humidity, atmospheric densities, rainfall and seasonal sequences. For example, the sweet manufacturer would not market some of his products in a very hot, humid climate as the sweets would reach the buyer in rather a sticky mess. Climatic conditions are best examined alongside such matters as distances from ports, types of communication, gradients location of population, airports, etc.

7. *Business practices and creditworthiness etc.* This embraces enquiry into the code of legal practice regarding the conduct of business in the overseas country. For example, it would include the giving and implementation of guarantees and warantees connected with

the suitability of the goods and performance, for a certain period after sale. Additionally, one would confirm the importer administered his business in an honest and fair way without a taint of corruption.

8. *Scope of market research.* The extent and area of the market research must be determined. It may be one country or simply an area or region within a country. Cost and remit terms will play a large part in reaching the decision. None of the foregoing items can be taken for granted in any market abroad. Research must be necessarily undertaken to establish the conventions of the market which is not easy to undertake and bring to a successful outcome. The scale of the market research undertaken is influenced by the exporter's budget and his estimate of the market potential. To be effective, the market research must be well-planned and well-executed. It must have a defined objectives and it is advisable to spend some time on reflecting the terms of the remit to ensure it adequately meets what is required to produce the desired market research results. Ideally, it is desirable to undertake a pilot survey of the assignment to eradicate any unforeseen problems which may emerge. Ultimately, this also ensures that a more meaningful report produced.

In some circumstances, it may be preferred to undertake multi-market research which involves conducting market research within several countries simultaneously with the same objectives in view. This is complex and can be difficult to administer, particularly when several languages are involved and the countries differ in their local idiosyncrasies.

A further point to bear in mind is the scope of the research which can vary by individual country. Pilot exercises would tend to reduce misgivings and avoid a simple market research exercise being transformed into an inquiry.

To conclude, the following points must be evaluated, ideally by a manufacturer, to decide whether or not to enter an overseas market.

1. Growth trends, particularly embracing production and apparent consumption aspects.
2. Details of leading competitors, market shares, promotion techniques, services and facilities offered.
3. Actual channels of distribution and destination cost.
4. Legal requirements, standards etc.
5. Adequacy of transportation, particulary bearing in mind speed, frequency, and overall service cost.
6. Degree to which the product is subject to official technical regulations or standards.
7. Tariffs, quotas and import licences impositions/obligations.
8. Estimate of market size segregating production, imports and export elements.
9. General political/economic stability of the market.
10. Adequacy of products currently available.

Various methods of conducting market research exist and the final choice depends on many factors particularly the nature of the product and the money available to conduct the assignment. The latter will be much determined by the likely market share potential of the product etc. to be researched.

One techniques is to use desk research. Usually, this simply involves a study/evaluation of public/trade statistics and reports/surveys. This may concern data produced by HM Government, agencies, trade associations, international organizations, the press etc. and the more important sources are detailed below:

1. The major banks, particularly Barclays International, Midland International, National Westminister, and Lloyds International, produce booklets on trade prospects in various countries. Additionally, some of them produce quarterly bulletins through their economic and commercial departments dealing with economic trends,

fiscal policy and world trade prospects. All such publications are usually free.

2. *The Times* and *Financial Times* produce surveys from time to time in various countries highlighting trade prospects particularly to the British exporter.
3. The Economic Intelligence Unit produces reports on various industries/countries and long-term developments.
4. The various trade associations produce useful reports on their commodities and opportunities for the exporter.
5. The EEC and OECD, particularly the former, produce numerous reports on trade prospects and related subjects.
6. The Department of trade and Industry weekly journal contains much statistical data and overseas trade news.
7. The Confederation of British Industry produces a monthly report on overseas markets.
8. The major UK based Chambers of Commerce and Industry produce monthly journals on overseas markets and related matters. Moreover, British Chambers of Commerce are situated in many countries overseas to encourage trade and have available extensive data on trade prospects. Further details can be found in Appendix D of *Elements of Export Marketing and Management.*
9. The Central Statistical Office produces regularly extensive international trade statistical data.
10. The Central Office of Information circulates details of British achievements overseas and gives data on British products available for overseas importers.
11. A computerized intelligence service is also operated under the aegis of the British Overseas Trade Board dealing overseas contracts available for which the UK exporter can tender.

12. The *Economist* produces much useful statistical and international trade data.

Finally, the exporter can if he wishes ask the British Overseas Trade Board (Export Services Division) to undertake a survey in a particular commodity/country. Advice can also be sought from the local Chamber of Commerce. (See *Elements of Export Marketing and Management*, pp. 238-44, where a comprehensive list of all UK Chamber of Commerce addresses is found).

Another method is the official overseas Trade Mission, for example, a 'British Week' in Utrecht. The British Overseas Trade Board encourages such assignments which helps the businessmen in two ways. Firstly, it enables him to meet Government officials and local businessmen to ascertain at first hand the market opportunities available together with its constraints. Secondly, it is a means of obtaining actual business by taking exhibition space. This technique is much on the increase and many small exporters have started their overseas markets in this way. The local Chamber of Commerce can also help and the BOTB provide financial assistance to British businessmen to visit overseas markets or official trade missions.

Another technique, which is not always recommended, is the personal visit. An ill-planned visit/programme overseas can produce indifferent results to appraise market potential. A much better assignment is a visit to the trade fair or exhibition, which can provide a useful insight into the overseas market to establish product market potential. It could be a book fair or furniture exhibition. Much export business through the skilful entrepreneur exporter is secured by exporters visiting overseas markets themselves, defining/identifying the market and then exploiting it. Details of such trade fairs are available from BOTB and the local Chamber of Commerce.

The businessman planning such a trip is well-advised to obtain one of the *Hints to Exporters* booklets issued by the

British Overseas Trade Board. Individual copies are available for over one hundred countries.

The final method is, of course, the properly planed and correctly executed market research assignment. It can be in four ways, as detailed below:

1. It can be undertaken by the merchant. Advantages of this method include:relative secrecy (only the merchant and the manufactururer know reserach is proceeding); speed of execution and report presentation; and convenience, which facilitates collaboration between the two parties and, if the merchant has a resident agent or branch manager in the territory, time and money can be saved in that part of the enquiry which must be made in the market. Major disadvantages include absence of any market research skill or technical knowledge of the product; the merchant may be biased in sales outlook towards the producer; and ultimately, such an exercise could result in friction between manufacturer and merchant.
2. The director or senior executive of the manufacturing company may be given the task of conducting the survey and submitting the report. In some large companies, market research staff are employed full-time, In others, the export manager or export sales manager is entrusted with task. Advantages of this technique include: confidentially of survey and report content (only manufacturer is aware of such facts); speed of compilation, execution and report presentation; and finally, convenience, particularly in keeping cost of assignment to a minimum and avoiding consultant' fees. Disadvantages include: absence of adequate market research skill in the overseas product market involved to appreciate all the elements involved; production of a possibly biased report; and finally, when the report is published, it may be treated with suspicion as it is not produced by an independent source.

3. An independent organization may be engaged to render a specialized service of the market research exercise. This will produce a fairly unbiased report which is well-researched, as the personnel are likely to be efficient in their technique. It could result in cost savings of the survey, when compared with advertising agency. Disadvantages include: possible inadequate consideration of technical products, specification and risk of previous research for another sponsor being rehashed.

4. Advertising agency containing a market research organization. Often the manufacturer who engages an advertising agency tends to form a long association thereby permitting a continuing interest to be made. This encourages a good relationship between the two parties with beneficial results, particularly understanding the technical specification and potential of any products manufactured. Advantages include a completely unbiased approach to the survey, professionally undertaken at a reasonable cost. A major disadvantage is the length of time sometimes taken to produce the ultimate report and the risk that it may stem from ulterior motives towards justifying promotion of their advertising turnover.

Market research is undertaken usually through the technique of question-and-answer based on a well-though-out questionnaire. The questions must be explicit and not ambiguous. Ideally the 'yes'/'no' or pre-choice type of answer produce the best results. Politically loaded questions should be avoided. Overall, the latter technique (*viz.* 'yes'/'no') tends to aid answer classification and thereby enables a more meaningful report to be produced. Moreover, it is desirable the questionnaire be tested in the field to eradicate any misgivings in its content which later could prove costly. Above all, the questionnaire should be so formed to produce all the relevant data required of the market research remit, and be confidential in processing.

Basically, three methods of market research exist and these are detailed below:

1. By personal interview from a questionnaire. This involves engaging trained personnel to conduct field interviews. It is costly but reliable. Moreover, a greater number of questions can be asked to produce an 'in-depth' interview. Such a survey usually involves fewer questionnaires being completed but produces a good response rate with genuine answers. This person responding to a field interview tends to give more truthful answers than with a self administered questionnaire. It can be associated with product sampling.

2. The self-administered questionnaire. This may be despatched to the recipient by post, or picked up at the local retail outlet or other prescribed place. In some cases, it could accompany a company's product to establish the buying market characteristics and what motivated the purchase. This could help in preparing promotion in other areas. The self-administered questionnaire tends to contain no more than ten main questions. Longer questionnaires tend to discourage the person completing it and thereby produce a poor response rate. The questionnaire is usually returned by post. The cost of obtaining this data on each completed questionnaire is modest compared with the field interview but the response rate tends to be low.

The planning of such field interviews and questionnaire distribution is important. It is desirable that a good cross-section of the populace be obtained relevant to the survey remit terms, and techniques such as random sampling be adopted in the household selected, rather than a complete blanket coverage in one area which may produce indifferent results. For example a survey on baby foods is best directed toward couples of child-bearing age and not amongst old age pensioners. This could be devised by establishing the child-bearing couples in an area and having a random survey conducted.

The completed questionnaires received are edited and processed, usually through a computer to provide a presentation of statistical data in aggregate terms. This forms the basic data on which the report is written. It is for consideration whether all the questionnaires are processed or merely a selection of them randomally taken. A report promptly produced following the survey is essential as material quickly becomes out of date and thereby loses its significance.

3. By organized group discussion. In such circumstances up to fifteen people led by a chairman would discuss the merits of particular product. For example, a new car may have been on the market for some fifteen months, and the manufacturer may wish to determine in a overseas country the market attitude towards its design, general competitiveness, comfort, reliability, maintenance cost, availability of spares, price competitiveness, etc. Participants in the group must, of course, have some experience of the product and it is usual for them to be all of the same social class/group, that is, A/B. Details of the social class grouping are given in Table 12.1. Moreover, such participants would be

TABLE 12.1

Social Class Groupings

Social grade	*Social status*	*Description*
A	Upper middle class	Higher management, administrator or professional.
B	Middle class	Middle managerial, administrative or professional.
Cl	Lower middle class	Supervisory, clerical, or junior management.
C_2	Skilled working class	Skilled manual workers.
D	Working class	Semi-skilled and unskilled manual workers.
E	Those at subsistence level	Pensioners, casual or lowest grade workers, unemployed.

paid a modest fee and a psychiatrist would be present to help the discussion form meaningful conclusions. Overall, such a method determines attitudes and trend of a particular product in a specified market. The discussion usually lasts for up to thirty minutes or longer if required and is taped throughout. It is later analysed by the research company for report-writing purposes.

Another market research technique can be of an omnibus nature involving several companies/manufactures participating in the exercise and each bearing a proportion of the cost thereof. For example, several manufacturers of washing machines may wish to find out more about the market in which they are selling/competing in a specified country. Alternatively, it may involve several unrelated products and companies such as case, televisions, kitchen furniture, household utensils etc. It may involve price, design, reliability, aftersales service, advertising response with individual manufacturers particular but not common questions to thereby form a composite questionnaire. Each company would, therefore, receive only the data which he requested originally, such as 'answers to questions 1, 4, 5 and 7 of a ten-answer questionnaire'. Overall, it helps to reduce cost of such market research and can also be used in items (2) and (3) described in the following paragraphs.

Associated with market research is research conducted into the product, distribution arrangements, customer satisfaction, or promotion.

1. Product research emmbraces the development, design and testing of products. It also concerns acceptance of the packaging, colour and general identification of the product.

2. Distribution research concerns testing the adequacy of the transport arrangements of the consignment ana its related elements. This includes conducting test transits to establish areas where delays occur and the service is adequate to the importer.

3. Customer research establishes what the consumer thinks of the product purchased. It is particularly useful as it determines consumer motivation towards buying the product and the indequacies of the product.

To conclude, market research is an essential ingredient in the successful development by the exporter of overseas markets. The product should be well though out and advice sought when in doubt, particularly through the British Overseas Trade Board or local Chamber of Commerce and Industry. The subject is treated more extensively in Chapters 2, 3, and 4 of the companion volume *Elements of Export Marketing and Management*, and by the definitions in *Dictionary of Commercial Terms and Abbreviations.*

STATISTICS

Our study of export research would not be complete without consideration of statistics which is tending to play an increasingly important part in the technique of facilitating the development of overseas markets. In our brief evaluation of statistics, it is important to bear in mind that the statistical techniques should be used skilfully, and the exercises undertaken should be continuously costed, to ensure one obtains 'value for money' in relation to the benefits to be derived from such data, particularly in terms of export trade development/market share potential etc.

An examination of the various statistical aids available to the exporter now follows.

1. Sampling has become a very popular technique to determine the results of a survey or similar exercise. For example, the market research operator may initiate a self-administered, postal questionnaire programme in a particular area or region overseas to determine the adequacy of a product launched some two years ago. Each questionnaire circulated would be consecutively numbered. To avoid editing and processing all the questionnaires through a computer, a random selection can

be taken on a 'first come, first served' basis. Alternatively, one can process every fifteenth questionnaire—which would be called selective sampling. In such circumstances, the questionnaire would be so collated as for each one to be bundled in numerical order.

2. Graphs and diagrams form an important part of statistical presentation today. It aids the viewer to comprehend them better, rather than studying a series of statistical tables. Moreover, it facilitates such comparisons being made as, for example, one year's export results compared with another. Details of the various type of graphs/diagrams are given below:

(i) The histogram and bar charts present statistical data in a bar type of formation with each bar for example, representing a particular product's results in one year. One could have one bar representing bicycle sales, another motor mowers, another washing machines, and so on. Separate bars placed alongside each other could be produced to show one year's results compared with the preceding one.

(ii) The histogram graph is ideal for presenting a time series of statistical information. For example, the monthly results of sales in an overseas territory could be plotted every month on a graph. This could be related to the budgeted forecast.

(iii) The pie diagram is merely a circle split up into various segments proportionate to the statistical data presented. For example, the total cost of running the export office for one year could be assessed and ultimately broken down into components. For example, telephone calls may represent 10 per cent, stationery 5 per cent, wages 70 per cent, and all these elements could be reflected in the pie diagram formation. It is ideal for poster presentation and simple to understand.

(iv) Again suitable for poster presentation is the pictogram where a symbol represents a certain statistical value in the presentation. For example, if the exporter sold 1500 washing machines to a particular country in a month, this could be represented by a one and half washing machine pictogram symbol, each pictogram symbol representing 1000 units. This technique greatly facilitates statistical data presentation comprehension.

(v) The ogive is a useful diagramatical presentation which is basically the cumulative total plotted on a graph against the time interval. Thus, during a twelve-month period, each month's results would be added to the previous cumulative figure. Hence, by October the graph would reveal the cumulative figure from 1st January to 30th October. Such aggregation of data also be plotted against budget. Hence, by April it would be the first four months' results against budget, by May the first five months' results against budget and so on.

(vi) A further diagram is the logarithmic graph. This is not widely used but requires special log paper, for the data to be plotted thereon. It is ideal for time series involving extreme values such as recording on the same graph the figures 17,500, 1600,900 etc. in logarithmic terms.

(vii) A further diagram is the frequency polygon. This is ideal for presenting a time series. It is plotted on the basis of the actual result against the midpoint of the time interval. Thus, for example, the sales results for the years 1983 and 1984 were £1.2m and £3.5m respectively. The £1.2m figure would be plotted to cover the period mid-1982 to mid-1983, and the £3.5m the period mid-1983 to mid-1984.

(viii) The scatter diagram is merely the presentation on a graph of each entry within a group. For example, it could be customers passing through a shop during period 0800 to 1900 hours, and the amount each client spent. Thus the result may involve 250 customers which would be each recorded on the graph relative to the time of purchase and the amount. The purchases could range from 10 to 450 Dutch guilders. An examination of the completed graph may suggest the bulk of the customers made purchases between 100 and 150 Dutch guilders. Such data could produce a trend and many statisticians endeavour to draw a straight line through the plotted data to produce a statistical analysis.

(ix) Finally the Z-chart is a useful diagramatic presentation and in profile conforms to the shape of the letter 'Z'. The bottom part of the 'Z' records the monthly results on a time series basis, whilst the top portion portrays the annual total of the commodity. The diagonal linking the two takes the form of an ogive and gives the cumulative figure on a monthly basis for one year. Thus the Z-chart could produce on one diagram the commodity sales results for one year embracing on the bottom line the monthly sales results, the top line the moving annual total, and finally the ogive diagonal the aggregated results throughout the twelve-month period.

3. The word 'average' in statistics has a wide meaning and the more common types of statistical averages in use today are given below:

(i) The mode is regarded as the most popular/representative item in a group. For example, if some ten types of diesel engines are sold in an overseas market, the modal one would be the one which has the largest sales.

(ii) The arithmetic mean (AM) is widely used in statistics and it emerges on the basis of the aggregate of the group divided by the total participating in the group. Hence, if the aggregate totals 1200 and the number of participants is 20, the AM would be 60.

(iii) Allied to the AM is the dispersion of the range of items in the group. This can be measured by using either the mean deviation or standard deviation technique. For example, if the AM is 60 the mean deviation may be 6.7 suggesting the group is not widely dispersed. In broad terms, dispersion is a measure of how the group is dispersed, which takes account of the group range and how it is composed. For example, the group range may be from 1000 to 5000 thereby giving a range of 4000. However, the AM may be 2700 and nearly 70 per cent of the items within the group emerge within the band 2500-2900. This would suggest the mean-deviation technique of measuring the group dispersion would be most ideal as found in the mean deviation of 6.7. A group more widely dispersed with only 25 per cent coming within the band 2500-2900 would require a standard deviation measure as it gives less prominence to the extreme value of the group. In broad terms the mean and standard deviation is a measure of how the group is dispersed when related to the average such as the AM. If, for example, the AM is 60 and the mean deviation is 6.7, it suggests the group is concentrated around the AM.

(iv) The median is the value of the item situated at the half-way stage in a series. For example, if a group of 49 persons are placed in order of age graduation, the median age of the group would be the age of the 25th person in the group. This may be 34.5 year, although the actual group ages may range from 15-72 years.

(v) A further dispersion measure is found in the quartile deviation. The quartile deviation would be achieved by establishing the age of the 13th person in the group (in the above example) and the 38th. The former may be 27.5 years which is the lower quartile, and the latter 55.5 years, termed the upper quartile. The quartile deviation is obtained by subtracting the upper and lower quartiles (55.5—27.5=28.0 years) and dividing by two. This would give a figure of 14 years as the measure of how the group is dispersed from the median. A useful statistical technique widely used.

4. Published statistices both by Government and commercial organizations are numerous. This includes trade associations, banks, Central Statistical Office etc. Such data should be used critically otherwise the wrong conclusions can be reached

from the data used. In particular, the source and how the statistics are made-up should be ascertained if practicable. Particular care should be taken when calculating derivatives and comparing varying sets of figures, some of which be unrelated and collated in a different way. Usually, the local Chamber of Commerce and Industry or BOTB can help the exporter obtain the requisite statistical data required. This is particularly relevant to market surveys.

MANAGEMENT INFORMATION

Management information involves the preparation and presentation of satistical data on a regular basis (perhaps monthly). For example it could present, each month throughout the year against a budget forecast, the total number of radios sold in a particular country. These data aid management to measure how the business is progressing in a particular, market, and in the event of any fall-off in the results against budget, remedial measures can be taken. For example, poor local distribution arrangements may be one of the reasons for disappointing sales results or inadequate sales outlets.

Management information is an important area for scrutiny to ensure the right type of information is being produced promptly, and in the form required by management to ensure competent running of the business. Computers can play a useful role in the provision of such data. Overall management information is an aid to measuring business efficiency and development.

INDEX NUMBERS

The use of index numbers in statistical analysis is very much on the increase.

The basis of the formulation of an index is the selection of the base year/month/period etc. which ideally must be reasonably typical and not extreme, and relating all subsequent calculations to it. The index may represent one item or a group of items each with a consistent proportionate representation through the life of the index. Thus, when devising an index of retail prices in a particular overseas country, it will comprise numerous items. Food may represent 30 per cent, housing 10 per cent, transport 15 per cent, clothing 10 per cent, etc. Hence, if the price of food went up 50 per cent in one year, and all the other items remained unchanged, the index would not rise 50 per cent but 25 per cent (125)—representing the proportion of the food element in the index. Such a system is called weighting and is in common practice. If one item is involved, like the retail price of particular commodity, it is merely the relationship of the price in a particular year relative to the base year. An example is given below:

Retail price index of bicycle—Base year: 1978

Year	1978	1979	1980	1981	1982	1983	1984
Dutch guilders	400	440	464	468	472	488	484
Price index	100	110	116	117	118	122	121

The importance of the base year cannot be overstressed as needing to be representative; in all subsequent years the product must not change in specification otherwise comparisons are not valid.

CORRELATION

Correlation is the relationship or degree of harmonization between two groups. For example in a particular area the higher the temperature in the summer months, the greater the sales of ice cream products. This would be a positive correlation. Similarly, it would arise if a government increased expenditure through compulsory inoculation for a particular disease resulting in less patient-care in the long term. This is due to the reduced likelihood of the populace having such a disease.

Negative correlation would arise when the correlation is askew and had no consistent relationship. This could arise through consumer choice of a product which is primarily based on personal circumstances, income group and prejudices with no real pattern emerging.

Overall correlation is an important aspects to evaluation in statistical and market analysis.

SKEWNESS

Skewness is the technique of assessing how the group is dispersed. In the ideal group distribution situation it would be reasonably evenly dispersed on either side of the average which may be the mode, median or arithmetic mean. In such a situation the data plotted on a graph would take the form of a bell profile. This statistical facility is useful when examining how a group is formulated.

SEASONAL TRENDS AND MOVING ANNUAL TOTAL

Statistical analysis frequently involves a determination of trends which may involve a forward projection of up to five years. Such predictions can be obtained by calculating the trend emerging over a five/ten year period and projecting it into the future. This usually involves a tabulated or graphical presentation and ideally it should be based on a mothly or quarterly basis to aid meaningful production requirements and promotion strategy.

It is important to consider in such an evaluation seasonal trends and exceptional circumstances. For example, a very severe winter could substantially improve the sale of indoor heating appliances, whilst a very wet summer could increase the sale of rainwear. A further example is found in a change in fashion when in a particular year to celebrate a certain event, people were encouraged to wear a garment green in colour.

The moving annual total already mentioned in our consideration of the Z-shart is very much on the increase in terms of its use. It is ideal for sales data and reflects how the total sales performance is progressing. It is calculated on the basis of the aggregation of twelve consecutive months' figures. Thus for the twelve-month period ending 31st March, it would embrace all the twelve individual months' results from the preceding April until March (both months inclusive). The next month's result would include May until April (both months inclusive) and so on. Such data can be tabulated or recorded on a graph. It is particularly useful to produce market trends but care must be exercised to ensure it does not include any exceptional circumstances to produce a sudden sales increase surge, otherwise to base judgements on such data could produce a false picture in the future.

Statistics is a specialized subject and, in broad terms, is a science. Great skill should be exercised in the choice of statistical technique used and particular regard must be given to their need and use. Statistics wrongly used can produce false impressions and the production/presentation of statistical data should be regularly reviewed by those involved in the presentation, with personnel requiring such data. Particular attention should be given to the cost of providing such data and the time-scale of production. Data should be produced as currently as practical, as out-of-date information is of little value to management to aid their decision-making process. Additionally it must be born in mind statistical data are basically relative, with one set of figures compared with other. In such circumstances it is essential one compares like with like and accordingly special attention is given to definitions by both the personnel producing the data, and by those using it.

EXPORT PROMOTION

Export promotion is an important activity of the development of international trade and to be successful it must be professionally planned and executed. It comprises all those activities undertaken by an exporter, by direct or indirect appeal, with a view to persuading general buyers (the public) or specific buyers to purchase the exporter's products or service in preference to other products, or services offered by other companies, either locally or from overseas.

Various techniques exist regarding such promotion and the more common ones are now examined:

1. All forms of mass advertising media service selected from those offered in the actual market with a view to securing optimum impact. Each of these is now examined:

   (i) Radio and TV Visually orientated products are ideal for TV advertising but it must be borne in mind that not all countries permit commercial advertising through such a media. Radio, on the other hand, is ideal for products which are easy to describe and do not have a strong visual impact. Moreover, in underdeveloped countries it is often the only means of communication, particularly when illiteracy is high.

   (ii) Cinema, involving slides or film presentation, is tending to become more popular, particularly with local presentation/promotions. It is most effective when the dialogue is limited, thereby overcoming the language barrier and permitting the presentation to have a wider international market appeal. Although the film cost may be high, it can be adequately recouped if the film is shown in several countries.

   (iii) Press advertising involving national or local newspapers, consumer or trade magazines and technical journals is a very popular method of promotion. Each newspaper, magazine etc. has a specialized market and this should be evaluated together with its circulation to determine its adequacy for the product promotion. The exporter must establish whether the publication has any political or religious allegiance, its compatability with the product and manufacturer's promotion.

   (iv) Advertising sites situated on hoardings, transport vehicles, public lounges/areas at railways stations or airport passenger terminals. Such sites, some of which can be permanently illuminated, are ideal for a wide range of consumer products.

2. All forms of sales aids such as leaflets for use at point-of-sale with supporting posters, price tickets and other display material, stickers and pelmets, and well-designed retail support items such as catalogues and instruction leaflets. This includes window display material.
3. All forms of merchandising—more usual with consumer products—such as premium offers, special bonus deals and specimen layouts designed to enhances sales appeal such as showroom displays.
4. Direct mail which involves sending sales literature direct to selected potential buyers. This is best undertaken locally rather than by the UK-based exporter thereby saving heavy postage charges. Moreover, it needs to be adequately researched to ensure it reaches only householders who can be regarded as potential buyers. It is best used in industrial countries where a high degree of literacy.
5. The use of trade fairs, public exhibitions and any means of displaying products to visitors at such shows. The technique is very much on the increase.
6. Public relations involving the release to the mass media, *viz.*, press, TV and radio items of 'news' about the export company or its products in such a way taat free publicity is secured. This includes measures taken to promote the brand image amongst employees, agents and distributors abroad, suppliers and other contacts, and shareholders.
7. Education of personnel having influence on sales of the product, directly or indirectly, *viz.*, salesmen, service engineers etc. This virtually constitutes product support—often of a technical nature—involving users, distributors and service engineers.

The first step in planning export promotion is to formulate an advertising budget. An examination of the various methods is detailed below:

1. The exporter can base the budget on a percentage of the price structure such as 5 per cent of CIF or FOB per unit price. Hence, if the exporter forecast to sell 10000 units each at £100 CIF, it would produce an advertising budget of £50000. The percentage would be higher than 5 per cent when the product is launched and in the initial years, thereafter depending on its success and the degree of competition.
2. As an alternative to the foregoing, the exporter prepares the budget based on a percentage of the previous year's turnover.
3. A further method is to allocate advertising money to be used when the market opportunities arise. This is usually called the 'task' method. The exporter calculates what expenditure will be necessary to accomplish a given objective. Care must be taken to ensure that tasks are not set which require expenditures way beyond what one can reasonably hope to earn. Such tasks are gared to anticipate sales in order to keep a reasonable ratio between expenditure and earnings.
4. The investment method regards all expenditure as an investment exactly as if it were new plant or the purchase of shares in an associate company, that is, an allocation of capital to the project promising an income flow in the future. The accountant might justify this course by adding the amount to the 'goodwill' item in the firm's balance sheet at the time it is laid out, for gradual amortization in later years. Provided adequate sales result, this method can work well if a realistic amount is allocated to the promotional purpose—not a sum so small as to be derisory.
5. Many exporters have a standard form of agency agreement which requires the agent to contribute to

promotion expenditures. This is more common where the agent is in fact an importer/distributor than where he is a commission selling agent. This may require the agent to share in all such expenditure, or it may only relate to advertising in the market with the possibility of sharing 50/50 expenditure for exhibitions or fairs leaving sales aids to be supplied at the exporter's expense. The prime advantage is that the agent, as the 'man on the spot', shares the promotional expenditure and should be able to judge the impact of promotional measures quicker and perhaps more accurately than may the exporter several thousand miles away. It is important the exporter exercises adequate supervision over the agent.

Overall, there are four methods in which export promotion can be handled and each is now examined:

1. It can be left to the agent to undertake all forms of advertising in his market. This involves making premium offers and bouns deals at his own discretion, to exhibit at fairs etc. in his country if he thinks it worthwhile, and to embark on such public relations activities as may appeal to him.
2. The principal's publicity department could assume responsbility for promotional activities abroad as well as home. The smaller type of manufacturer is unlikely to employ enough staff in its publicity department for them to have adequate time to devote to export. Moreover, they are likely to lack adequate expertise. In the larger manufacturing company however, the publicity manager with staff qualified in the foreign field can export manager's prescribed objectives. This method can be a viable one although one must be conscious of the risk that home market promotional material can partially subsidize the international market.
3. Where the exporter does not have adequate resources available for export promotion, an advertising agency

can be engaged. It is advocated that one chooses an agency with local offices or associates through whom they work. Care needs to be exercised in the choice of agency to ensure it is of repute and capable of carrying out the assignment. It is important for the exporter to check on the effectiveness of the agency by requiring its foreign sales agent to include comments on the promotional efforts in their periodical reports. For example, when tne selling agent considers that advertisements launched in his market do not adequately support his sales activities, it supported by facts and remedial measures suggested.

4. When the exporter cannot undertake his own export promotion or does not wish to engage an advertising agency, a further option exist—namely the employment of a part-time consultant. This is ideal for the small exporter.

The services offered to the advertiser by the advertising consultant are somewhat different from that offered by the advertising agency. Although the consultant is unlikely to take part in the physical operation of any advertising plan, his very broad experience of all aspects of advertising enables him to offer a very comprehensive advisory service.

The consultant is normally fee-earning and will prepare the advertising plan and recommend the nature of its execution, leaving the actual detailed work to be effected by the advertiser. The consultant's real function, which comes from an in-depth knowledge of his client's business and the markets in which he operates, is the initiation of the advertising plan. However, his advice may extend to areas such as product and package design, and method of distribution, as these are influenced by the plan which he has formulated. The consultant is likely to assess the advertising plan during its operation to determine its effectiveness and to suggest remedies for any weaknesses which reveal themselves.

MARKETING PLAN

The marketing plan is the basis on which all the overseas promotion is formulated. To devise the marketing plan involves reconciling the export strategies and objectives of the manufacturer into marketing terms. It should be produced by the export director or most senior person responsible for the export market.

The marketing plan embraces many elements including market research projects, promotion/advertising details, products involved, distribution arrangements, and total volume/value of goods by individual product/country. Where relevant, various costing information should be included particularly the research and advertising budget. An appraisal of the viability of the plan should be given, and all the timing of the elements of the plan should be inserted. For example, the actual periods the advertising programme will operate. Overall, the marketing plan must have the approval of all the departments involved. Above all, the plan must be realistic and should have a clear sense of purpose and direction. It should be reviewed perhaps quarterly throughout its one-year life to reflect change in circumstances.

VISITS TO OVERSEAS MARKETS

Our study of export marketing would not be complete without brief consideration of planning an overseas trip. Whenever a foreign trip is planned it is imperative to establish a very clear picture of its object(s) and to prepare a brief accordingly. The trip could be for one or more of the following purposes:

1. Initial market research—to carry out to completion the prior desk research investigations.
2. Continuing market research.
3. To appoint an agent from those short-listed.
4. Finding a replacement agent when the existing one retires, dies, or whose paid services are terminated.

5. Discussing with an agent differing marketing approaches better distribution arrangements, improved documentation arrangements, etc.
6. Examining with agents the prospects of improved sales, better advertising, new opportunities within the market, improved sales training for staff, etc.
7. 'On-the-spot' investigation with the agent to enquire into customers' complaints.
8. To examine prospects of setting up a local company.

One needs to be adequately briefed before undertaking such a trip and the following points must be borne in mind relative to the overseas visit:

1. Obtain sound advice on personal conduct. Such information can be found in the *Hints to Exporters* series of booklets which cover most of the markets in the world. Each contains regularly up-dated information on currency and exchange regulations, passport and entry formalities, methods of doing business, and so on. The booklets cover individual countries extending to over one hundred overseas markets and are available from the British Overseas Trade Board.
2. Time the visit to ensure one does not arrive during any legal or religious holiday period as most businessmen are likely to be away.
3. Conclude/confirm as far as practicable all hotel reservations, travel arrangements and currency needs. Credit cards can help with regard to the latter. Air travel is expensive and, in certain circumstances for near Continental countries, the overnight sea journey with cabin accommodation and the accompanied car can prove to be a cheaper and more flexible operation, particularly when the exporter is visiting a number of areas over several days. A modest amount of loose change is desirable for the individual countries to be visited.

4. Plan the itinerary allowing adequate time for travel and for seeing the various peoble with whom contact has to be made. Allow a modest amount of time for any journey delays. All necessary visas must be obtained before leaving including 'transit visas' when merely stopping *en route*. All journeys should be booked in advance through an airline, ship operator or accredited travel agency. A valid passport is essential.

5. Ensure all the clients on your itinerary are aware of your visit and its purpose so that they are adequately prepared and the senior personnel are available.

6. Ensure adequate insurance is arranged in all relevant areas. Personal baggage should be modest proportions and clothes should be compatible with the climate/circumstances. Always appear smartly dressed when on business. If the exporter cannot speak the language competently, an interpreter should be present at meetings. The visit should allow adequate time for relaxation and the usual health precautions should be adopted including any vaccinations prior to departure.

7. The export salesman should take an adequate amount of sales literature and, when practicable, samples.

8. Prepare notes of all meetings conducted recording salient points within the remit terms of your visit. Report and observe when relevant the customs and idiosyncrasies of the populace. Give particular attention to detail and when necessary have it checked.

9. Ensure one's family has details of the visit and contact is made with them, such as, a telex or telephone call, on arrival. Also the appropriate family arrangements should be made before departure particularly adequate finance and payment of bills.

Arrangements to call on the Commercial Officer at the Embassy should be made through the Department of Trade and

Industry. Likewise, the businessman should visit the exporter's bank which may be the head office to discuss any mutual problems relative to existing or future trade. The subject of businessment's strips to overseas markets is dealt with exhaustively in Chapter 11 of the companion volume *Elements of Export Marketing and Management*.

13

INDIAN ENGINEERING EXPORTS

A.P. SINGH

Indian engineering industry is one of the most important sectors of the Indian economy. It employs over 20 lakh people and accounts for nearly 30 per cent of the productive capital and 35 per cent of the value added in the organised sector. While details of select products between 1981-82 and 1983-84 appear in Annexure I, production of engineering goods increased from Rs. 3,474 crores in 1970-71 to Rs. 20,102 crores in 1980-81. Further, the engineering industry accounts for 14 per cent of all-India exports and tops the list of items exported from the country (Annexure II). That its exports rose from Rs. 5 crores in 1956-57 to Rs. 1,170 crores in 1983-84 speaks of the way it has grown over the years (Table 13.1).

Sectorwise exports of engineering products in 1982-83 are: capital goods (Rs 530 crores); primarily steel and pig iron-based items (Rs. 177 crores); nonferrous-based items (Rs. 21 crores); and consumer durables (Rs. 522 crores). Of all these categories, capital goods recorded the largest increase, followed by consumer durables. Exports of steel and non-ferrous-based items did not rise much and showed an erratic trend. Sector-wise details of engineering exports between 1956-57 and 1982-83 are given in Table 13.2.

TABLE 13.1

Exports of Indian Engineering Products (1956-57 to 1983-84)

(*Rs crores*)

Year	*Amount*
1956-57	5.16
1978-79	716.93
1979-80	706.68
1980-81	900.00
1981-82	1,042.74
1982-83	1,250.00
1983-84	1,170.00

Source : Engineering Export Promotion Council, Calcutta.

TABLE 13.2

Sectorwise Exports of Indian Engineering Products

(*Rs crores*)

Sector	*1956-57*	*1980-81*	*1981-82*	*1982-83*
Capital goods	0.62	371.00	368.00	530.00
	(12.1)	(41.2)	(34.7)	(42.4)
Primarily steel and iron-based products	1.70	173.00	197.00	177.00
	(32.9)	(19.2)	(18.6)	(14.2)
Non-ferrous products	1.10	32.00	22.00	21.00
	(21.3)	(3.6)	(2.1)	(1.7)
Consumer durables	1.74	324.00	473.00	522.00
	(33.70)	(36.00)	(44.6)	(41.7)
Total	5.16	900.00	1,060.00	1,250.00

Note : Figures in brackets show percentage to total.
Source : Engineering Export Promotion Council, Calcutta.

As against exports of Rs. 1,170 crores during 1983-84, the target fixed for 1984-85 is placed at Rs. 15,00 crores. Major items of Indian engineering exports and their value in 1982-83 are:

Electronics (Rs. 95 crores), complete vehicles (Rs. 65 crores), diesel engines and parts (Rs. 60 crores), bicycles and bicycle parts (Rs. 40 crores), sanitory castings (Rs. 32 crores), auto parts (Rs. 54 crores), hand-tools and cutting-tools (Rs. 47 crores), electric power machinery and switch-gears (Rs. 42 crores), cement machinery (Rs 3.0 crores) steel instruments (Rs. 30 crores), wires and cables (Rs. 52 crores), and machine-tools (Rs. 28 crores).

TERRITORIAL PATTERN

West Asia dominates the show with its share standing at Rs. 275.66 crores (26.33%). It is closely followed by South-East Asia with imports valued at Rs. 190.89 crores (18.23%); Europe, Rs. 210 crores (20,98%); and Africa, Rs. 191.76 crores (18.32%). Details of regionwise export of Indian engineering exports are given in Annexure III.

The principal markets far Indian engineering products are; USSR (Rs. 180 crores); USA (Rs. 95 crores); Iran (Rs. 65 crores); Nigeria (Rs. 55 crores): Iraq (Rs. 55 crores); Saudi Arabia (Rs. 50 crores); Egypt (Rs. 45 crores); and Sri Lanka (Rs. 35 crores). Although India's exports of engineering products have shown a spectacular growth over the past decade, particularly after the oil boom, India's share in world exports amounts to 0.2 per cent (Annexure IV), If the situation is to be improved, exports of Indian engineering products will have to grow at a fairly rapid rate.

COLOSSAL DEMAND

Viewed in the context of the colossal overseas demand and the expertise and resources available within India, the Engineering Export Promotion Council had fixed an export target of Rs. 9,000 crores by 1990-91. This projection was based on the assumption that the exports of engineering products and projects would grow at the rate of 25 per cent per annum or a real growth rate of 15 per cent per annum. Even at this rate, India's share in world exports of engineering products will touch only one per cent by 1990-91.

Considering the dismal situation on the export front in recent years, this target has since been scaled down to Rs. 6,000 crores. Incidentially, over 1980-84, engineering exports increased by 6.2 per cent year against the target of 10.2 per cent for the Sixth Plan period. Indeed, from 1978-79 to 1983-84, the realised export growth rate was only half of the target rate for a number of engineering items, namely metal products, machinery, electrical and transport equipment. Against the buoyancy of project exports during the '70s, the figures suddenly slumped by almost 75 per cent between 1981-82 and 1982-83.

Realisation of exports of such a magnitude will require expansion in markets, involvement of additional units, exportable products and production capacity. It would, however, be interesting to note that nearly 78 per cent of engineering exports are accounted for by only 19 countries and 86 per cent of these exports emanate from a few identified items. While diversifying markets products, total availability will have to be steadily enlarged through appropriate investment and pragmatic production policies and without increasing domestic demand. To ensure that growth of exports leads to maximum benefit in regard to improvement in quality and greater use of modern technology at crucial points of production and assembly, it should ensure the maximum possible increase in employment. In addition to this, there must also be greater participation in the export effort by a large number of manufactures especially belonging to the small-scale sector.

Further, industrial units must upgrade their technology to be able to compete in international markets. Instead of spreading too thin, greater attention will need to be given to a few selected markets. At present, hardly 230 units account for almost 85 per cent of the total engineering exports. In India, there is a large number of manufacturers, who provide a wide range of products such as automobiles, heavy electricals, cables, machine-tools, electric motors, transformers and switch-gears, motor vehicles and a host of consumer durables, which have enormous export potential.

FAVOURABLE EFFECTS

While aiming at the expansion of engineering exports, adverse effects of the emergence of China on the world economic scene, growth of protectionism among industrialised countries, mounting oil requires, mounting oil requirements and political changes in some of the countries of West Asia and Africa cannot be ignored. Another problem confronting exports of Indian engineering exports, particularly those to the South-East Asia, relates to counter-trade. Under this system of trading, importing countries stipulate certain conditions for exporting countries to purchase specified items from the former. It would be equally important not to forget the favourable effects of the new prosperity of oil-rich countries and of rapid industrial development taking place in some of the non-oil producing countries of South-East Asia and Africa.

Indian technology is best suited to the requirements of these countries and the costs of innumerable services that India can provide in the engineering field are highly competitive. In fact, there are a number of labour-intensive products, which India can manufacture with considerable comparative cost advantage for export markets of both developed and developing countries. The Engineering Export Promotion Council has, however, done some exercises in this context and identified the following items, which have sizable labour content:

> Automobile parts, bicycles and bicycle parts, machine-tools, hand-tools and cutting-tools, diesel engines and pums, heating and cooling equipment, electric fans, sewing and knitting machines, and electrical appliances and accessories.

PROJECT EXPORTS

India has already earned a good deal of foreign exchange through consultancy, project engineering, and irrigation and construction services. Our export earnings from such services should also rise significantly over the next decade. Till recently, a sizeable share of project exports was directed to West Asia. but the pace of development has slowed down in that region. Any revival of project exports will depend upon India's capacity to diversify the areas of its penetration. According to present expectations, India's earning from projects and construction should be around Rs. 3,000 crores in another six to seven years. To reach this stage, India has to make headway in terms of infrastructural base, especially in technology, finance and marketing.

For solving this problem, the Government of India has decided to strengthen and reorganise the privately sponsored Overseas Construction Council on the pattern of the Export Promotion Council. In another proposal put forward for generating larger exports from projects, the Association of Indian Engineering Industry has called for the establishment of an Inter-Ministerial Project Export Board, which should act as a single-point clearance for project exporters. With a view to upgrading the tools and techniques employed by the indigenous industry and helping it to catch up with the developed world, twenty large construction companies in the country have set up a National Institute of Construction Management and Research.

TEAM WORK

Team work is another factor, which can help raise exports of engineering products. This is particularly relevant in the case of turnkey projects, where too many functions are involved and it becomes absolutely difficult for a single agency to execute the job single-handed. With a view to successfully completing the entire job and taking full benefit of the project business available abroad, it would be desirable for various

Indian units especially in different activities, to come together and form consortia, The question of export consortia becomes equally relevant in product exports made by small-scale units because of their limited production capacity and financial resources.

AFTER-SALES SERVICE

Yet another constraint holding up expansion of engineering exports relates to after-sales service. Scant regard for such a vital export activity stems from ignorance of modern industrial culture, which is further reinforced by the protected domestic market. In fact, the neglect of after-sales services is basically due to absence of customer-orientation in our marketing system, which has seldom gone beyond the production disposal operation. This serious lacuna has, in many cases, spoiled the image of our engineering products abroad.

DELIVERY SCHEDULES

Strict adherence to agreed delivery schedules is another problem in the export of our engineering goods. It is often found that once exporters are not able to ship their goods in time, they start explaining their defaults in deliveries. In fact, no explanation can be a substitute for despatch of goods in time. Delivery is the chief factor in international trading and involves the name of the country as a whole. There could be instances, when delivery schedules are upset owing to disrupted sailings, power cuts and industrial strikes/lock-outs, but the overseas buyer, who has option to procure his requirements from anywhere in the world, is hardly concerned with it. Other ingredients for strengthening exports of engineering products include a stable policy for export incentives, larger trade among developing countries and completion of the existing projects undertaken in West Asia and other countries.

Although it is necessary to participate in trade fairs and exhibitions and improve our trade relations with various markets for strengthening exports, it is equally important to adopt such domestic policies, which generate the required export surpluses for products, for which there exist markets instead of simply looking for, as we have done, products in which we have some surplus capacity. Exporters should not suffer for want of power or transport bottlenecks, which completely upset the export plan of individual exporters and spoil the overseas image of our country.

ANNEXURE 1

Production of Select Engineering Items (1981-82 To 1983-84)

Item	*Accounting unit*	*1981-82*	*1982-83*	*1983-84*
Steel castings	Th. tonnes	81.1	87.7	89.9
Transmission towers	Th. tonnes	96.7	113.4	118.8
Structurals	Th. tonnes	121.5	130.6	130.7
Steel pipes and tubes	Th. tonnes	806.2	808.4	817.4
MS bolts and nuts	Th. tonnes	27.6	11.1	18.8
Wire ropes	Th. tonnes	23.7	29.9	31.1
Boilers	Rs. crores	346.7	435.9	482.4
Diesel engines	Th. nos.	174.5	156.5	156.1
Cranes	Th. nos.	22.7	22.7	23.0
Power driven pumps	Th. nos.	373.0	460.6	491.6
Agricultural tractors	Th. nos.	84.1	62.9	75.8
Machine-tools		249.9	269.6	272.4
Domestic refrigerators	Th. nos.	324.3	380.0	494.8
Sugar machinery	Rs crores	26.3	41.5	49.8
Mining machinery	Rs crores	64.2	65.6	68.6
Power transformers	Mill. kva	21.5	18.6	23.1
Electric motors	Mill. hp	5.29	4.81	5.5
Motor starters	Th. nos.	1,468.7	1,441.0	1,518.0
Railways wagons	Th. nos.	17.8	15.3	17.4
Commercial vehicles	Th. nos.	91.1	86.0	88.3
Cars	Th. nos.	42.5	43.6	46.7
Jeeps	Th. nos.	20.2	21.8	23.2
Scooters	Th. nos.	201.2	264.9	279.8
Three-wheelers	Th. nos.	25.8	31.9	38.5
Bicycles	Th. nos.	5,051.0	4,781.3	5,830.1

Source: Association of Indian Engineering Industry, New Delhi.

ANNEXURE II

Share of Engineering Exports vis-a-vis All-India (1972-73 To 1983-84)

(*Rs crores*)

Year	*All-India exports*	*Engineering exports*	*% age share of engineering in all India exports*
1972-73	**1,971**	**141**	**7.1**
1973-74	**2,523**	**193**	**7.6**
1974-75	**3,329**	**349**	**10.5**
1975-76	**4,043**	**408**	**10.1**
1976-77	**5,142**	**552**	**10.7**
1977-78	**5,408**	**624**	**11.5**
1978-79	**5,726**	**717**	**12.5**
1979-80	**6,418**	**737**	**11.5**
1980-81	**6,711**	**900**	**13.4**
1981-82	**7,806**	**1,043**	**13.4**
1982-83	**8,834**	**1,250**	**14.1**
1983-84	**9,396**	**1,170**	**12.4**

Sources: **Department of Commercial Intelligence and Statistics, Calcutta, and Engineering Export Promotion Council, Calcutta.**

ANNEXURE III

Regionwise Engineering Exports

(Rs crores)

Region	*1956-57*	*1979-80*	*1980-81*	*1981-82*
Asia	3.76 (72.86)	373.44 (50.69)	425.74 (48.70)	466.55 (44.56)
South-East Asia	1.77 (34.26)	199.81 (27.10)	232.63 (26.61)	190.89 (18.23)
West Asia	1.99 (38.58)	173.83 (23.59)	193.11 (22.09)	275.66 (26.33)
Africa	1.20 (23.23)	143.13 (19.43)	172.58 (19.74)	191.76 (18.32)
Europe	0.01 (0.21)	127.28 (17.28)	173.35 (19.83)	219.62 (20.98)
East Europe	—	40.55 (5.50)	78.67 (9.00)	140.56 (13.43)
West Europe	0.01 (0.21)	86.73 (11.78)	94.68 (10.83)	79.06 (7.55)
America	0.02 (0.36)	76.10 (10.33)	80.31 (9.19)	70.42 (6.73)
Oceanic Islands	0.10 (1.96)	2.70 (0.37)	2.19 (0.25)	5.67 (0.54)
Australia	0.07 (1.38)	14.03 (1.90)	12.37 (1.42)	17.56 (1.67)
Others (service & software)	—	—	7.63 (0.87)	75.41 (7.20)
Total	5.16 (100.00)	736.68 (100.00)	874.77 (100.00)	1,046.99 (100.00)

Note: Figures in brackets show percentage to total.
Source: Engineering Export Promotion Council, Calcutta.

ANNEXURE IV

India's Share in World Exports of Engineering Goods

Year	*World exports*	*India's exports*	*% age share of India in world exports*
1970	100,737.56	258.21	0.3
1977	347,840.27	894.37	0.3
1978	419,050.71	951.69	0.2
1979	490,419.30	881.83	0.2
1980	565,466.72	1,164.57	0.2
1981	546,377.39	1,102.62	0.2

Source: Association of Indian Engineering Industry, New Delhi.

14

EXPORT PROMOTION AND MARKETING TECHNIQUES

LESSONS FROM JAPAN

Japan is poor in natural resources which are indispensable for the development of the economy. Therefore, for many years, promotion of international trade has been one of the most important problems of acting the country which has been taking various measure for export promotion. There are some measures taken *exclusively* for the promotion of export of commodities produced by small business. Because of scarcity of necessary funds, most small enterprises find it difficult to get correct information and trends in foreign markets and also no developing a new market abroad. In order to make up for such handicaps of its small business and to promote their exports, the government takes the following measures:

1. To find local products which are suitable for foreign tastes and modes and to improve their quality and design so as to meet foreign requirement, the government invities designers and other experts from abroad, who go around the country to give advice and guidance.

   When it is necessary to improve the quality of those local products which are discovered by foreign experts, the government gives subsidies to their producers.

2. All Japan Export Merchandise Fair is organised once a year to introduce and advertise products of smaller enterprises. The Government gives financial assistance for the opening of the Fair, Merchandise of superior quality selected at the Fair are to be displayed at special booths in the International Trade Fair which is held every year in Tokyo or Osaka.
3. For qualitative improvement of export products of smaller enterprises and to encourage trial production of new commodities, technical advice and other assistance is given to small business.
4. Various measures taken by JETRO (Japan External Trade Organization), such as market research, advertising, intermediation of trade, consultation on foreign trade, have contributed much for the export of small business products.
5. As to financing, the Small Business Finance Corporation supplies plant and equipment funds at lower rates of interest (7.5 to 7.6%) for enterprises which have concluded long-term export contracts or for enterprises which belong to designated lines of business and have given actual results of exporting more than 20 per cent of their total production.
6. In order to facilitate borrowing of Operation funds by small business connected with export, some credit guarantee rates of premium.
7. As to taxation, extra depreciation is allowed on machinery and other fixed assets owned by small enterprises which have income through foreign trade. Besides, 1.5 per cent of income through foreign trade transaction can be exempted from corporate tax when it is kept as 'foreign market development reserve.'

PACKAGING FOR EXPORTS

Quality goods which are exported from India in excellent condition often reach their destination in a damaged state. They may be returned and cause considerable loss to the seller, or they may be retained to the disadvantage of the buyer. In either case, they give the exporter—and even the country of their origin a bad name. So acute the problem that was the Government of India has set up an Indian Institute of Packaging which concentrates on problems of Packaging.

Packaging for the domestic market need not only be attractive; for export purposes it has to be strong and protective as well. Insurance studies indicate that about 80 per cent of the losses in respect of export cargo can be prevented by proper packaging.

Export packaging has three major functions to perform:

Protection against water and moisture, against breakage and against theft. Covering that is impervious to moisture should be used to protect goods that are affected by water which can cause rust, stains, mildew rotting, delamination, swelling or warping.

Breakage may be prevented by proper choice of container. Articles which do not fill the container should be braced, fastended, blocked or otherwise held in place to prevent interior movement. Great attention should be paid to inner packaging.

The container and the interior packing should be such as to absorb shocks and cushion external pressure. To prevent pilferage, new well constructed containers should be used, made of fibre board or nailed wooden boxes. The contents should not be described on the outside.

Costs can be kept down considerably by the use of the appropriate material. Indian packaging tends to be haphazard in the choice of material and their quality, and accordingly more costly.

Another factor to be borne in mind is that in some countries and for some items charges on imports may be levied according to the number of containers, so that a larger number of boxes will attract a higher levy. This can be an important cost item. Some governments have stringent regulations on the use of internal packaging material. Care should also be taken to ensure that packaging material does not contain anything offensive to reliegious sentiment.

While the word trade in fish and fish products expanded from over 5 million tonnes in 1954 to 15, million tonnes in 1963, India's exports fell from 25,000 tonnes to 17,000 tonnes. Indias's share in the world trade accordingly declined from 0.47 per cent to 0.1 per cent. Similarly, world production of fish rose from 24.6 million tonnes in 1951-53 to 44.6 million tonnes in 1961-63, an increase of 84 per cent. But in the same period, Indian production expanded by only 30 per cent from 0.77 million tonnes to 1 million tonnes.

In a study, the National Council of Applied Economic Research, India, had recommended measures for improving the size of the catch, increasing the processing capacity, improving the quality of packaging, making market surveys, publicity and diversification by producing new specialities. These recommendations merit careful study by fishing interests. Offsore and deep sea fishing were neglected for lack of mechanised boats, ancillary equipment and other facilities such as fishing harbours, cold storages, ice factories and transport vehicles. There was also the problem of supplying the requisite technical know-how to fishermen in the trade, on the one hand, and the prejudice among educated men against the fishing occupation on the other; both have to be resolved if fishing is to develop into a flurishing industry. If appropriate measures are taken, it should be possible both to increase India's export of fish and fish products and to produce enough fish for the internal and external markets.

A sizable portion of the marine fish landings in India consists of seer fish. 11,151 metric tons were landed in 1954. With improved trolling and the operation of long lines, it is certain that the catch of seer will rise appreciably in the future.

At present the fish is salt cured and exported to the Middle East and Far Eastern countries. The prospects for exporting canned seer should be quite as good as mackere, sardine and tuna. The quality of the product will be the deciding factor.

Processed foods are in very great demand in Switzerland which has one of the highest living standards in the world. Fish consumption (of all products, excluding crustaceans and molluses) for 1964 was 23.86 kilos per inhabitant, and increase of 3.62 kilos over the 1963 figure of 20.24 kilos. The total consumption of fish and fish products for 1964 was around 136 million kilos. The per capital consumption of crustaceans and molluses was approximately 2.80 kilos, and increase of 0.60 kilos over the 1963 figure of 2.20 kilos.

Frozen foods are becoming increasingly popular. Deep-freeze units for storage of frozen foods are available all over the country and commercial deep-freezes are installed in 2500 villages. Consumption of frogs' legs is probably in the region of 125,000 kilos per annum, of which only half is produced locally. Consumption has been rising, particularly in the restaurant trade which takes some 50 per cent in the domestic production. Imports of frozen frogs legs come mostly from Rumania, Czechoslovakia and France.

There is good scope for Indian exports, though transport costs from India are higher than from Eastern Europe. Canned prawns and shrimps are another important import item. Consumption has more than doubled over the last few years. About 25 per cent of the volume of imports consists of shrimps. The rest is prawns. Shrimps, however, constitute 50 per cent of the value. India exported 17,000 kilos of prawns and shrimps in 1963, the highest so far; in 1964, there was a sharp decline.

There is also scope for the export of frozen shrimps to the U.S. Imports into California and Arizona of shrimps from India for 1969 were 1.022,921 pounds against 613.877 pounds during 1964. Imports of frozen shrimps (peeled and deveined) went up 15 times as compared with 1964.

Swiss importers have complained that the prices of Indian timber are usually high, though the quality is good. The main variety imported from India is Palisander, of which 1,13,000 kgs., valued at 2,27,000 francs were imported in 1964. Much less expensive is Brazilian Palisander, of which Switzerland imported 181,000 kgs., valued at 208,000 Francs. Swiss importers also by Indian timber indirectly from Italy. The Italians import it in large quantities and veneer it for local consumption and for export to foreign countries. Though Italian prices are high, the Swiss prefer to import it from Italy because they are certain of the quality. Indian exporters would do well to try and market veneered palisander, teak and walnut. The acceptable dismensions of sheets are 0.6 centimetres thick, 6 ft; or more long and as wide as possible. There is no Customs duty on the import of sawn timber into Switzerland.

As an official commercial representative, you can provide support to your suppliers at home who are competing for contracts in your post country. Winning contracts for the supply of goods or services through international competitive bidding can be a lucrative business. A major contract, or even an important subcontract, awarded to one of your exporters at home may earn millions of dollars in foreign exchange for your country. Most countries purchase at least part of their goods and services through international competitive bidding. The purchasing entity may be central, regional or local government authorities; public utility companies; or private organizations. As an official commercial representative posted in a foreign market, you can help your country's exporters participate in international tendering operations.

THE TENDERING PROCESS

To know how and where you can most effectively intervene to your country's advantage in the complex and competitive business of international bidding, you must understand the tendering process.

For a major procurement, the call for tenders is the final outcome of a lengthy process. Many decisions on the tender may have already been made well before the publication of the call for bids. Calls for tender and the subsequent bid evaluation and contractor selection are frequently undertaken only to comply with a legal formality.

The various stages of the process of the development of a major project for international tendering, in chronological order, are:

Identification of a possible requirement (*i.e.* the supply of goods or services).

Draft proposal outlining in broad terms how this requirement should be addressed, including financial possibilities, that is, a pre-feasibility study.

Feasibility study, to determine the project's viability, both financial and technical.

Project definition.

Preparation of detailed specifications, with all supporting documentation.

Preparation of the inquiry document or "bid package."

Call for tenders, with its own series of procedures.

The terms used many vary from place to place and from project to project; steps may be skipped; and the time required from start to finish may be very long or quite short. But the sentence itself is generally invariable.

The first rule of competing in the international market for tenders, then, is to try to involve your potential suppliers in the tender process at the earliest possible stage, in order to exert the maximum influence on the evolution of the project, including the direction of the final award. For example, a machinery supplier may try to have a detailed specification "written around" its equipment, so that it will be the only logical supplier when the award is made.

The second rule is to identify the stage or stages at which your intervention is likely to have a favourable result. Some possible actions are described in the box on page 350. Clearly, if you simply wait for stage 7 in the box, you will long since have lost the game, unless you are dealing with an unusually straightforward purchase.

ACTION ON ARRIVAL AT YOUR POST

As your country's commercial representative, you can play an active role in helping to generate bussiness for suppliers at home for projects carried out in your post country or administered through institutions located in your country of assignment. As a first step, as soon as possible after your arrival at the post, study national agency laws and tendering regulations. Digests of these can usually be obtained from either the appropriate ministry or the local chamber of commerce and industry. In particular, you should review the following requirements:

Registration and pre-qualification requirements. These concern the extent to which potential contractors or suppliers from your country must be registered and pre-qualified before they are allowed to submit bids.

Pre-qualification of bidders is now required for most foreign companies that wish to bid for major works or supply contracts. Moreover, many calls for tender are not publicized but are issued, as requests for proposals, to a short list of suppliers whose qualifications have already been ascertained to the satisfaction of the issuing authority.

It is therefore, particularly important that you obtain full information on the requirements of the prospective buyer for the pre-qualification of bidders, and that appropriate organizations in your country be informed of these requirements as soon as possible, to enable them to take steps to comply with the deadline. Otherwise they will not be given the opportunity to bid.

Agency and joint venture requirements. It is often necessary for your engineers, contractors and suppliers either to be represented by local agents or to enter into a joint venture with a local contractor. But even where this is not a legal or customary requirement of the issuing authority, the assistance of a local agent or partner is frequently essential to:

Ensure that the tender is submitted to the right office on time.

Lodge any bonds and guarantees required by the tender authorities.

Participate in all discussions on specifications, quality or prices. (When a bid is of interest but not precisely according to the tender requirements, negotiations and modifications are often necessary before a contract is awarded. Also re-tendering has become common in many countries, that is, cancelling a previous tender and calling it again.)

Provide technical support.

Ensure that your firm's interests are fairly represented at the opening of tenders, to report the results of the competition and to provide guidance for the submission of future bids.

Undertake follow-up action at various stages of contract implementation.

Expedite payment and assist in resolving any disagreements to the satisfaction of both parties.

It is essential that the local agent who presents a bid on behalf of a foreign principal be acceptable to the authorities concerned. Bids made through a firm that is not on their approved list are never considered. Those responsible for tendering or the local chamber of commerce and industry will usually be able to provide a list of approved agents. If not, it may be necessary to examine the results of previous bids for similar requirements of the same authority and to ascertain whether any of the agents who have been successful in the past are in a position to make offers on behalf of your exporters.

In the case of a partnership with a local firm for the tendering process, it may or may not be necessary to register such an arrangement.

SETTING UP YOUR TRADE INTELLIGENCE NETWORK

When you have familiarized yourself with the rules and regulations, study the country's development plan, if any, to determine possible areas of future project activity. Your first objective is to identify the organizations in your territory, in both the public and the private sectors, that have the authority to issue tenders and that are likely to do so in the foreseeable future. During the initial phase of establishing your contracts, introduce yourself to various agencies to ascertain which of them may be inviting bids from time to time for goods and services that your country can supply and to ensure that you are placed on their mailing lists for any press releases on prospective invitations to tender or requests for proposals. The ministry of planning, or its equivalent, will usually be able to provide you with the names of tendering agencies. The chamber of commerce and industry can also be of help. Make a concerted effort to develop at least one special or key contact in each identified organization if possible, but in any event from among individuals on the local scene who are particularly knowledgeable about how such business is conducted.

In addition, it is important to establish and maintain close relations with officials of the ministries responsible for planning development and finance, as well as officials of other ministries concerned with project planning and implementation (agriculture, telecommunications, industries, light and power, transportation and so on). You should also get in touch at an early stage, and maintain contacts, with key persons in trade associations, the specialized trade and export press, and international and domestic banks who are able to provide advance information on forthcoming projects.

Be particularly alert to, and investigate immediately, any news of a current or forthcoming visit to your territory by any international aid agency mission. These "programming" missions often provide the first indication of a future project.

PLANNED PROJECT LIST

Any information on tender opportunities that you may uncover should be transmitted immediately to your headquarters and to any of your country's potential suppliers who are known to you, as well as to your country's commercial representatives in posts to which the matter may be of potential interests. (The information you should transmit is described in the next section.)

As soon as you have the time to do so, compile a "Planned project list" for your territory, broken down by agency, with details of each project, the consultants, the contractors and subcontractors, if known, and the approximate value. Compiling this information will give you an early "feel" for the market as well as an insight into who is buying what from whom, and in what circumstances. Provide, in a "Remarks" column on this list, official or unofficial information you may have on any of the projects that might be of interest to your suppliers.

The list should be classified "commercial confidential" and be made available only to your country's suppliers and to your ministry or trade promotion organization (TPO) and your colleagues in other posts. It should be reviewed frequently, and relevant, fresh information should be added immediately.

Draw up a separate but associated "List of contacts" related to tendering opportunities and procedures. The list should contain the following information: names of authorities or agencies; postal address; cable, telex, telefax and telephone numbers; and names, titles and positions of contacts in these organizations. This list should be available for consultation by your country's authorities and potential suppliers.

CHART A

Possible Action to Take at Different Stages of the Tender Process

1. *Identification of a possible requirement*: Study development plans. Establish a network of contacts. Be alert to the possibilities inherent in the local environment. If possible, put forward your suggestions to the appropriate authority on what can be supplied; for example suggest some unique technology from your own country that will benefit a project.

2. *Draft proposal, or pre-feasibility study.* Suggest to the appropriate authority a possible means of financing a study, either by the authority itself, a national or international financing agency or your own country. Try to ensure that the study is undertaken by your country's consultants.

3. *Feasibility study.* Try to ensure that the work is undertaken by consultants in your country; arrange for it to be financed by your country if necessary and feasible.

4. *Project definition.* The same as (3) above.

5. *Detailed specifications.* the same as (3) above.

6. *Preparation of inquiry documents* ("*bid package*": the same as (3) above.

7. *Call for tenders.* Try to ensure that your suppliers are given full consideration throughout the following steps:

(*a*) *Invitation to contractors to pre-quality.* Rush requirements to potential tenders in your country who wish to pre-quality.

(*b*) *Issue and submission of pre-qualification documents.* Rush the documents to your potential tenderers if the documents are not sent direct. Ensure submission before the deadline.

(*c*) *Analysis and notification of selected tenderers.* Notify your colleagues in other posts of tenderers that are selected so that they can identify possible subcontracting opportunities for firms at home.

(*d*) *Issue of Inquiry documents ("bid package").* Ensure that these are sent as soon as possible to qualified tenderers at home. Send an extract of details to your colleagues as in (c) to reinforce their subcontracting efforts.

(*e*) *Amendments (if any) to Inquiry documents.* Monitor and assist as necessary.

(*f*) *Tenderers' queries or tenderers' Conference.* Transmit information or assist in attendance. Continue to monitor.'

(*g*) *Submission and receipt of tenders.* Ensure submission before deadline and in the proper form.

(*h*) *Opening of tenders.* Attend if possible and report fully to your ministry or TPO, as well as to firms at home submitting bids.

(*i*) *Evaluation of tenders.* Monitor to the extent possible. Offer assistance to make your country's bids more responsive to requirements.

(*j*) *Award of contract.* Report fully on the successful bidder, other competitors and so on. Report to other commercial representatives for further sub-contract follow-up.

SUBMITTING ADVANCE PROJECT INFORMATION

If you are able to obtain advance information on invitations to tender, alert your ministry or TPO and potential contractors in your country who have the requisite technical and financial capacities.

Provide as much detail as you can on the project, such as the following:

Nature of the project or anticipated requirement.

Present status of the project, its prospects of implementation and the anticipated cost.

Source of proper finance.

Potential for international participation and the prospects for your country's exporters as suppliers of any part of the requirement, either as prime contractors or as subcontractors.

Name and address of the agency and the contact person, if known.

Special procedures or conditions, for example, closing dates for submissions, whether offers must be submitted direct or through a local agent, method of payment, language of tender, bond requirements, guarantees, the cost of tender documents and so on.

Stress in your notification that the pre-qualification notice, tender, call for bids or inquiry documents will specify the contractual conditions and the information required, both at the tender stage and at various phases of the contract.

PRE-QUALIFICATION OF BIDDERS

As mentioned above, pre-qualification is now a standard requirement for potential bidders for major works contracts. This is increasingly the case for supply contracts as well. The tender authority usually requests the following information to prepare its short list of qualified bidders:

The experience of the firm with work of the same type, and its experience in the country or a similar country or region.

Its capabilities with respect to personnel, equipment and plant.

Its financial position.

In order to submit their proposals for pre-qualification, firms need at least a summary of the specifications of the project. The tender authority usually issues or publishes an invitation to tender. When the potential bidder responds to this, it will be sent the summarized specifications, if these have not already been advertised, and a questionnaire to be completed and returned to the tender authority together with any requested supporting evidence, references and so forth.

The tender authority then verifies the information, analyzes it and establishes a short list of companies to be invited to submit their offers. These companies are asked to confirm their intention to submit a bid.

THE TENDER DOCUMENTS

In due course, and usually against payment, the tender authority will send a complete set of inquiry documents, also known as "tender documents" or the "bid package," to the firms on the short list. These documents are in most cases sent direct to the firms, rather than through your office. Nevertheless, you may in some circumstances consider it advisable for such bid documents to be sent to the companies concerned through your TPO via your office and the diplomatic pouch to ensure receipt.

A limited number of sates of tender documents—specifications, drawings, and terms and conditions—are sometimes made available to government agencies free of charge. When this is not the case, the cost of documents and the number of sets to purchase are relevant considerations. As the time allowed for the submission of a tender is frequently short, you could run up heavy costs dispatching the documents by express mail to make sure they get there in time. Before incurring those costs, it is a good idea to keep track of the outcome of previous invitations. In particular, it is desirable to know such details as whether customs duties will be applied, the competition normally involved, the prices submitted and whether historically a particular supplier has been preferred. The published outcomes of previous tenders for similar products, supplemented by discussions with the authority concerned, will usually provide and indication of pattern.

Transmitting the documents: If you are called upon to transmit tender sets to your potential suppliers, send them by the fastest possible secure route, after checking them carefully for completeness. Write a short covering letter ro attract attention. The letter should provide, or describe:

The material or equipment required, and quantities.

The reference number assigned by the issuing authority.

The tender deadline.

The name and address to which the tender must be sent.

The language in which corresspondence and documentation must be submitted.

The number of sets of documents to be submitted.

A reminder that all instructions must be followed precisely.

Guarantees or bid bonds, if and, to be furnished with the tender.

A summary of any special conditions or other essential data.

Emphasize the importance of strict adherence to the tender documents' requirements. Surprisingly, surveys show that over half of all proposals are rejected for technical errors, such as having been written in a language other than that specified in the tender, having been received after the due date, not having been received after the due date, not having enough local content when this has been specified and so on.

THE EVALUATION PROCESS

Once a proposal has been submitted in response to a call for tenders, the buyer carries out:

A technical evaluation. This determines the bid's conformity with the specifications and drawings. A comparison of proposed alternatives is made if they are put forward. Methods of construction are examined. The implementation programme provided is studied, and particular attention is given to work proposed for subcontracting and how that fits in with overall requirements. The amount and quality of manpower, plant and equipment suggested are also studied.

A financial evaluation. A number of factors are looked at; capital cost; discounted cash flow; programme of payments and their financing arrangements; suppliers' credits, if any; the currency in which the contractor wishes to be paid; the bonds and guarantees submitted; interest rates; down payment sought: retention monies; daily work rates; and the final contract price.

An evaluation of overall arrangements. This entails determining whether the bid conforms to instructions and to qualifications and exclusions that may have been stated or implied. Insurance provisions have to be checked, as well as the administrative expertise offered (as regards shipping, customs and transport, working hours, labour and so on).

It is often helpful for bids in developing countries to include offers of technical traiding, costed separately so as to keep the price offer as low as possible.

If any of the required information is missing, the proposal is likely to be rejected.

Controversy frequently arises when the contractor that has submitted the lowest bid is not awarded the contract. But the winning bid should be the one evaluated to be the most economically effective. Inevitably, certain clarifications will be necessary, and negotiation (for instance, on price reduction) is common.

FOLLOW-UP

When your country's suppliers bid for an important contract, you should try to be present at the opening of tenders, or follow up when the contract is awarded, both to indicate your official interest and to report on the outcome. Details of the successful tender, the reasons for acceptance, local views and government or private announcements relating to the award, as well as any other significant political or economic background that may have affected the issue, can be of considerable guidance is subsequent submissions. Moreover in some circumstances subcontracting may be possible.

SUB-CONTRACTING

The value of sub-contracts can, in many cases, be very large. No major contractor does all the work itself. Its own particular interest may be in the sale of engineering services, in systems integration, project management or construction management, or the supply of one particular item of equipment or service out of the many required under the contract. In an important project, a lead contractor may take overall responsibility for what is in effect, a consortium. If the bid is successful, this firm becomes the "prime contractor."

The prime contractor is responsible for contracting out parts of the work that it itself does not wish to perform, to one or more subcontractors, which may, in turn, farm out part of their assigned work to a subcontractor at the so-called second "tier" or level, and so on to the third and even lower tiers.

FINANCING

All stages of the tendering process involve costs that have to be financed in some way. The key to successful invention at any stage is often an acceptable and viable financing proposal related to that stage. In certain situations, you may wish to consult your authorities at home to determine domestic possibilities for financing one or more stages of the process.

USING BUYER'S GUIDES

Buyer's guides can be a useful fool for promoting products in foreign markets. Some suggestions on how to produce and disseminate them. For exporters with limited promotional budgets, investment in an overseas sales mission may pose financial difficulties, particularly when markets are located far from the supplying country. Other techniques can, however, provide some of the same benefits as marketing missions—and at lower costs. One of these is buyer's guides. Such booklets, focused on specific product lines, can give foreign buyers a concise idea of what the exporting country can offer and encourage them to contact the suppliers concerned.

BASIC FEATURES

Overseas buyers are often approached by a large number of foreign suppliers and therefore have limited time to spend looking at each piece of sales literature that arrives on their desks. A buyer's guide should thus be attractive and concise, so that, first, the buyer is stimulated to read it and, second, can rapidly absorb the essential facts in it.

Each buyer's guide should deal with one product line only, as buyers are usually specialized in a single line or merchandise category. In general, the booklet should provide answers to the main questions that a buyer asks before visiting a potential supplier.

The booklets should be small in format, for case of handling, with no more than a dozen or so pages of text, in addition to listings of suppliers. The should include one or more attractively designed maps pointing out major supply centres, especially those that are not generally famliar to foreign visitors. The guides should contain the following information:

1. Background on the exporting country's supply possibilities in the product line, including the types of items available, production techniques, the main production centres for the products covered, and names addresses of manufacturers and exporters supplying them.

The supplier listing should provide not only the address and telephone and telex numbers of the firms but should also describe the functions of the enterprise as a manufacturer, agent or exporter and offer a breakdown of products handled. For example, a garment importer will be interested in knowing if a manufacturer handles men's women's children's wear, to identify the lines of his import speciality.

2. General information on trading with the supplying country, such as marketing practices, trade regulations or tariffs that affect exports in that line (such as concessional tariffs in exports markets applicable to those products), currency, regulations, terms of sales, standards applied in production, quality control services, procedures for sending product samples (when goods are be produced accounting to sample), shipping arrangements, insurance facilities and so on.

3. Usefull details for buyers eventually visiling the supplying country concerning its geography, climate, communications facilities, banking services, visa requirements, hotels, transport, official holidays and other related information.

4. Addresses of the supplying country's official commercial representation offices and diplomatic missions in foreign markets.

5. A table of contentes, listing the main secetons, for quick reference.

PRODUCTION

Either the national trade promotion organization (TPO) or the national chamber of commerce could undertake the production and distribution of the guides. Through their trade promotion activities and contacts with the private sector they will probably have most of the required information at hand and will simply need to organize it and arrange for publication.

The TPO or chamber will, of course, have to select the priority product groups on which the guides will be produced. The TPO in particular should have a good indication of the product groups to be promoted, especially if it has drawn up an export development programme that outlines these.

There is no limitation on the number of guide book comprising a series, but it is advantageous to focus on product groups that have a broad supply base consisting of a number of established manufacturers and exporters.

A selection will also need to be made of the firms to include in the listing of suppliers at the end of the booklet.

Criteria for choosing the firms to be mentioned include:

1. Adequate export management know-how and suitable communication skills for responding to overseas trade inquires.
2. Legal character as a registered manufacturer, a co-operative or an exporter with limited liability.
3. Adequate sales materials and catalogues for responding to inquires, including pricelists and policies for terms of sale and delivery.

A graphics designer should be hired to do the basic layout for the guide, unless the agency has such a professional on its own staff. Different colours can be used on the cover of each booklet in the series. It is not necessary to include photographs in them, as these can be supplied by individual exporters at a later stage.

The number of copies to be produced will depend on the number of target markets and the number of potential buyers, among other factors. In some cases several hundred copies may be sufficient, while in others a thousand or more may be needed, for instance it the guide will be distributed at trade fairs.

DISTRIBUTION

The guides can be distributed in several ways. One is through the country's official commercial representatives posted in foreign markets. The guides can be given out in response to requests to these offices from buyers in their host country.

Another way to distribute the booklets is at specialized trade fairs in which the supplying country is represented by either the trade promotion agency or a group of exporters. The booklet can be handed out to buyers wishing more information on suppliers not represented at the fair.

The guides can also be given to buyers requesting information from the TPO or chamber directly, either through correspondance or by visits to the organization. They can likewise be part of an information kit distributed to key foreign importers and trade executives through mailings.

INDONESIAN EXAMPLE

A series of buyer's guides is being produced through an export promotion project that ITC is carrying out with the Government of Indonesia. Indonesia's National Agency for Export Development (NAFED) has published two such booklets, one on Indonesian textiles and apparel and a second on Indonesian home furnishings. Others planned will cover builders' woodwork and industrial timber products, leather products, rattan products and processed foods.

The budget for the two guides was approximately USS 4,000, which covered both design and production costs. Two thousand copies of each guide were produced in English.

The guides have been distributed by NAFED to over 30 of the country's embassies and commercial offices overseas, which in turn have made them available to interested buyers.

In addition to stimulating written requests from buyers for more information on potential suppliers, the guides are intended to encourage foreign buyers already planning to visit the region to include Indonesia on their itinerary. Because many major foreign importers schedule regular buying trips to Southeast Asia, the stop in Indonesia does not usually involve any considerable extra expense.

As a result of the guides, a number of buyers have already planned trips to Indonesia to visit specific supplying firms. In addition, some of the firms listed in the guides have been contacted by letter for more information on their products. The publications have therefore been an effective tool in stimulating increased exports from the country in the two product groups covered by the buyer's guide series.

MEETING THE RIGHT VISITORS AT TRADE FAIRS

To get the most out of trade shows, you should concentrate on meeting only those visitors with a real interest in buying your products. Most exhibitions attract large numbers of visitors, and at peak times you and your colleagues working on the stand are likely to come under considerable pressure trying to meet all of them. It is especially important at those times to be able to identify and classify visitors quickly in your mind so that you can offer each one the attention that he or she deserves. Only some of the visitors are likely to be potential customers. You should focus your attention on that group. But unless you can readily spot these people, you are in danger of wasting a great deal of time.

Generally speaking you can classify trade fair visitors into three board categories:

1. Those who may be curious or show an interest but are not potential customers.
2. Those who demonstrate a genuine interest: some may be potential customers.
3. Those with a keen interest in your products or services now and who are definitely prospective customers.

INTERESTED BUT NOT CUSTOMERS

The first category includes several different types—the "nulsance" visitor, the "inquisitive" visitor, the "old friend" and the general public.

The nuisance visitor. This is someone who comes to your stand simply to put his feet up, engage in casual conversation or avail himself (hopefully) of any free refreshments that may be offered. Try to avoid wasting time with these persons. Often the solution is a polite yet firm excuse. Say something such as, "I expect to have an urgent meeting shortly" or "Can we set up a meeting in an hour's time?" (Hopefully this will deter the nuisance visitor and he or she won't come back again.) Alternatively try asking, "Which product are you interested in?" or see whether the remark "Can I assist you in some way?" will deter the person.

The inquisitive visitor. Such people are similar to nuisance visitors. They are not interested in any of your products of services but stop by in order to kill time. They typically ask general questions and are also often avoid collectors of all leaflets within reach! You will have to find ways of dealing with such visitors. One approach that usually works is to ask them, "Which company do you represent?" or "What line of business are you in?" Hopefully you will be given an answer or lead that enables you to terminate the conversation quickly.

The old friend. We all know about the old friends or acquaintances who just happen to drop in on your stand. They are usually not interested in doing business. They either know you or somebody in your organization or are sending you greetings from someone you mutually know. They may want to discuss the "good old times," the economic or political situation or the weather, or just have friendly conversation about their recent holiday. Whatever the reason, they can take up a great deal of your time chatting away amicably. You must remember that this is not why you are at the exhibition. If they really are good friends and you want to meet them, try to arrange a social meeting one evening after the exhibition is closed.

The general public. If you are dealing with consumer goods you are most likely to welcome the general public to your stand. However, in trade or specialist exhibitions you are usually trying to appeal to business people. A number of exhibitions these days attempt to appeal to both the trade and the public at large by setting aside certain days (or times of the day) when the general public is admitted. (Often name badges are colour coded to enable you to distinguish the various categories of visitor readily).

Be wary of distributing expensive catalogues and leaflets to everyone who comes by. There may indeed by a number of genuine and interesting inquiries from non-trade sources, but you certainly need to guard against the keen "catalogue collectors" who pick up numerous copies of all glossy literature within reach. Much of this is discarded on the way out, and some exhibition organizers even go so far as to provide waste bins just for this purpose!

POTENTIAL CUSTOMERS

This group includes visitors who show some interest in your products but are unlikely to be customers in the near future. Also in this category are journalists who are looking for stories about new products, as well as known personalities (VIPs), students and so on.

Journalists. They are mainly interested in new products and stories about product successes and failures. If you have an unusual stand or are staging demonstrations, for example, you may also provide the background for a newsworthy story. Inquisitive journalists may sometimes take up a lot of your time, but it is usually worth-while.

Remember that journalists are busy people and it will, therefore, be advisable to have attractive press folders available containing news, leaflets and photographs. Always give the name, address and telephone number of someone from whom further information can be obtained.

Press folders not only save you time but they also ensure that journalists take with them the sales and technical information you want them to have. Whether you will subsequently like the piece they write about your products is another matter. Hopefully, what you read will at least be based in part on data included in the press folder. It should also mean that errors are kept to a minimum.

Journalists from the specialist or trade press should be made particularly welcome, because what they write will be read by an important market segment. Most journalists working for the technical press have considerable experience and background knowledge. Therefore be prepared for more searching questions than a journalist from a general publication and, if appropriate, have further detailed literature available for them. Remember that good editorial coverage is valuable promotion for your activities and costs you absolutely nothing! The same amount of space in the advertising columns would cost you a great deal of money and may not be so effective.

VIPs. These days nearly all exhibitions attract some VIP guests and visitors. They range from government ministers to local' officials. Usually the exhibition organizers notify exhibitors of key VIP visits. But if well known persons do come along without prior warning, they can usually be easily recognized by their large entourage and their identification tags.

While few VIPs are likely to be prospective customers, they demand full attention and a warm welcome. Be prepared to talk about all kinds of topics that have little or nothing to do with your specific stand or products. Also be prepared for photographers. If a VIP does stop at your stand, seize the opportunity to take your own photographs: They can be useful for newsletters and future brochures.

Students. Generally speaking students are likely to be interested in new prospects and technology. They can easily take up a lot of your time, but remember that some may become your customers in future years. How much time you give them depends on the pressures you are under at your stand and what value you attach to longer term goodwill and public relations. If you have made prior arrangements for an organized group

visit, ensure that you are available. Make your presentation succinct and interesting, bearing in mind the age and interests of the students.

REAL CUSTOMERS

The third broad category of visitors—the "professionals" and trade customers—are the group you are trying to attract to your stand. Experience shows that this, too, is a diverse group. You should soon be able to spot various types of real customers, however, and recognize the most likely prospects.

How can you pick out visitors who are genuinely interested in your products or services? By:

Their appearance?

Their visitor's name tag?

Their accent or language?

The interest shown in your literature?

The time spent on your stand?

The kind of questions asked?

Some or all of these factors (and, of course, others) may help you to assess the different visitors, but it is helpful to go into a little more detail and try to group your prospective customers into the following categories.

The purchasing initiator. These may include scientists, researchers, laboratory staff, engineers, designers, architects and so forth. All of these persons are likely to be interested in your products, initiate further inquiries and recommend purchase. Be prepared to answer a broad range of detailed questions from them on, for example:

Technical matters.

Quality standards.

Material specifications.

Maintenance.

Your literature.

Names of other users.

This group of visitors will except you to demonstrate a high level of professional and technical know-how in answering their queries. If you develop a rapport with such visitors, you will find that most will readily share their know-how and experiences with you. They are also usually only too willing to refer you to other useful colleagues and contacts.

These with influence: These visitors tend to come with a diverse range of job titles—it may be a person in charge of puschasing at a public institution (such as a hospital), a buyer from a private company or a purchasing manager from a large industrial plant. Whatever their job title may be, all of these visitors will show an interest in prices, terms of payment discounts and so on, but they generally disclose very little else.

You should have well prepared commercial information readily available to answer the kinds of questions that such visitors are likely to ask. How do your prices compare with the competitors? What credit facilities are available? What are your terms of business? And so on.

Consider whether it would be advisable to try to meet your visitor again after the exhibition. You may need to spend more time finding out precisely what he or she requires and how the machinery, for example, fits in with other existing plant and prscesses. Another meeting can also help to build up confidence and perhaps produce a firm order. Before arranging another meeting, however, determine carefully whether it is likely to be productive.

The end user These persons may be technical staff or in some cases the managers or supervisors who actually want the product. They have considerable practical experience and usually know all about raw materials, production processes and the like. They are, in the main, professionals who, if approached properly, are prepared to talk freely about their business. If you manage to arouse their curiosity and encourage them to compare the advantages and drawbacks of materials and products, there is a good chance that they will go on to discuss the methods and processes used in their plant quite openly. It is important to gain the goodwill and interest of this group of visitors, since their views may well determine the final decision about purchasing. If you are; for example, selling printers' inks, it is the machine operate or foreman who is likely to decide whether to use your inks or not.

The decisionmaker. Again this group comes in all guises:

> The visitor may be the owner of a business, the plant manager, the project manager or in another position in the company. He or she may come to your stand accompanied by a professional adviser, a sales manager or financial expert.

These visitors usually show an interest in the overall advantages of the product, details of ordering and delivery, servicing, maintenance, storage and promotion. Even though they generally make prior appointments, they are likely to show up at your stand unexpectedly.

The buyer with the purse strings. Sometimes a company chairman, managing director or finance director may come to your stand. However, senior this person may be, remember that even top management has to (or should have to) work within budgetary controls or obtain the consent of the head of finance (or similar department).

Although you may have been successful in your negotiations with the person you thought was a decisionmaker when he or she called at your stand you may not have been talking to the person with the budgetary authority to purchase. Often with person with the budgetary responsibility does not go to exhibitions at all. Many promising sales leads get stuck," linger on indefinitely or simply just "die." The moral is to try to establish who really holds the purse strings. It is certainly not uncommon for a keen prospective customer to find on return to his organization that his purchasing suggestion is overruled by colleagues for a variety of reasons.

Remember that sometimes two or more of the characteristics outlined above may be found in one persons. The owner of a small business may be not only the initiator, but also the end-user, the decisionmaker and the controller of finance all combined into one. As a general rule, the larger the company, the more complex its purchasing process. Also usually the more expensive the prospective purchase, the more people will be involved in the buying decision.

OTHER KINDS OF VISITORS

Visitors to your stand will not all be in the categories discussed above. Be prepared to deal with a range of other visitors, some of whom will be interested in representing your company in other countries or perhaps selling you something.

The prospective agent. At many exhibitions you will be visited by people offering to represent you or act as an agent in the country where the exhibition is being held or elsewhere. The key piece of advice in such circumstances is not to sign any agreements on the spot:

> You must give such offers careful consideration and visit the people concerned in their offces so that their facilities can be properly evaluated.

If you are actively interested in finding new agents or distributers displaying a sign at the show," Agents wanted." The exhibition organizers should also be informed, as they usually provide a service of putting exhibitors and prospective agents in touch with each other. On the other hand, if you already have representatives or agents covering certain countries or market segments and do not want to be pestered with calls from would-be agents, say so. Display a simple sign saying, "Our agent (s) in...is (are)...." This will avoid wasting everyone's time.

Salesmen. Whether you like it or not, some callers at your stand are likely to offer to sell you something. It may be raw materials, equipment or a wide range of services in the legal, technical, financial and marketing fields. Be patient! You may not have come to the exhibition to be sold products or services, but you never know what possible opportunities may arise in such cases. You may find a suitable product to import or a worthwhile service you are looking for. Take any relevant leaflets offered and get full details of prices, delivery and so forth if the product looks interesting. Try to keep such meetings brief and friendly.

Other visitors interested in cooperation or investment. Again there are a wide variety of possibilities. Some people may be interested in your products and want to manufacture them locally. They will need know-how, special tools and equipment that you can perhaps provide. Others may be interested in adding your product to their marketing base. You may also have a visit from a financier who is looking for investment opportunities and may suggest ways he might finance the further development of our products.

It sometimes happens that you feel under pressure in such situations, especially if the closing date for the exhibition is approaching and you want to return home with tangible results. It should be a rule in these and similar cases that you do not come to any decisions on the spot. Such proposals demand thorough investigation and above all satisfactory answers to many questions. You will also need to examine and check various facts and figures before you can come to a decision on whether and how to proceed. You have to check the legal, financial, costing and other issues. Above all you must find out a lot more about your potential partner.

The professional industrial spy. Be wary of those who come to visit your stand several times and show considerable interest in the construction of your product and associated production mrthods. They may be industrial spies. They are likely to take a keen and close interest, make detailed notes of every aspects, ask for technical literature and perhaps even seen permission to take photographs in a static or operating mode. They may even go as far as suggesting using some of your equipment on a trial basis with the sole intention of copying your products.

Usually an industrial spy will have a carefully prepared cover story. You must try to discern the real situation as soon as possible. Start by asking detailed questions about the person's identity. Ask for business cards and inquire about the size of the company he or she represents. Ask questions about other organizations with which you are familiar in his country. Find out what he knows about other people operating in your field. If you have asked the right questions about identity, the amateur spy will usually give up, while the professional spy will usually persist.

Try further questions. Start with questions of quantity—how many items are required per year? How many similar products are sold in his country or area? From which country are they imported? What does he know about prices? If all this does not uncover the professional spy, start talking about patents. For example, begin by saying something such as:

"We registered a patent for our product in your country and we don't wish to provide extra work for local law-years..."

Discourage his willingness to purchase a sample with the excuse that transport and other allied costs force you to sell in quantities of at least one full container load or for a minimum sum of money. If your product is complex, stress that professional after-sales service is required and that essential spares must be bought and held in stock. Ase whether he can provide you with introductions to other customers.

If after all these and similar questions you receive satisfactory answers, you may indeed have found a real customer.

AUSTRALIAN OFFICE PROMOTES SOUTH PACIFIC EXPORTS

The South Pacific Trade Commission, set up by the Australian Government, helps promote and develop exports from the South Pacific Islands. Among the various import promotion offices set up in recent years to promote products from developing countries into major markets, one of the most unique is the office set up by the Australian Government nine years ago to stimulate exports from South Pacific Islands into Australia. Through product development and international marketing services, the South Pacific Trade Commission (SPTC) has worked with traders in these countries and territories to broaden their range of exports and diversify their target markets. Exporters in the region who are not yet familiar with the SPTC may wish to contact the Commission for assistance in expanding their foreign trade. The experiences of the SPTC may also be of interest to organizations in other regions responsible for promoting exports of small Islands.

ESTABLISHMENT

The SPTC was set up in Sydney in 1979 because of the Australian Government's awareness of the need to increase imports from the South Pacific Islands into Australia. Although funded entirely by the Australian International Development Assistance Bureau, the Trade Commission works for and is responsible to the Islands that are members of the South Pacific Forum. This includes the Cook Islands. Fiji, Kiribati, Nauru, Niue, Papua New Guinea, Samoa, Solomon Islands, Tonga, Tuvalu and Vanuatu.

The South Pacific Trade Commission is headed by a Senior Trade Commissioner of the Australian Government. He is supported by a small team of four persons who maintain active links with the Island business communities. All staff are involved in the SPTC's major projects, and their continuous personal contacts with the Commission's business clients enables rapid and effective response to requests for information and follow-up to trade development opportunities.

SERVICES

The commission provides a base in Sydney for businessmen visiting Australia. Facilities such as secretarial assistance, conference and display rooms, and communications facilities are available. Advice and assistance are given to prospective Pacific Island trades visiting the market, including introductions to presidential business partners.

Recently the aims and objectives of the South Pacific Trade Commission have broadened, with the emphasis today being on projects to develop new export production in the Islands, upgrade their existing exports, promote their export products in Australia and elsewhere, and stimulate export-oriented investment in them. The Commission thus takes the initiative in developing new business ventures or new export products and working with consultants, supplies ongoing management support to new export oriented firms.

PRODUCT DEVELOPMENT

One of the Trade Commission's major areas of work, as mentioned above, is to undertake projects to develop export projects in the Forum Island countries and territories. Examples of such projects currently being implemented are the manufacture of cane furniture in the Solomon Islands, yacht building in Tonga, snack food production in Western Samoa and clothing manufacture in Tuvalu. Similar projects are also under way in other locations. In these activities the Commission gives special emphasis to export development schemes designed especially to involve the women in the Islands. The SPTC's role in these projects has been to suggest sales openings for these products in the Australian market; obtain expert advice on matters such as labelling requirements, appropriate packaging, quarantine requirements and so on; have factory layouts drawn up; help put together a financial package; help develop a marketing plan, and offer other advice as appropriate.

PROMOTIONS

The Commission is responsible for organizing promotions of Pacific Island products through displays and exhibitions. Its showroom is used by trade promotion officials from the Island states and prospective agents in Australia, many of whom have taken advantage of this facility on several occasions. Exhibitions are also organized in other places, including markets outside the region.

The exhibition "Stamps of the South Pacific", which attracted much favourable publicity when it was staged at the Rockefeller Center in New York, is an example of a successful Pacific Island promotion outside the region coordinated by the Trade Commission. Stamps are one of the main exports of these Islands, as their attractive designs and colourful illustrations make them widely appreciated. (This particular stamp exhibit has since been displayed in Sydney, where it was a special feature at the University of New South Wales Open Day and at the Newcastle Philatelic Society Stamp Exhibition.) As a result of this promotion, the exports of the stamps have increased.

The Trade Commission regularly participates in an exhibition that is staged to promore food and beverages, the Australian International Fine Food and Drink Exhibition. This trade show, held alternately in Sydney and Melbourne each year, promotes sales to Australia's AS23 billion food and beverage marked. The Commission exhibits products from a number of Islands at the fair. Last year the SPTC sponsoreda group of 15 participants at this event from the Cook Islands. Fiji, Papua New Guinea, the Solomon Islands, Tonga, Vanuatu and Western Samoa, and many orders were placed for these islands' products during the five-day exhibition.

In addition the SPTC coordinated a display of Tongan Boats at the 1987 Sydney Boat Show. Dinghies, runabouts (light motor boats), surf skis and oars were among the products displayed from the islands, and these items attracted widespread interest. All goods from the Islands on exhibit were sold early in the show, and a number of orders were taken for furure delivery.

Last year the Trade Commission also participated on behalf of Island exporters in the Holiday and Travel Show in Sydney, the largest travel promotion held in Australia each year. The participation focused on promoting individual tourist operations in each Island. SPTC funded and operated a "Polynesian Shop" in the Pacific Village at the show. This shop sold food and other goods produced in Forum Islands. The results for these exhibitors were excellent. Most Islands take part in this promotion every year.

IN-HOUSE TRAINING

One of the Trade Commission's most innovative and successful schemes is its Attachment Programme, which is open to both government officials and business people from the Islands. It offers an opportunity for the participants to get firsthand experience in the operation of the Trade Commission during the period of four to six weeks they are based in the Commission's Sydney office. They also gain experience under the programme by meeting their counterparts in Australian companies working in export production, marketing and sales. A work programme is tailored to the needs of each person participating. Accommodation and living expenses are covered by the SPTC.

In 1987 the Trade Commission sponsored 20 persons on programmes of this kind. Participants came from Tonga, Vanuatu, Papua New Guinea, the Solomon Islands, Micronesia, Kiribati and Fiji.

The Trade Commission also offers other types of assistance when possible to business executives and government officials from the Pacific Islands. For example, forestry officers from Tonga's Ministry of Agriculture, Fisheries and Forestry were recently in Sydney to examine the potential market for red

cedar timber from their country. While in Sydney the SPTC arranged for them to meet with major timber merchants and leading furniture manufacturers to discuss sales of this potential export.

INVESTMENT

There is growing interest in investing in the South Pacific Islands, among Australian as well as other foreign business partners. The Trade Commission plays an active role in promoting export-oriented investment in Forum Islands. Some of the ways it helps are to organanize investment seminars: arrang programmes for government officials of Forum Islands to promote investment; look for potential investors, including joint venture partners, help put together a financial package for such projects, arrange for specialist advice and for critical assessment of investment proposals; and provide ongoing management advice.

RADIO PROGRAMME

Some of the main problems in expanding exports from the South Pacific Islands are their long distances from major markets, and their limited transport and communications facilities. Consequently, development of an effective communications network in the South Pacific has high priority.

As a part of that network, the Trade Commission, in conjunction with Radio Australia and the Australian International Development Assistance Bureau, has just started producing a weekly radio programme entitled "Pacific Sunrise" that is broadcast by Radio Australia to the Pacific Islands. The programme focuses on a number of trade and investment topics each week including trade development news, product export programmes, financial and marketing advice for the small business operator, new business opportunities, market analysis and other subjects of commercial interest. Interviews with people from the region, as well as with representatives from the SPTC, are also carried on the programme. The radio programme and an associated monthly newsletter are intended to help keep listeners abreast of the latest developments in regional trade and investment.

NONGOVERNMENTAL ORGANIZATIONS

From time to time the Trade Commission also works with nongovernmental organizations to develop the export trade of the Islands. Special projects have been developed to use the resources of these organizations and the Commission jointly.

Trading Partners in Australia is one such non-profit group that imports and sells handicrafts from developing countries. With support from the Trade Commission, the Trading Partners Craft Exhibition travelled throughout the state of New South Wales in Australia for two months last year, attracting much publicity and interest. The Commission offers assistance for promotions and publicity for activities of this type that will benefit the exports of Forum Islands.

MORE INFORMATION

Firms in the South Pacific Forum grouping that wish to obtain information on the SPTC's activities should contact the Commission at the address below. Inquiries from business organizations regarding trade and investment opportunities in the region are also welcome.